A CULTURAL HISTORY OF THE HOME

VOLUME 6

A Cultural History of the Home
General Editor: Amanda Flather

Volume 1
A Cultural History of the Home in Antiquity
Edited by Andrew Wallace-Hadrill and Joanne Berry

Volume 2
A Cultural History of the Home in the Medieval Age
Edited by Katherine L. French

Volume 3
A Cultural History of the Home in the Renaissance
Edited by Amanda Flather

Volume 4
A Cultural History of the Home in the Age of Enlightenment
Edited by Clive Edwards

Volume 5
A Cultural History of the Home in the Age of Empire
Edited by Jane Hamlett

Volume 6
A Cultural History of the Home in the Modern Age
Edited by Despina Stratigakos

A CULTURAL HISTORY OF THE HOME
IN THE MODERN AGE

Edited by Despina Stratigakos

BLOOMSBURY ACADEMIC
LONDON • NEW YORK • OXFORD • NEW DELHI • SYDNEY

BLOOMSBURY ACADEMIC
Bloomsbury Publishing Plc
50 Bedford Square, London, WC1B 3DP, UK
1385 Broadway, New York, NY 10018, USA
29 Earlsfort Terrace, Dublin 2, Ireland

BLOOMSBURY, BLOOMSBURY ACADEMIC and the Diana logo are trademarks of Bloomsbury Publishing Plc

First published in Great Britain 2021
This edition published in Great Britain, 2024

Copyright © Bloomsbury Publishing, 2021

Despina Stratigakos has asserted her right under the Copyright, Designs and Patents Act, 1988, to be identified as Editor of this work.

Cover image © Amaia Arozena & Gotzon Iraola / Getty Images

All rights reserved. No part of this publication may be reproduced or transmitted in any form or by any means, electronic or mechanical, including photocopying, recording, or any information storage or retrieval system, without prior permission in writing from the publishers.

Bloomsbury Publishing Plc does not have any control over, or responsibility for, any third-party websites referred to or in this book. All internet addresses given in this book were correct at the time of going to press. The author and publisher regret any inconvenience caused if addresses have changed or sites have ceased to exist, but can accept no responsibility for any such changes.

A catalogue record for this book is available from the British Library.

A catalog record for this book is available from the Library of Congress.

ISBN: HB: 978-1-4725-8430-4
Set: 978-1-4725-8441-0
PB: 978-1-3504-1232-3
Set: 978-1-3504-1235-4

Series: The Cultural Histories Series

Typeset by RefineCatch Limited, Bungay, Suffolk
Printed and bound in Great Britain

To find out more about our authors and books visit www.bloomsbury.com and sign up for our newsletters.

CONTENTS

List of Illustrations   vii

Series Preface   x

    Introduction   1
    Despina Stratigakos

1   The Meaning of Home: Defining Domesticity in the Modern Age   13
    Rachel Hurdley

2   Family and Household: A Century of Bedrooms   39
    Annmarie Adams

3   The House: The Global Age of Housing   63
    Kenny Cupers

4   Furniture and Furnishings: Material Culture and Making the Modern   91
    Pauline Garvey

5   Home and Work: Household Labour and the Making of Inequalities   113
    Rosie Cox

6   Gender and Home: (Re)scripting Domestic Life and Design   137
    Barbara Penner

7   Hospitality and Home: British and American Cultures of Entertaining   161
    Grace Lees-Maffei

8	Religion and the Home: Sites of Sanctuary and Suspicion *Pamela E. Klassen*	185
Notes		205
Bibliography		207
Notes on Contributors		239
Index		243

ILLUSTRATIONS

INTRODUCTION

0.1	Heinrich Hoffmann, photograph of Hitler escorting a young girl to his house	4
0.2	The interior of the 1920s Schröder house, Utrecht	8
0.3	Geoff Sloan, home theatre, 2010	10

CHAPTER 1

1.1	The homely porch, Eugene, Oregon	14
1.2	Advertisement page from *Selling Electricity*, 1907	20
1.3	Suburban dwellings in Vanves, France, 2016	23
1.4	Mantelpiece in a 1992 detached house in Efail Isaf, Wales	28
1.5	Mantelpiece in a 1910 terraced house in Pontypridd, Wales	31
1.6	Porch 'bedroom' of a homeless man in Cardiff, Wales	35

CHAPTER 2

2.1	'The Palos' house published in *Homes of Moderate Cost*, 1941	40
2.2	Master bedroom of an Eichler house	44
2.3	Post-war house design by Norman M. Klein	46
2.4	1952 advertisement for Utica sheets	48
2.5	Philip Johnson reading on the bed in the glass house	53
2.6	Parents' bedroom in Mr Hadrill's house, Montreal, 1924	57
2.7	Patient in Children's Memorial Hospital, Montreal	58
2.8	'Selfie' photograph of Lindsay Mazliach in her bedroom, shared on Instagram	61

CHAPTER 3

3.1	Catalogue home from Sears, Roebuck, and Co.	68
3.2	A detached house in Belgium	69
3.3	Mass housing in Michanzani, Zanzibar	78
3.4	King Ming Estate, Hong Kong	80
3.5	Eugène Atget, The 'Zone' of Paris, 1913	82
3.6	PREVI housing project, *c.* 1976	85

CHAPTER 4

4.1	Marcel Breuer's B3 Chair	97
4.2	Contemporary view of the kitchen of the Haus am Horn in Weimar, Germany	99
4.3	Bedroom interior display at the Stockholm Exhibition, 1930	103
4.4	Alvar Aalto's Armchair 400	104
4.5	Bride and Home Exhibition, Stockholm, 1944	106

CHAPTER 5

5.1	Woman washing clothes in a copper, Melbourne, *c.* 1935	116
5.2	'The more WOMEN at work, the sooner we WIN!' Second World War recruitment poster	118
5.3	The housewife and mass consumption	120
5.4	Class at the Household Workers Training Project, San Jose, California, *c.* 1940	124
5.5	A typical single-storey New Zealand house	129
5.6	DIY and masculinity	133

CHAPTER 6

6.1	Calvert Vaux, 'Design No. 21: Irregular Wooden Country House', 1864	142
6.2	Asher B. Durand's engraving, 'The Wife', 1830	143
6.3	Christine Frederick, *The New Housekeeping*, 1913	148
6.4	Margarete Schütte-Lihotzky's Frankfurt Kitchen, 1926	149
6.5	'New Kitchen Built to Fit Your Wife', *Popular Science*, 1953	151
6.6	Cover of Matrix, *Making Space: Women and the Man-Made Environment*, 1984	157

CHAPTER 7

7.1	Emily Post, *Etiquette in Society*, 1922	166
7.2	Utility Furniture Exhibition, London, 1942	168
7.3	Illustration by James Kingsland in *Guide to Easier Living*, 1950	173
7.4	Contemporary kitchen design with hatch by MTB Schreinerei	174
7.5	LAN (local area network) party in Montreal, 2016	181
7.6	Instagram post by D.J. Huppatz, 2020	182

CHAPTER 8

8.1	Illustration by Leonard Weisgard in *My Book of Prayer*, 1959	192
8.2	*The Mennonite Treasury of Recipes*, 1980	192
8.3	Family at the dinner table in Los Angeles, *c.* 1916	193
8.4	Christmas event at the home of Superior Court Judge Earl C. Broady, Beverly Hills, *c.* 1950	195
8.5	Fort Qu'Appelle Indian Industrial School in Lebret, *c.* 1885	200

SERIES PREFACE

A Cultural History of the Home is an authoritative, interdisciplinary, six-volume series investigating the changing meaning of home, both as an idea and as a place to live, from ancient times until the present. Each volume follows the same basic structure and begins with an overview of the cultural, social, political and economic factors that shaped ideas and requirements of home in the period under consideration. Experts examine important aspects of the cultural history of home under eight main headings: the meaning of home; house and home; family and home; gender and home; work and home; furniture and furnishings; religion and home; hospitality and home. A single volume can be read to obtain a thorough knowledge of the period or one of the eight themes can be followed through history by reading the relevant chapter in each of the six volumes, providing an understanding of developments over the longer term.

Individual volumes in the series will cover six historical periods:

Volume 1: *A Cultural History of the Home in Antiquity* (500 BC–800 AD)
Volume 2: *A Cultural History of the Home in the Medieval Age* (800–1450)
Volume 3: *A Cultural History of the Home in the Renaissance* (1450–1650)
Volume 4: *A Cultural History of the Home in the Age of Enlightenment* (1650–1800)
Volume 5: *A Cultural History of the Home in the Age of Empire* (1800–1920)
Volume 6: *A Cultural History of the Home in the Modern Age* (1920–2000+)

Amanda Flather

Introduction

DESPINA STRATIGAKOS

If the home has traditionally been a place associated with growing up and feelings of comfort and belonging, how does our awareness of living in a rapidly transforming modern age shift our perceptions? Does the home become a bulwark against change or, instead, a steering gear in the turn towards the new? We can well understand how certain aspects of the home – such as the materials and methods used in the physical construction of the dwelling – might lend themselves to processes of modernization. But the ways in which we structure our identities and social practices within the home are just as much subject to change, a reality that is lamented by some and embraced by others.

In the past century, gender roles have often been at the centre of debates concerning the home and the forces of economic, technological, and social progress. In Europe and North America, the shortage of male labor during the First World War prompted the recruitment of women for jobs in munitions factories and for other occupations, such as bank clerk and streetcar conductor, usually reserved for men. When hostilities ceased, re-domestication policies thrust women out of their jobs in order to employ war veterans and thereby rebalance the 'natural' order of the sexes (Grayzel 2013: 106–9). Women were also offered incentives to re-embrace their traditional roles as housewives and mothers. In Weimar Germany, such efforts included state-sponsored housing settlements. Modernist dwellings erected in Frankfurt am Main featured rationalized kitchens that promised housewives factory-like efficiency in the preparation of meals. Created by Austrian architect Grete Schütte-Lihotzky, the Frankfurt Kitchen's scientific design aimed not only to ease household drudgery, but also to lend a professional air to women's domestic work (see Figure 6.4). Its tiny size, however, and physical isolation from the rest of the home meant that women worked alone and unseen (Henderson 1996: 231–36). Thus, despite radical pretensions, modernist architecture in this instance ultimately reinforced traditional gender roles.

At the same time, the 1920s also witnessed the proliferation of novel types of homes that challenged conventional gender and family roles. Women's emancipation movements in the later nineteenth century had expanded educational and career opportunities for women, transforming their conventional life paths. As more women lived independently, their need for housing grew pressing. Residences for single women emerged in European and North American cities in the late nineteenth century, but became increasingly visible in the period following the First World War. In Frankfurt am Main, the new housing settlements included apartment blocks for single women who stood outside the nuclear family order (Henderson 2009). Social conservatives viewed such homes as evidence of society's moral decay. *The House of Single Women*, a 1932 novel by Swiss writer Johanna Böhm, drew on modernist models for its fictionalized setting of an apartment block for single women, which the author portrayed as a house of horrors, teeming with lesbianism, suicide, and murder (Stratigakos 2005: 152–58).

Yet another type of home caught the public's attention in the 1920s and 1930s: the dwellings of the rich and famous. The advent of new technologies in broadcasting, recording, and film brought entertainers and politicians into the everyday lives of people. Celebrities were both larger-than-life and a part of the family, creating a voracious market for information on the lives of these intimate strangers (Henderson 1992: 52). Curiosity about celebrities' homes dominated the public's desire to see beyond the mask of fame to the 'real' person within. Since the nineteenth century, American and European middle-class cultures had come to focus on the domestic milieu as the site of the authentic self. Hollywood fan magazines and newspaper gossip columns gushed about what the famous did at home – 'what they ate, what their beauty secrets were, what pets they pampered, what cars they drove, what they wore' (Henderson 2005: 44). Articles on movie stars' houses typically blended details about the architecture and interior decoration with details about the occupant's personality, thrilling readers who believed they were getting to know the actor on more intimate terms (Abrams 2008: 119–20). Beyond fan magazines and gossip columns, the mainstream media also embraced the popularity of celebrity homes. In the 1930s, *Architectural Digest* began to run a regular feature on the homes of Hollywood movie stars and directors.

The growing interest in visualizing the domestic spaces of the rich and famous also had a physical dimension. Specifically, the 1920s and 1930s witnessed a dramatic rise in the popularity of house museums, where one could experience first-hand the homes of history's 'great men' (Coleman 1933: 18). In a 1932 essay, Virginia Woolf noted that 'London, happily, is becoming full of great men's houses, bought for the nation and preserved entire with the chairs they sat on and the cups they drank from, their umbrellas and their chests of drawers'. The owners of these houses, she continued, may have had little artistic taste when it came to decorating, 'but they seem always to possess a much rarer and more interesting gift – a faculty for housing themselves appropriately, for making the table, the chair, the curtain, the carpet into their own image'. Here, amid their possessions, Woolf contended, one could get to know the great men of history far better than from any biography ([1932] 1975: 23).

In the 1930s, the growth of celebrity culture and interest in the houses of 'great men' combined to produce a fascination with the private home life of Adolf Hitler. German- and English-language newspapers and magazines sympathetically portrayed the off-duty Führer as a modest and good man as well as a peaceable neighbour. In 1934, the National German Press Association, reporting on national and foreign markets for German photojournalism, revealed that photographs of Hitler at home playing with his dogs and with children were the most popular (Figure 0.1). These domestic portrayals, widely distributed and consumed by global audiences, helped to soften the dictator's image and to deflect attention from the hatred and violence of his regime (Stratigakos 2015).

The physical destruction of cities and mass dislocations of population during and after the Second World War in Europe left millions of people homeless or in exile. In Germany alone, nearly one-third of the nation had lost their homes (Bessel 2003: 28). Although the scale of homelessness was unprecedented, the loss of home through war and political turmoil was nothing new to the twentieth century. Indeed, it stands as a defining characteristic of our modern times. The mass migrations of this past century, whether voluntary or forced, have fuelled the nostalgic longing for home. For those many millions, home is a painful absence, a self and way of life that can never be recovered.

In the period following the Second World War, the desire for a return to normalcy expressed itself in domestic design. West German interior design of the 1950s harkened back to the modernism of the 1920s, and particularly that of the Bauhaus, the avant-garde art school that had been vilified and closed by the Nazis. Modernism became a symbol for resistance to fascism, and of progress and democracy, its earlier leftist roots forgotten. A similar political reuse of modernism took place in the United States, where leading Bauhaus teachers such as Walter Gropius, Ludwig Mies van der Rohe, and Marcel Breuer had migrated in the 1930s. Their functionalist style came to be associated with the values of freedom and democracy, and served as a tool of Cold War diplomacy (Betts 2004: 12–13).

Such politics were on view in the famous 1959 'kitchen debate' that occurred in Moscow between Soviet Premier Nikita Khrushchev and American Vice

FIGURE 0.1: Heinrich Hoffmann, photograph of Hitler escorting a young girl (Rosa Bernile Nienau) to his house on the Obersalzberg, from Heinrich Hoffmann's book *Youth around Hitler (Jugend um Hitler)*, 1934. Heinrich Hoffmann Collection, Picture Archive, Bavarian State Library, Collection number: hoff-9448.

President Richard Nixon. Standing in front of the exhibit of General Electric's modernist, appliance-filled kitchen, part of a model home on display at the American National Exhibition in Moscow, Nixon lectured Khrushchev on the consumer advantages of capitalism over communism. For Nixon, consumer choice represented a democratic freedom and expression of individual liberty. Moreover, American technology and consumption, he insisted, made American women's lives easier and more comfortable. Before the exhibition, Khrushchev had set the stage for the ideological debate by calling the model home a capitalist deception, an attempt to mislead the Soviet people by presenting as typical a level of consumption that average American workers could not afford (Carbone 2009: 59, 72; Reid 2009: 87, 89).

Khrushchev was not entirely wrong. The American good life on view in Moscow, which presented the road to freedom and happiness as being paved with consumer goods, was one to which many Americans aspired in the post-war period. Low-interest government loans, an increase in car ownership, the building of highways and the development of inexpensive tract housing in new subdivisions on the periphery of cities ushered in an era of mass homeownership. Mass homeownership, in turn, stimulated the mass consumption of household goods to furnish and maintain these new homes, thereby fostering a new consumer culture (Cohen 2003: 195). But this prosperity was not shared by all, despite today's often nostalgic representation of the post-war period as one of abundance. When the kitchen debate took place in Moscow, almost forty million people were struggling with poverty in the United States, including a third of the nation's children (Anderson 2015: 213; Coontz 1992: 29).

Nor did all American women feel liberated by what Nixon saw as the comfort and ease of their modern homes. After the Second World War, government propaganda urged women who had been employed in wartime industries to return home and redefine their identities as full-time homemakers. Many women hoped to continue working, but found the range of jobs open to them and salaries offered much reduced. For young women, the strain of balancing family and work was not always worth the meagre rewards. Their departure, however, made space for older women to enter the paid labor force, refuting a simple picture of retrenchment in the post-war period (May 1988: 76–77). Nonetheless, by the early 1960s, many women felt disillusionment with the domestic dream peddled in Moscow, and when Betty Friedan's *The Feminine Mystique* was published in 1963, a book critical of middle-class women's suburban lives, eager readers propelled the book onto the *New York Times* bestseller list (Friedan 1963). Friedan would later be taken to task for having defined inequality around her own privileged concerns, neglecting the different needs and experiences of women of colour, lesbians, and poor and working-class women (hooks 1984; Crenshaw 1989; Coontz 2011).

Despite these limitations, Friedan's book came to serve as a manifesto for what became known as the second wave of the feminist movement, which gathered steam in the late 1960s and emerged as a major social force in the 1970s. In seeking access to the public realm on terms of greater equality with men, women increasingly questioned traditional domestic roles and, particularly, their unpaid work. Women sought collaboration from their spouses in housework and childrearing as well as new forms of living that made the sharing of domestic labor possible. In the 1970s and 1980s, feminist architects proposed new models of domestic living designed to liberate rather than restrict women. In 1986, for example, as part of a multi-year urban renewal project in Berlin (International Building Exhibition Berlin), Christine Jachmann and Myra Warhaftig designed model apartment buildings on the principle of 'emancipatory housing'. Their goal was to create dwellings that enabled residents to combine employment outside the home with childcare and housework by rearranging traditional floorplans and designing communal spaces to allow for the sharing of domestic labor (Jachmann 1992).

Such attempts by women to design more equitable dwellings and urban environments have a long history. In 1916, for example, Alice Constance Austin laid out plans for Llano Del Rio, a socialist colony in southern California, with the intention of liberating women from isolation and household drudgery. Her town plan interwove homes with parks, community centres, and commercial pedestrian zones, and offered communal domestic services, such as central laundries and kitchens run by professional staff. Transported through underground tunnels, meals would arrive from the communal kitchens and would be enjoyed by the family on their dining patio; the houses themselves had no kitchens. Dirty dishes would then be returned to the central kitchen for cleaning (Hayden 1981: 242–43; Hayden 1976: 300–8).

Revolutionary at first glance, the potential power of Austin's designs to reshape women's daily existence was in fact restricted by deeply entrenched social norms. Among them, and typical of many new communities established by American builders in the twentieth century, Llano Del Rio only admitted Caucasian residents. In a 1916 advertisement published in *The Western Comrade*, a Los Angeles-based socialist magazine, the settlement's founders attempted to justify this exclusion: 'We have had applications from Negroes, Hindus, Mongolians and Malays. The rejection of these applications is not due to race prejudice but because it is not deemed expedient to mix the races in these communities' (Shor 1997: 166). The continuation of segregation policies into the mid-twentieth century limited the access of African Americans and other minorities to new housing developments and the ability to accumulate wealth through homeownership, with effects still felt today (Harris 2013; Rothstein 2017).

Austin's plans for Llano Del Rio were never realized, and subsequent feminist interventions in domestic design have similarly found little resonance with commercial builders. Instead, many families have come to rely on consumer goods, such as instant meals, to alleviate housework. Fast food restaurants – a massive industry that generates hundreds of billions of dollars in revenues globally – have become an integral extension of the modern home in a way that would have been unimaginable in the nineteenth century, when family meals were rarely taken in public. By contrast, 69 million people in more than 100 countries will eat today at a McDonald's restaurant (McDonald's Corporation 2015). But few are likely to call it home.

Socialist-minded Austin would have been dismayed with the commercialization of fast food, but she would have understood the impulse to free up time for other things. What mattered most in her imagined utopian community were the familial relations within a home, and especially a woman's relationship to her husband and children, which Austin believed would be strengthened by eliminating the time and energy spent on domestic work. Thus, despite Austin's desire to liberate women from housework, her idealization of motherhood and insistence on the nuclear family as her model remained conservative. Indeed, Austin's visionary plans did not include any of the communal childcare facilities that already existed in Llano del Rio. They also did not provide housing for the single adults who were living there at the time and who had been attracted to the colony by its socialist experiment (Hayden 1976: 301).

Today, Austin's plan for a town composed solely of nuclear households, with a male breadwinner and a stay-at-home mother, might strike some as heavenly and others as a dystopian nightmare. Family ideals differ radically across the social and political spectrum of Western societies. Within heterosexual nuclear families, more fathers are staying at home to raise children while their wives serve as the family breadwinner. The legalization of same-sex marriage in Western countries has brought state recognition to families led by same-sex couples. With the rise of divorce rates in the twentieth century – in the United States, 'one eighth of all marriages ended in divorce in 1900' compared to one-half by the end of the century (Amato and Irving 2006: 48) – many families no longer reside under one roof, with children moving between parental homes and living in 'blended' families that may include step-parents and step-siblings. More and more people are living in single-occupant households. In the past century, the proportion of Americans living on their own has increased steadily from about five percent in the 1920s to 27 percent in 2013. The phenomenon is most pronounced in large urban areas; in Manhattan and Washington, about half of all households have just one occupant (Henderson 2014). The premise of the enormously popular American television show *Friends*, which aired from 1994 to 2004, was that home and family are a choice, based more on close ties of friendship than on blood.

Friends is also notable for the informal domesticity it celebrates; much of the show takes place in the friends' Greenwich Village apartments, and the casual ways in which they socialize and occupy those spaces defines, for many, the culture of home in the twenty-first century. This contrasts with earlier Victorian ideals, when the hierarchical arrangements between family members were reflected in domestic habits and spaces that reinforced the authority of the parents – especially the father. The social and political upheavals that followed the First World War began to challenge those power foundations.

The Schröder house in Utrecht in the Netherlands represents a singular, but telling, example. The radically modernist home, designed in 1923–24, emerged from a collaboration between a young widow, Truus Schröder, and Gerrit Rietveld, a Dutch designer involved with the avant-garde De Stijl art movement. Schröder had previously lived with her older husband and their young children in a conventional bourgeois home, where they had fought about his authoritarian methods of childrearing. When her husband died, Schröder worked with Rietveld to design a different kind of home that supported her vision of an egalitarian and even playful household. The two-storey white-cube structure,

FIGURE 0.2: A contemporary view of the second-floor interior of the Schröder house in Utrecht designed in the early 1920s by Gerrit Rietveld and Truus Schröder. Photograph by Stijn Poelstra. © Artists Rights Society (ARS), New York, c/o Pictoright Amsterdam.

with its hovering planes and red, blue, and yellow elements, stood out dramatically in a neighbourhood of traditional brick row houses. The family lived largely on the upper floor, which swept away the confined and overstuffed interiors of the traditional Victorian home with its open spaces, large expanses of windows, moveable partitions, and brightly coloured built-in furniture (Figure 0.2). Here the children listened to conversations among visiting artists and intellectuals, and socialized in a space designed to encourage creativity, freedom, and joy (Friedman 2006: 64–91).

Schröder and Rietveld did not invent the open plan. It had emerged decades earlier in the United States, aided by the development of central heating, which allowed large spaces to be comfortably heated, and of reinforced concrete construction, which eliminated the need for interior weight-bearing walls. Frank Lloyd Wright's Prairie-style houses, designed at the turn of the twentieth century, dispensed with interior walls to create dramatic, freely flowing interiors for a prosperous clientele. After the Second World War, the new suburban communities popularized open plans on an unprecedented scale. New house types, such as the split-level ranch, did away with formal rooms, including entrance halls and parlours, which in well-to-do homes had enabled formally receiving and entertaining visitors. In the new suburban houses, kitchen, dining, and living spaces were often combined in an open plan (Lane 2015: 6–9). Such changes were encouraged by the search for more affordable housing, which resulted in smaller dwellings. Merging living areas provided occupants with a more expansive atmosphere. But the new plans also expressed and enabled the desire to occupy domestic spaces with greater informality and freedom of movement, promoting the easy-going togetherness of family, friends, and neighbours (Jacobs 2015: 134–37).

The lack of domestic servants also contributed to the growing popularity of open plans. Most nineteenth-century middle-class homes employed servants to assist the housewife with the heavy physical work of maintaining a home, from hauling coal for fires to the weekly laundry. This labor, and the servants themselves, were kept largely invisible and inaudible through the separation of the workspaces of the home, such as the kitchen, from the family's living areas. After the turn of the twentieth century, employment of domestic servants declined as the working classes turned to other job opportunities. Middle-class housewives thus became increasingly reliant on their own labor to maintain their homes. Already in the 1920s, the Frankfurt Kitchen had attempted to alleviate that burden with its rationalized design. In keeping with earlier visual and spatial practices, however, housework remained hidden: a sliding door isolated the wife in the kitchen from other rooms, whose inhabitants, notably the husband, were left undisturbed by cooking noises or smells (Henderson 1996: 236). In post-war suburban settlements, by contrast, the kitchen was integrated into the family's living spaces (Jacobs 2015: 140–45). Although the labor of the housewife was now apparent, she was expected to carry it out with conspicuous ease in keeping with the new casualness of domestic life and with the help of appliances, envisioned as her 'electronic servants' (Holliday 2001: 108). In the 1980s and 1990s, spacious, richly equipped kitchens assumed a new status as the social heart of the home, where an entire evening of informal entertaining might take place. The kitchen, with its sophisticated appliances and users, who regarded cooking as a creative event, thus transformed from workroom to theatre. In affluent households, this focus on creativity was enabled by the renewed availability, in a globalized workforce, of paid domestic laborers, to whom the more menial side of housework could be assigned.

Other spaces in the home have also become, quite literally, more theatrical. With the advent of radio and television in the twentieth century, public entertainment was delivered directly to the home. Movie theatre attendance plummeted in the United States from 1947 to 1957, in part because televisions became more common in homes. Technological improvements, including larger screens, stereo sound, and the adoption of colour and even 3D film, turned the modern movie experience into a spectacle that encouraged people to return to public theatres (Valentine 1994: 163–69). Technologies for improving

FIGURE 0.3: A dedicated home theatre, assembled and photographed by Geoff Sloan in 2010. Credit: Geoff Sloan, Flickr.

entertainment experiences at home began to catch up in the 1970s and 1980s with VHS and LaserDisc players. The introduction in the 1990s of the DVD, followed by Blu-ray discs and high-definition digital television brought higher quality cinematic experiences into the home. Today, home theatres are proliferating and may feature surround sound, large-screen display, popcorn and vending machines, and movie-theatre style chairs. Attendance at public theatres in the United States has dropped once more as people choose the convenience and comfort of watching at home (Schwartzel and Fritz 2014).

Modern technologies that have allowed the home to become an increasingly sophisticated site of leisure and entertainment have also enabled it to function as an office. An estimated one in five workers globally telecommute regularly, and the numbers are expected to rise, boosted by the relatively low cost and widespread availability of personal computers, cell phones, and internet service (Reaney 2012). The Covid-19 pandemic, which forced businesses and schools around the world to operate online, may also accelerate the trend (Guyot and Sawhill 2020). Working from home is not a new phenomenon (Hollis 2015); in nineteenth-century European and North American cities, women often took in piecework, and many men, including professionals, proprietors, and artisans, also had their workspaces at home. Today, however, home-based workers in the United States are more likely to be in management and business, and the telecommuting workforce is split equally between men and women (Mateyka, Rapino, and Landivar 2012: 15; Global Workplace Analytics and Flexjobs 2017: 9).

The merger of office and home in recent years has raised concerns about the erosion of boundaries, with work seeping into home life. Telecommuting's ability to lower overhead costs for businesses and increase worker happiness and productivity has promoted its acceptance among many employers (Rapoza 2013). For employees, the flexibility to set one's own work hours and the convenience of working at home also make it an attractive option. But these benefits may come at a cost: on average, telecommuting adds five to seven hours to the work week compared with working exclusively at the office. Telecommuters are also more apt to work on weekends, vacations, and when they are ill (Noonan and Glass 2012: 40, 45). While scholars have long disputed the ideal of the home as an isolated retreat from the wider world, the spatial integration of domestic and professional spheres makes it difficult for telecommuters to leave work behind.

Even so, telecommuters report being less stressed by working remotely, in part because they can avoid long commutes, which increase health risks, such as anxiety and obesity (Gajendran and Harrison 2007: 1528; MacMillan 2015). Yet as white-collar workers are thus improving their quality of life, low-wage employees are seeing their commutes grow ever longer. Many low-earning jobs, such as cleaning or security, cannot be done remotely, and as housing costs rise in Europe and North America, low-income families are forced to relocate to urban peripheries (Tu 2015). The working poor thus spend more of their time on the road and away from family and home.

Rising housing costs are not only adding to the long commutes that keep low-income employees away from home. In the United States, they have also contributed to the dramatic increase in evictions in low-income communities. The majority of poor households that rent spend at least half of their income on housing costs, leaving them vulnerable to misfortunes, such as job loss or illness, which can make it impossible to pay their bills. Single mothers with young children are especially at risk. Evictions take a heavy psychological toll on children, who may have to change schools, and live with constant disruption and loss. But it also affects families and neighbourhoods, which grow increasingly fragmented socially, undermining informal networks of support (Desmond 2016: 298). As economic inequalities grow, a home nestled within a community has become an elusive dream for many poor citizens, even in the wealthiest of nations.

The essays in this volume explore the home's centrality to debates of the past century about our identities, resources, hopes, and anxieties as individuals and communities. They focus on developments in Western countries, while also considering broader global connections. To their analyses, the contributors bring the perspectives of their respective academic disciplines, spanning anthropology, architectural and design histories, gender studies, geography, history of science, religious studies, sociology, and urban history. Three shared interests nonetheless unite the authors' different approaches. The first is the acknowledgment that meanings of 'home' are complex and elusive. Accordingly, there is a commitment to interdisciplinary investigation and marshalling the insights of diverse fields. Finally, and reflecting broader trends in the humanities and social sciences, the physical materiality of the home – its objects, spaces, and layout – comes under close scrutiny. Across the essays, a rich and colourful mosaic emerges of a place that seems familiar but also strange and unexpected: the modern home.

CHAPTER ONE

The Meaning of Home: Defining Domesticity in the Modern Age

RACHEL HURDLEY

INTRODUCTION: SHELTER, FOOD, AND WARMTH?

Well, another thing that is important to me is my house. It gives me shelter and whenever if I was sleeping out with the stars probably I would get cold for one thing, and animals and ants would be crawling all over me.

—Scott, schoolchild in a homeless shelter
(Percy 2014: 25)

What does 'home' mean? What on earth does 'the meaning of home' mean? How is it possible to make any claims of meaning when, for Scott, his prime concern is survival; his parents are most important to him because they provide his means to live – food. For others, home is not a building, but a road island (Kiddey and Schofield 2011), a cup of tea and conversation (Hurdley 2013), or a (theoretically) mobile home (Hart et al. 2003; Richardson and Ryder 2012). For reasons ranging from trauma to tourism and extreme wealth, the modern notion of a single fixed abode is becoming detached from the 'idea of home' or 'dwelling' (Heidegger [1954] 1971; Rybczynski 1986; McIntyre, Williams, and McHugh 2006; Harrison and Taylor 2008). 'Mobility', 'globalization', and 'urbanization' constitute our twenty-first century zeitgeist (Urry 2007; Ritzer 2010; United Nations 2018). Amidst the effervescence of this networked

FIGURE 1.1: The homely porch, Eugene, Oregon. © Rachel Hurdley, by permission of Joan Haran and Gary Fleming.

human world, is there a still, quiet place where we can find the desired, longed for, remembered place called 'home'?

This volume covers a century of technological and social changes that have transformed everyday life in many parts of the world. The beginning of the period is marked by the Great Depression, rise of Hitler, foundation of the USSR and of the Independent Irish Free State, and early victories for Mao Zedong. There was famine in Russia, civil war in Spain, an abdication crisis in Britain, and the Salt Marches in India. The 'first wave' of feminism succeeded in gaining women's suffrage in many developed countries (although New Zealand women were the first to gain the right to vote in 1893). Tutankhamen's tomb was discovered, Lindbergh flew the Atlantic, the first 'talkie' played in cinemas, and the 'Charleston' swept the dance floors. The beginnings of slum clearance, subsidized housing, cheaper building costs, and home loans improved housing for both the poor and middling classes in North America, Britain, and other Western European nations (Green and Wachter 2005; Lowe 2011; Scott 2013). Towards the end of the period that concerns us, there is global economic depression, war, thousands fleeing state-supported torture and abuses of human rights, popular protests and democracies in crisis, terrorist attacks, epidemics, and starvation. In some areas of North America and Western Europe, houses, even whole streets or villages, can be bought for less than the price of a coffee. Others are experiencing housing shortages and booms so extreme that adults are living with their parents or on friends' sofas, while families live in emergency accommodation. And yet, transformations in technologies, in the lives of many women, and in migrations and personal travel have made this world seemingly unrecognizable from that 'old' world balancing between the two World Wars, before global power tilted from Western Europe to the United States (de Grazia 2006). And now, the balance of power is shifting again, poised between the United States, China, other emerging economies, and global corporations (Mahbubani 2013).

Is it possible to understand what home means to others across such disparate places, times, and social worlds? To encompass continuities and changes through one year in one street, let alone a century across the world, would fill a book (Miller 2008). This chapter will focus on one central argument: culture – meaning-making – defines what matters, and therefore who matters. Who makes the 'meaning of home' is a critical question, since 'home' is so closely connected to 'identity'. Until research into 'the meaning of home' began in the last quarter of the twentieth century, there were no rigorous contemporaneous studies of the symbolic importance of whatever 'home' is. And the various histories of house, home, and dwelling are subject to constant revision and debate, since these can never be statements, but rather contributions to an argument.

THE INVENTION OF 'THE MEANING OF HOME'

Think of it: *heym*   and   *home*   the meaning
the same   of course   exactly
but the shift   in vowel   was the ocean
in which I drowned.

—Excerpt from 'Fradel Schtok' by Irena Klepfisz
(in *A Few Words in the Mother Tongue*, 1990: 228.
By permission of the author)

The 'cult of domesticity' was a nineteenth-century invention, coinciding with first-wave feminism. This ideology separated the feminine, sacred space of home from the male industrializing, public sphere, at least in terms of cultural representations and expectations. Women's everyday lives changed in the inter-war period, with new domestic technologies and (for some) the 'servant problem' altering household routines and roles. The Second World War (and to a limited extent, the First) led to women taking up unfamiliar 'male' work outside the home. Following the war effort, home and family were inextricably connected with peacetime and patriotism, with women – now cast as 'consumers' – once again expected to be 'homemakers' (Cohen 2003). Second-wave feminists, such as Betty Friedan (1963), reacted to this renewed 'cult of domesticity' by challenging cultural, legal, economic, and political patriarchies, at least for white heterosexual women in developed countries. By the 1970s, feminist academics were doing research into domestic labor, consumption, and architecture as serious political, economic, and social concerns (Oakley 1974; André 1981; Matrix 1984). At the same time, 'the meaning of home' became a topic for academic study (Hayward 1975). And now, in the early 2020s, the latest 'new domesticity' (Matchar 2013) is flourishing, while social media such as Pinterest offer new opportunities for sharing 'dream homes' and stimulating décor envy (Turner 2017).

'Home' is imbued with cultural, social, and affective meanings, holding a special place in the individual and popular imagination, memory, and everyday life. Until recently, though, the study of housing in developed countries focused primarily on policy, economics, and architecture. Geoffrey Hayward (1975) is attributed with producing the first list of meanings of 'home': physical structure; territory; locus in space; self and self-identity; and social and cultural unit. In the late 1980s, two academics instigated a distinct Housing Studies cross-disciplinary topic, considering the house as a crucial space of interaction (Saunders and Williams 1988). Home was not just bricks and mortar, but a place for building and maintaining social relations and meanings. They drew on Anthony Giddens' (1984) conception of locale. This interest in the meaning of home and its place in the constitution and maintenance of identity, social, family, and gender relations came, therefore, at a time when new approaches to modernity were coming to the fore.

In what is regarded as a key contribution, Carole Després (1991) produced a critical review of academic literature on the home for the period 1974 to 1989. From her examination of these studies, she identified categories of meaning which encompassed both the psychological and social/cultural. Peter Somerville went on to state that sociological research had shown a recurrent set of meanings of the home around family life: 'shelter, hearth, heart, privacy, roots, abode and (possibly) paradise' (1992: 532). However, he later argued that the categories of meaning are not generated by any particular body of theory, and are thus arbitrary (1997), while Jeanne Moore (2000) proposed that the generation of lists of meanings by previous studies has been of only limited value. She suggested a greater contextual understanding and an emphasis on culture and symbolism for future study of the home.

Many disciplines have undertaken research on the home over the last four decades (Benjamin, Stea, and Saile 1995; Moore 2000; Mallett 2004; Blunt and Dowling 2006). There have been tensions in approaches towards house and home, which have tended to revolve either around large-scale, policy-based quantitative analysis or small-scale, qualitative study. However, ethnographically influenced research into the meanings of home (an understanding of 'home' as more than four walls and a roof) has broadened attitudes to tenure and property (Saunders 1989). Critiques of housing, transport, and social policy have demonstrated the often flawed social engineering and/or profit motives driving house-building and planning, such as 1930s suburbia and the move to small kitchens and domestic electricity (Oliver, Davis, and Bentley 1981; Ravetz and Turkington 1995), and the political economy of the car (Ingrassia 2013). Furthermore, just as non-Western houses had been scrutinized for decades (Bourdieu 1990; Oliver 1976, 2003), anthropology increasingly turned towards familiar cultures of the 'West' to argue that nothing in the 'Western' house should be taken for granted (Strathern 1987; Cieraad 1999; Miller 2001). 'Home' in Western post-industrial societies is entangled with global networks of agribusiness, industry, and communications, increasingly complex relations between globalizing homogeneity and local processes of differentiation, as well as with debates on what exactly constitutes 'the West' (Kumar 2009).

Recent sociological and historical research focuses on the everyday, looking for meaning in what people do, rather than treating home and family as structures or fixed institutions (Morgan 2011). The Museum of the Home in London, St Fagans National Museum of History in Cardiff, the DDR Museum in Berlin, and exhibitions such as 'Within these Walls' at the Smithsonian in Washington, DC, all explore this interest into national cultural domains. Studies into the everyday and, in particular, the lives of women, have contributed to the proliferation of books, papers, magazines, television programmes, and social media platforms engaging with what home means.

Home is perhaps most meaningful when it is lost or faraway. Even the commonly used term in English, *nostalgia*, derives from ancient Greek epics about *Nostoi*, the returns or homecomings of Greek heroes, such as Odysseus after the Trojan War, through many *algea* (pains). Related both to melancholy and homesickness as recognized medical conditions by seventeenth-century European doctors, nostalgia is now considered a late modern pathology (Boym 2008). In many languages, words roughly equivalent to homesickness, of uprootedness, and/or loss are untranslatable, emphasizing the deeply cultural, embodied experience of home and its absence: *dépaysement*; *heimweh*; *hiraeth*; *saudade*; *toska*. Since home-sickness requires home to be always deferred, is 'home' a space, waiting for boundaries and contents to lend it fleeting meaning?

And has it been forever ephemeral, with the growing post-Enlightenment status of the personal, intimate, of the ordinary and everyday merely adding plangency to this paradox of home?

How can we root through all these variations to the meaning of home? Amid its complex links with macroeconomy, gender, heteronormativity, corporate influence, political economy, wars, and abuse, where is 'home'? Can home be defined by its absence or what it is not? On the cusp of the period covered in this volume, Freud wrote about the inextricably uncanny character of home:

> In general we are reminded that the word *heimlich* is not unambiguous, but belongs to two sets of ideas, which without being contradictory are yet very different: on the one hand, it means that which is familiar and congenial, and on the other, that which is concealed and kept out of sight . . . Thus *heimlich* is a word the meaning of which develops . . . towards an ambivalence, until it finally coincides with its opposite, *unheimlich* . . . In this case, too, the *unheimlich* is what was once *heimisch*, homelike, familiar; the prefix 'un' is the token of repression.
>
> —Freud [1919] 2003: 4–5

Homeliness thus contains within it the strange, hidden, unfamiliar – even dangerous. Freud recounts tales of unnerving coincidences, ghosts, hauntings, and maleficent creatures, which enthral and horrify. A sudden chill, bumps in the night, and the odd shadows cast by ordinary household objects can throw the familiar place of home into that other realm of childhood fears and unspoken thoughts. A century later, house buyers and estate agents talk of the 'character' or 'atmosphere' of a house in terms of basic binaries: warm/cold, light/dark. In a study I conducted about the meaning of home, people spoke of how a house 'felt' (Hurdley 2013). 'Homely' usually equated with 'warm' and 'gleaming'; unhomely with 'cold', 'dark', and 'dusty nooks'. There was also a strong analogy, or homology, with 'mother' or 'grandmother' (not always positive). For example, one woman swore never to have a mantelpiece like her mother's, displaying untouchable breakable ornaments, 'mother's precious things'. Mother's house can be fragile, unhomely, in other ways. More mundane than repressed desires and hidden terrors is the practice of domestic violence. Concealed, often suffered silently, abuse marks the lives of one in three women globally, and is often witnessed by children (WHO 2017). The 'meaning of home' may conjure dream homes and childhoods, but its emergence as a topic for research at the same time as the recovery of silenced and hidden histories demands that we move beyond nostalgia. The next section will look at domestic technologies to demonstrate how little relation they have to technological developments, but rather are underpinned by political economy and culture.

TECHNOLOGY, TOAST AND FROZEN PEAS

I should like to let you know how important sliced bread is to the morale and saneness of a household. My husband and four children are all in a rush during and after breakfast. Without ready-sliced bread I must do the slicing for toast – two pieces for each one – that's ten. For their lunches I must cut by hand at least twenty slices, for two sandwiches apiece. Afterward I make my own toast. Twenty-two slices of bread to be cut in a hurry!

—Forrester 1943

Following a ban on sliced bread as a wartime conservation measure, this letter appeared in the *New York Times* from a distraught housewife. Six weeks later, on 8 March 1943, the ban was rescinded. Sliced bread had become an essential time-saving measure in the space of only fifteen years (as had pop-up toasters), and is now the paradigm for brilliant inventions. A slice of toast or a peanut butter sandwich are easy food even children can make for themselves if they are home alone and need a quick snack. But these – the first convenience foods – are part of a complex history of social change over the inter-war period. Broadly speaking, this was a process of widening access to goods and technologies, together with mass media, communication, and transport.

In November 1920, the first commercial station broadcast live results of the United States presidential election. Six years later, radio signals reached almost the whole country. 'No other event of 1920 would have more of an effect on the future than the birth of radio, which was in turn the birth of American mass media' (Burns 2016). In the same decade, Clarence Birdseye developed the methods of freezing fish he had learnt from the Inuit into a factory process (Kurlansky 2012), and a bakery in Chillicothe, Missouri, sold the first machine-wrapped and machine-sliced loaf of bread (Bobrow-Strain 2012). By 1929, 60 percent of American families owned a car (Parissien 2013); by 1946, the same proportion owned a telephone, although this growth in use occurred mainly in cities (Cumo 2007: 95). Mass production of modern refrigerators began in earnest after the Second World War. By 1950, more than 80 percent of American farms and more than 90 percent of urban homes had one (Nagengast and Meckler 1994). In 1928, Alexander Fleming discovered penicillin. Once mass production became possible, from 1945 onwards, it transformed our world (Bud 2009).

After the Second World War, the 'functionalist' paradigm in social science (Murdock 1949; Parsons and Bales 1956; Parsons 1959) emphasized a shift from the household as a site of production to one of consumption. This further separated the public male realm of work from the private, domestic space of the 'consumer' housewife (Giles 2004), as if the home were detached from the social, economic, and cultural capitals associated with production. Since the late twentieth century, however, cultural histories of domestic technologies

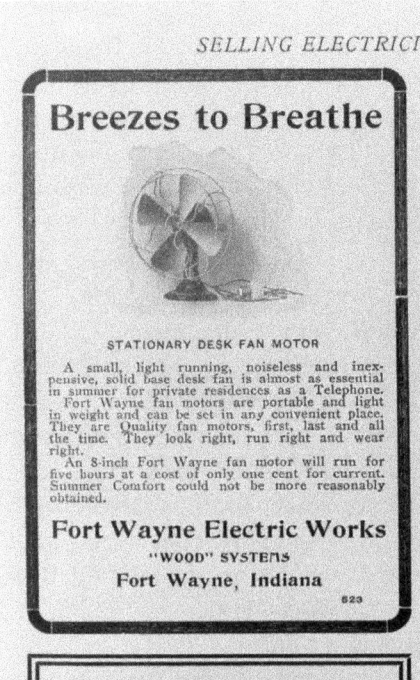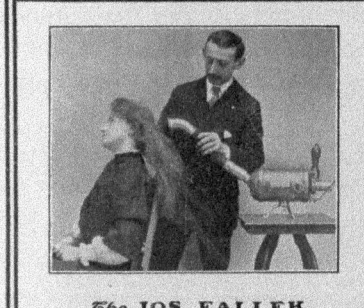

FIGURE 1.2: An advertisement page from *Selling Electricity* (New York: McGraw-Hill, May 1907) showing the uses of electricity and its products. Library of Congress, Washington, DC, reproduction no. LC-USZ62-110407.

have revised this perspective, demonstrating how machines, cleaning products, convenience foods, and personal hygiene items have not simply reflected but also shaped gender, class, and cultural identities. The appearance of kitchen goods changed with the loss of domestic servants, from a factory 'look' to a new smooth aesthetic to attract buyer-users (Forty 1986). At the same time, the 'cult of domesticity' that flourished in the nineteenth century was turning more towards industrial notions of efficiency, such as Taylorism and pseudo-medical attitudes towards cleanliness (Lupton and Miller 1992).

Although people may have been consuming domestic goods, they did not always buy the meanings attached to them; through usage, they sometimes produced altogether different meanings. The telephone, which initially spread in cities and was marketed to business users, quickly became dominated by women at home and teenage offspring. Men and people over seventy-five years of age were the least frequent users (Cumo 2007: 95). Consumers took possession of the telephone, regardless of its initial purpose, as it became a vital means for women to talk with friends and relatives, even though the (male) industry initially slighted this use as 'trivial gossip' (Fischer 1994). Richard John, in his book tracing the history of the telegraph and telephone systems in the United States, defines naturalization as the process by which 'the network was depoliticized through the constant repetition of the seductive dogma that existing institutional arrangements were rooted in technology and economics rather than politics and culture' (2010: 7). This resonates with Judy Wajcman's (2013) argument about the success of other household technologies. For example, the gas-powered refrigerator, predominant in the 1920s, was replaced by electric models in the United States due to aggressive investment, marketing, and government lobbying by General Electric and other corporations, which collaborated to push gas fridges out of history. In 1935, a technicolour film starred an electric kitchen, including an electric refrigerator, in a romantic comedy with Hollywood stars that was also a lengthy commercial (Cowan 1985: 210). The reason we have refrigerators that suddenly hum at all hours of the day and night, powered through costly electricity, with in-built obsolescence, rather than silent, cheap, and enduring gas fridges, is corporate profit, not consumers' benefit. In other words, people's comfort and convenience are not the principal reasons for adopting technologies: housework is not a private matter, but extends to social, cultural, economic, and political processes far beyond the front door.

Domestic work continues to be gendered through colour and appearance, such as black-box 'masculine' artefacts (for example, the all-in-one remote control) and white goods, like the washing machine (Kirkham 1996). After the cultural figure of the housewife finally became unmarketable in the 1990s, the 'busy mom' entered popular culture through endless marketing of, in particular, cleanliness and home-cooking to women who worked *and* looked after their families in clean houses (Neuhaus 2011). Although media images may now focus on lifestyle and the home as a site of leisure, to arrange exactly as we choose, the pressure is on to do precisely that: the effortful exercise of choice. As the influential cultural analyses of Pierre Bourdieu demonstrated (1984), people define themselves not only by what they have and do, aligning themselves with those who share their cultural, social, and economic characteristics, but also through distinction from those who do not. Taste and choice are, Bourdieu argued, for the bourgeoisie. Those on the margins either cannot exercise choice or, if they do, choose cheapness rather than quality. Frozen food and cheap white sliced bread are now the choice – or necessity – of those who lack not only economic but also cultural capital, as opposed to fresh vegetables and organic sourdough. Toasters are fraught with meaning; a 'white good' is, ideally, no longer white, but coordinated in a pastel or bold hue to match other status artefacts such as the 'American' fridge (as it is called in Europe), the food processor (to indicate home-baking, soup-making, juicing and any other current trend), and the latest style of coffee maker.

Ethnicity has entered the 'working mother' advertising paradigm, and queer and masculine domesticities are now receiving more academic attention (Pilkey, Scicluna, and Gorman-Murray 2015; Gavanas 2004). Despite this, middle-class women remain the focus; women – especially mothers – must still be as fragrant as their houses, providing care and up-to-date 'good food' for their families. Cleanliness, morality, class, nation of origin, and (to some extent) ethnicity are particularly closely connected, with the figures of 'chavmum', 'benefit queen', and 'smelly immigrant' standing in opposition to the busy working mother (Tyler 2008; Hancock 2004; Manalansan 2006). The feelings they arouse are visceral, with 'disgust' at their centre, demonstrating the way in which intersections of social inequality are reworked as moral deficiency.

Maintaining the cultural pretence that the home is a woman's domain is hard work. The 'ideal' Anglo-American single family home, with two cars and every imaginable appliance, may seem like the supreme realm of privacy, individual choice, and freedom. Yet the promoters of Taylorism and functionalism – essential components of modernist design – did not acknowledge the fatal flaw in their house and household efficiency plans. The best way to 'save labor' is to share goods and services, such as the laundry and the car. Suburbs distance consumers from goods and services, making individuals expend more effort and car ownership a requirement. Although cars were seen as emancipating women (Seiler 2009), their autonomy also made more work, with the rise of self-service super- and hypermarkets, rising expectations for 'soccer moms' to ferry children to numerous afterschool activities, and the marginalization of ex-urban bus services. As understandings of consumption have become increasingly nuanced (Miller 1995a), the old dualistic approach of production/consumption is now perceived as a network of complex processes and practices (Evans 2014). Requiring water, road, communications, and power networks, the house is a

FIGURE 1.3: Suburban dwellings, old and new, in Vanves, southwest of Paris, France, 2016. F. Lamiot via Wikimedia.org (Creative Commons).

greedy consumer, while modern expectations of cleanliness, freshness, privacy, perfection, and speed produce ever higher volumes of waste.

These escalating cultural expectations perversely parallel the growing number of people who lack adequate housing and sanitation (Laven 2014). Such differences materialize global social and wealth inequalities, which have never been greater (Piketty 2014). The physical labor from which domestic technologies have saved so many continues in developing countries (Lebergott 2014). Similarly, domestic goddesses (and gods) import consumables from, and export waste to, developing nations, where the dirty work is far away from clean, comfortable homes. In contrast to the invisibility of sweating bodies and vast rubbish dumps (Waste Atlas Collective 2014), global cultural hybridity is spectacularized in Western domestic aesthetics and cooking. Berber rugs are to be found in Ikea, Ganesh elephants on mantelpieces, and 'colonial' style houses in New England. With futon sofa beds in home offices, Fiji water in the refrigerator, and Bollywood on the smartphone, European and North American people sleep, eat, and relax in ways their ancestors would never have imagined. Department stores and museums, show homes, and various media bring it all to us. Yet the search for authenticity is stronger than ever, now that everything is available everywhere, for a price.

COFFEE CUPS AND FIREPLACES: WHY SMALL THINGS MATTER

> Neither the life of an individual nor the history of a society can be understood without understanding both.
>
> —Mills 1959: 3

Although the built house itself carries meanings, since location and style matter, it is the things and activities within that are the most powerful symbols of identity. Despite the growing capacity of technology to dematerialize the cumbersome stuff and laborious activities of everyday life, they persist. Through material culture and mundane domestic life, home becomes more than the sum of its functional parts. The idea that things have complex biographies is embedded in Western cultural history (Kopytoff 1986). Things are temporal curios, for they stay the same, whilst their meanings can change over time and in different spatial and cultural contexts. How they are used is as important as their appearance and form. Witold Rybczynski, beginning with a discussion of the chair, demonstrates how the relatively recent ideas of domesticity, privacy, and comfort are characterized by the uses, technologies, and positioning of furniture. As he comments, domesticity was 'an idea in which technology was a distinctly secondary consideration' (1986: vii).

In the next section, our focus on the cultural history of home turns towards fictional representation from novels published at the beginning of this 'modern' era: Agatha Christie's first novel, *The Mysterious Affair at Styles* and Sinclair Lewis's *Main Street*. In their different ways, these are both artefacts of their time, and contemporary cultural icons, much like the 'period pieces' that adorn modern homes. Think of a laundry mangle in a backyard or a reclaimed fireplace. An artefact that was ordinary in its original setting thus becomes extraordinary, and in turn stops us taking twenty-first-century homes for granted.

What is notable in both novels is the way plotlines and themes rely on ordinary household objects, taken-for-granted roles, and routines. In Christie's detective story, a woman is found dead in her bed, the remains of her bedtime cocoa on the dressing table.

> 'But now a fresh dilemma arises . . . Where can he hide this terrible slip of paper? . . . There are no means of destroying it; and he dare not keep it. He looks round, and he sees – what do you think, mon ami?'
>
> I shook my head.
>
> 'In a moment, he has torn the letter into long thin strips, and rolling them up into spills he thrusts them hurriedly in amongst the other spills in the vase on the mantelpiece.'
>
> I uttered an exclamation.

'No one would think of looking there,' Poirot continued. 'And he will be able, at his leisure, to come back and destroy this solitary piece of evidence against him.'

'Then, all the time, it was in the spill vase in Mrs. Inglethorp's bedroom, under our very noses?' I cried.

Poirot nodded.

—Christie (1920, ch. 13)

Thus began the 'golden age' of detective novels, set in an English country house, where, despite the exigencies of the First World War, servants gardened, cooked, cleaned, and served tea. Social classes and roles are clear. Hercule Poirot, a retired Belgian detective, makes his first appearance. Modelled on Belgian refugees Christie met in her home town of Torquay (Christie and Curran 2011), he stayed, unlike so many of his non-fictional compatriots, and continues to hold a special place in British cultural life, onscreen, in radio plays, and in books. Part of his appeal is the era his stories conjure, even up to his final appearance in the 1970s, from 1920s arts and crafts cottages, through 1930s streamlined modernist apartments, colonial Indian bungalows, ravishing hotels, and luxurious train compartments. Nostalgia for times that never were, except for the privileged few, and places that could not be, but for the constant behind-the-scenes work of so many, pulls hard at the twenty-first-century imagination. The material world that Christie creates is crucial, since it is that which provides the evidence for identifying how, why, and by whom the crime was perpetrated. In this case, the evidence includes a scrap of a green Women's Land Army armlet, a cut bell-wire, a charred paper in the fireplace, and strips of a letter concealed on the mantelpiece among fire-lighting spills. A bell to summon servants, women farm workers replacing men at war, and a bedroom heated by an open fire: as anthropologist Clifford Geertz stated, 'Small facts speak to large issues . . .' (1973: 23). These little things identify the time and the place in which they were situated: material marks of social class and gender relations, and telling, in a different way, of technological development.

To illuminate this last point, let us turn to a novel published in the same year on the other side of the Atlantic: Sinclair Lewis's (1920) *Main Street*, whose heroine, Carol Kennicott, struggles to adapt to small-town married life. Her arrival is celebrated with a party:

They did not bore Carol. They frightened her. She panted, 'They will be cordial to me, because my man belongs to their tribe. God help me if I were an outsider!'

Smiling as changelessly as an ivory figurine she sat quiescent, avoiding thought, glancing about the living-room and hall, noting their betrayal of unimaginative commercial prosperity. Kennicott [her husband] said, 'Dandy interior, eh? My idea of how a place ought to be furnished. Modern.' She looked polite, and observed the oiled floors, hard-wood staircase, unused fireplace with tiles which resembled brown linoleum, cut-glass vases standing upon doilies, and the barred, shut, forbidding unit bookcases that were half filled with swashbuckler novels and unread-looking sets of Dickens, Kipling, O. Henry, and Elbert Hubbard.

...

They fell upon the food – chicken sandwiches, maple cake, drug-store ice cream. Even when the food was gone they remained cheerful. They could go home, any time now, and go to bed!

—Lewis (1920, ch. IV)

For Carol, the food is small-town tedium; the newly built house a tasteless mixture of crass modernization, conservative genteelness, and cultural ignorance. Her home in Gopher Prairie and the people, like Main Street itself, are fashioned by her into a mass of backward ugliness requiring progressive 'reform'. Lewis's portrait of the politics of culture, gender, and class are particularly acute, represented through domestic practices such as eating, leisure, and housekeeping, and by the dwellings themselves. Carol aligns herself with 'outsiders' – immigrants, farm workers, and her servant – but eventually settles into Gopher Prairie and motherhood.

At six, when the light faltered in as through ground glass and bleakly identified the chairs as gray rectangles, she heard his step on the porch; heard him at the furnace: the rattle of shaking the grate, the slow grinding removal of ashes, the shovel thrust into the coal-bin, the abrupt clatter of the coal as it flew into the fire-box, the fussy regulation of drafts—the daily sounds of a Gopher Prairie life, now first appealing to her as something brave and enduring, many-colored and free.

—Lewis (1920, ch. XV)

For historian Glenna Matthews, Carol Kennicott exemplifies 'what Betty Friedan would call "the problem that has no name", that is, the pervasive emptiness of the middle-class housewife's life' as the home became increasingly associated in the 1920s with leisure and consumption, so different from the pre-war era (1987: 172). Initially raging at the conventions of small-town life, Carol learns her lesson and accepts the gendered routines of home, as her preference for a blazing fire is replaced by the ambient warmth of the furnace, emblematic of easy comfort rather than wild romance.

In a foundational study sixty years later, two American researchers explored the acquisition, possession, and disposal of things, and how violent dislikes and attachments pass as people age:

> Like some strange race of cultural gastropods, people build homes out of their own essence, shells to shelter their personality. But then, these symbolic projections react on their creators, in turn shaping the selves they are.
>
> —Csikszentmihalyi and Rochberg-Halton 1981: 138

Like Carol, younger people in their study treated domestic material culture as a means to display and perform identity. With age came a more transcendent approach to the world of objects. Moreover, as Csikszentmihalyi and Rochberg-Halton observe, connections between the meaning of home, family identity, and memory, particularly as these are manifested in domestic artefacts, are never one-way processes of people imposing meaning on their possessions. The next section will examine such 'stuff' in detail, drawing on a study I conducted exploring what people put on their mantelpieces, window sills, and other display spaces at home. Think of 'what children have to look at', as a child psychiatrist, John, pointed out in my fieldwork. The environments where they are fed, sleep, wake up, and play form their earliest ideas of what a 'normal' home is. Bourdieu's cultural analysis led to his conclusion that 'nothing, perhaps, more directly depends on early learning, especially the learning which takes place without any express intention to teach, than the dispositions and knowledge that are invested in clothing, furnishing and cooking . . .' (1984: 78–79).

WHAT HAVE WE BECOME? THE HEAVINESS OF HOME

> One theme underlying my method of tidying is transforming the home into a sacred space, a power spot filled with pure energy. A comfortable environment, a space that feels good to be in, a place where you can relax – these are traits that make a home a power spot. Would you rather live in a home like this or in one that resembles a storage shed? The answer, I hope, is obvious.
>
> —Kondo 2015: 43

In the mantelpiece study, it was notable how some people built up an accretion of objects over time – the kitsch souvenir, rather nice porcelain, pine cones, and invitations jostling together in a fine haze of dust. While this might have looked like a near-accidental accumulation of things, such *bricolage* was as painstakingly structured as more consciously curated collections, with perhaps the pure symmetry of candlesticks and vases on the mantelpiece, the carriage clock ticking fast or slow at the centre. Not just the overall form of the display mattered, but also its components and their particular arrangement. Although not everyone sharing a home might care about the display, that could in itself be a cause for conflict, as could differences in opinion. Similarly, a visitor may

FIGURE 1.4: Mantelpiece in a 1992 detached house in the village of Efail Isaf in Wales, UK. © Rachel Hurdley, by kind permission of Sioned Geraint.

share judgements of taste with their hosts, or, if not, find the variation telling, in terms of taste, class, and culture.

Let us look at some of the questions that a seemingly simple mantelpiece display raises. What kind of candlesticks are on that mantelpiece: Georgian or Primark? Are there three more carriage clocks in the attic: Dad's retirement present, the wedding gift, the heirloom from Auntie Gladys? Are the mementoes that sit in pride of place carefully chosen for their beauty, utility, or rather for remembrance of the giver? For some, the ugliness of a gift matters less than the heart's jump of love for the giver. And sometimes, there's a good story to tell about that tarry piece of ship's rope, papier-mâché owl, or rusty lamp. Particular sorts of stories, which remake us as adventurers, loving parents, or really working class because grandpa was a miner. All too often, the neat little site above the gas fire or under the flat screen television gets cluttered. Calendars of social ritual: Christmas, Diwali, Valentine's Day, Father's Day (for some); the tempo of lives – births, marriages, civil partnerships, deaths; family narratives; displays of cultural belonging proliferate. Then there is the card to be posted, the television remote, the coffee cup that leaves a ring. Sometimes, too, things take over, because of the stories that cling to them. A parent dies, and the house must be cleared, but memories cannot be cast out as easily as that old armchair. The paintings seen so often, they barely trouble the eye, suddenly spring out from the wall, bringing back the feel, the smell of childhood. And things that seemed not to matter now matter so much, because they bring back what would otherwise be forgotten. They are the stuff of memory. And even though memory might seem to be deeply personal, houses are materials of collective cultural memory and therefore expressive of identity, as we shall see.

Several participants in the mantelpiece study were women who lived in pre-1920 houses, none of which had all of their original fireplaces. A schoolteacher, Rhian, married to an accountant, commented that it was 'funny' that all their friends lived in old houses like theirs. Niki, who visited her friends in new houses, spoke of the 'silliness' of mantelpieces on their flat walls, rather than on an 'authentic' chimney breast. Yet all of these participants had either replaced the mantelpieces in their homes with reproductions and ones that 'looked authentic', as Rhian said, or knew that the mantelpieces were not original to the house before they moved in. However, Niki attached the 'silliness' to the house not the person. When they spoke of the 'other' – a visitor – casting their eyes over the things displayed on the mantelpiece or another space, they added that this gaze did not worry them at all. Therefore, there was hidden labor behind this relaxed attitude, and also to keeping 'silliness' away from anomalous behaviours, such as friends' lapses in taste, or their own purchases to achieve a 'look'. Some, such as Bryony, were concerned that the 'focal point' of the mantelpiece was clean, uncluttered, and had appropriate display objects on show for visitors. The vet's appointment card was on a side shelf, visible enough to remind Bryony, but not 'on show'. Thus, there is an etiquette to looking: unseen boundaries allow those flanking shelves to remain culturally invisible, in the same way that other anomalies are skimmed over.

Many informants cast themselves as this 'other', invoking friends' and relatives' houses to support a point they might be making, such as Niki referring to the 'snob value' of wedding invitations on display, in self-mockery of middle-class 'belonging' behaviours. Mary had visited a friend in a new place with a big display cabinet, who 'did not understand' why none of her friends liked it. However, when it came to talking about people in modern houses who had mantelpieces, and people who removed or restored mantelpieces in old houses, none of the informants directly criticized these 'others' who had done this. Barbara called it a matter of 'personal taste' and another casually called the mantelpiece 'just a nice feature'. Janet commented:

> It's something that just happens isn't it, you don't think, you know I sort of arrange those things on there and think that looks nice, and I thought well that looks nice, I don't know really, you don't sort of do it on purpose.

This idea of accretion over time was a particularly middle-class attitude. One woman, a senior academic, said the mantelpiece would always be cluttered:

> because we both just tend to put things up there . . . every shelf in the house is absolutely jammed with stuff and the attic is lined with shelving and every shelf in the attic is absolutely jammed with stuff. It's double and triple stacked, all the shelves . . .

In contrast to this attitude that such mantelpiece displays 'just happen' as people 'just tend' to place things, one participant, Rita, was explicit about her hard work in arranging her domestic environment, and particularly in 'trying to put back everything what I can' in the house (a 1920s semi-detached villa). She will 'never, never, no, never' change them, and is pleased to have restored the house from her husband's modernizing, who ripped out the fireplaces when the central heating was installed. Having lived in only two houses, she has never lived in a house without a mantelpiece, and has strong views about modern houses, saying they 'don't mean anything'. She equates the absence of a mantelpiece with modern houses, even though she backs this up with a story about a friend who lives in a modern house with a mantelpiece:

> She's got a fireplace with a stone surround and there's a mantelpiece and there's little bits of china . . . And I think there's a cocktail cabinet, a three-piece suite and two chairs. It's a huge dining room. It's nothing. The fireplace is nice there. I'll grant you that. But it, it's got nothing.

It is clear that the friend has all the material goods a house requires, that a person requires. All the conventional stuff of domesticity is there. Yet Rita negates this matter, absents it, because it is meaningless to her. In the context of the interview, it could be inferred that meaning for her was something that had to be earned over time, in terms of the age of the house and the age of the object, and also for her, the provenance of the object, as an inheritance and with a known narrative attached that has also been passed down. New houses and modernized old houses have no meaning, since they are not part of her culture. Her efforts 'trying to put everything back in', to regain what was lost, is a battle for meaning, for culture.

The extent to which this little place matters is elicited when control over space is under threat or lost. Llinos used to live in Royal Air Force housing:

> It was married quarters so you were given a specific residence and the fireplaces were terrible because they just had horrible, you know, electric fires, no character at all . . . Just put plants or something you know, just to get rid of it.

DEFINING DOMESTICITY IN THE MODERN AGE

FIGURE 1.5: Mantelpiece in a 1910 terraced house in the town of Pontypridd, Wales, UK. © Rachel Hurdley, by kind permission of Bethan Mason and Richard Reast.

Rowena, a wealthy woman who moved house frequently due to her husband's work was explicit about the need to make a house hers through displaying ornaments, even though many of their possessions had moved from house to house in boxes. In a new 'executive' house constructed by a large national housebuilder, she is horrified to see that the mantelpiece is barely an outline of the 'living flame' gas fire

> Because the ledge is so tiny, what on earth are you supposed to do with that? Is it because, whoever designed [it] thought that it didn't need to have anything sitting on it? But, as I say, I've lived in a hell of a lot of houses, and the mantelpiece has always been somewhere to put something, because the fireplace is always in the centre of the room. So when you walk into a room, the first thing you look at, whether you like it or not, is the fireplace . . . Because, you get a situation otherwise where you've got this thumping big black fireplace in this modern house, and how on earth are you ever supposed to personalize it? So is the intention to make it a visual thing in the room, and in which case, why should that be imposed on the person living in the house?

The imposition of a focal point dominates not just the visual; it is multi-sensorial and embodied. Mary, whose husband commissioned a stone fireplace for their elegant 1920s house, asks:

> ... what would I put there instead? Something cold and drab ... I don't know. You see I notice when they advertise hotels and olde worlde ones, they've always got the big log fires, haven't they? ... It's a fashion you've got to pay for. ... So they must think people like them still.

Although they now have only a moveable electric fire to put in the fireplace, it remains a warm, vibrant place. She justifies her liking for fireplaces by invoking hotels, which Mary Douglas considered a 'nonhome' since they follow 'criteria of cost efficiency', whereas a home is not a 'monetary economy' but a 'collective good' (1995: 263, 271). Yet the sensorial is also commodifiable.

As I mentioned earlier in the chapter, homeliness is equated with warmth, and, in this study, the mantelpiece was a metonym for the fire, the hearth, in houses where fires were rarely or never lit. As the literal *focus* (Latin for hearth and, by extension, the household gods, family and nation) of the home, the mantelpiece, where social rituals, biography, family history, and ephemera jostle, or where carefully chosen artefacts are very deliberately displayed, is the home in microcosm. My research supported Douglas's observation that 'home starts by bringing some space under control' (1995: 269). It seemed that whoever was 'in charge' of the display on the mantelpiece also organized spatial and temporal division in the home. This was almost always women, although in the case of a lesbian couple, one partner's taste was predominant, while a father who had renovated the family's 1900s house had also taken charge of the ornaments, since he was also an antiques dealer. In rental properties, where there is supposedly no one person responsible for the décor, the battle for space can become particularly fraught. In one case, an interviewee's deliberate placing of an ugly model building – a gift from her sister – on the mantelpiece was a declaration of war with a housemate that escalated, alarmingly, to the kitchen knives. Even Rhian, a middle-class woman in a large period property, was upset by the way her husband 'dumped' the contents of his pockets on the bedroom mantelpiece. Although she controlled the interior of the house, this brings home the way in which many women may have no space of their own in a family house, except for a bedside cabinet or wardrobe. The bedroom mantelpiece was what Rhian called 'my little space', and it was frequently transformed into a rubbish site by her husband. Her meaning was displaced by his.

The sense of possession, or desire for possession, is thus symbolic and affective. It is used in commerce to create a sense of homeliness, by coffee shops, bars, and hotels. At Christmas time in many countries, magazines and shop windows often show a mocked-up mantelpiece with traditional seasonal items. This particular event in the cultural calendar is central not only in memories of childhood homes but also in continuing routines of belonging, not only connecting individuals with family traditions, but also to national identity. In my study, British participants living on the eastern seaboard of the United States noted the seasonal rituals of 'Americanness', which included mantelpiece displays of 'family photo' Christmas cards, as well as extravaganzas on front lawns. As outsiders, their sensibility towards this was acute, seeing the familiar as strange. Like outsiders, the dispossessed are attuned to the 'symbolic power' of seemingly innocuous homely habits (Bourdieu 1991).

One study participant, Sarah, is Kenyan, but studying a university course in the UK. Her country was occupied by the British until 1963, and the 'symbolic violence' of cultural colonialism is clear in her narrative. The salience of the mantelpiece, as a metonym for the domestic fire, and, by extension, family and nation is especially sharp for her:

> So the mantelpiece now, collections that are on it start reminding us of where we came from, who are we as a people? . . . And you know our children who did grow up and didn't have any images of [our village in Kenya] . . . who just visit Grandma once in a while, our kids, we want to remind them of that. And when you bring in a new artefact from the village and they ask, 'What is that?', and you don't have an answer, that is such a sad question, Rachel, when you don't know anything about your culture. So what I'm trying to say is that the artefacts of our culture are starting to creep back because the shunning of the solutions from the West is starting to be reflected in the contents of the mantelpiece and the shape . . . Even Christmas cards now are made of banana leaves and natural things from our environment, sort of trying to draw back what we were losing. I don't know whether we've lost it, but it's coming back.

As Sarah's words show, the meaning of home in Kenya is changing, from one possessed by another culture, to one in which national history and culture can be regained. Although Bourdieu's work on taste focused on class, his arguments regarding cultural capital transpose to colonial rationalizations:

> [the] illusion of 'natural distinction' is ultimately based on the power of the dominant to impose, by their very existence, a definition of excellence which, being nothing other than their own way of existing, is bound to appear simultaneously as distinctive and different and therefore both arbitrary (since it is one among others) and perfectly necessary, absolute and natural.
> —Bourdieu 1984: 255

This concept of 'natural distinction', or 'naked taste', is laid bare when cultural definitions and distinctions are challenged. As Mary Douglas (1966) argued, 'dirt is matter out of place'. People judge others as similar to or different from themselves; cultural belonging is accomplished through belongings, be it a house, mantle, or Christmas card. 'Difference' is decided by the powerful; those who are displaced, or whose toehold on the margins of society is precarious – who are out of place – can be dismissed as different from 'us'. In this way, those who do not fit into or threaten cultural categories can be defined as 'dirty'. What Sarah's story shows is how, when power shifts, culture becomes mobile and these boundaries of belonging can be redrawn.

As I was reaching the end of writing this chapter, I left my homely office in my large university building to climb into my comfortable car and drive home to my family. The building supervisor helped me with my bags as it was raining, and we chatted companionably. I knew that my husband was cooking supper; my toddler would jump into my arms as my dogs swirled around, wagging their tails. Every day brings a joyous homecoming. Sitting between the fine stone pillars of the university building were two men, drinking beer and looking out at the downpour. The older man, Paul, was well-known by sight to my colleagues, a heroin addict who frequently takes shelter within the neo-classical colonnade. A greying duvet, a flattened cardboard box, a needle, a sandwich wrapper are among the things he sometimes leaves behind. He had been there all week, and was now entertaining a guest. If the two men were not moved on by university security, they would sleep there. I get into my car, and look around at the water bottles, biscuits, wipes, books, and crayons that my family leaves in its wake. A little home from home, rather than the precarious camp Paul and his friend have set up. Grabbing a waterproof picnic rug and a wide-brimmed hat, I approach the men. Paul flinches away, but his friend thanks me. 'How do you know we're homeless?' he asks. Thinking he is joking, I reply, 'Oh, there was just something about you . . .', managing to change my tone as I realize he is serious. He has moved so far beyond the bounds of what passes for ordinary, for 'homed', belonging to the mass of people who sleep in their beds within walls and behind locked doors, that it is my insight which seems extraordinary. At what moment did that reversal occur? He no longer recognizes himself, or his host as unordinary, in their unhomely stone settlement. Not a dwelling, since it could be uprooted any time, by them or those guarding the campus.

And at what moment did my reversal happen? In Britain, a house was once no more than a roof for the fire (Prizeman 1975), yet *home* now means longstanding walls, a roof, filled up with stuff. I do not want the lives of those men which brought them to here; nevertheless, they are companionable – just talking, and listening, sharing food and drink – in a way that makes anywhere homely. *Companion* is originally from Late Latin *com* – with and *panis* – bread: to break bread with. I am about to do the same thing with my family, after commuting alone in my car like millions of others, my smartphone wirelessly connected to the car, so I am always in touch. Houses are the ultimate status symbols; although the

FIGURE 1.6: Porch 'bedroom' of a homeless man, Cardiff, Wales. © Rachel Hurdley.

location and outward appearance are initially crucial for placing someone, it is the interior that provides guests the greatest opportunity for judging. In 1920, writers Christie and Lewis used domestic material cultures to enable judgements to be passed on criminality and on taste. The mantelpiece with its 'cut-glass vases standing upon doilies' and the cold fireplace tell Carol what sort of people she has found herself among. Poirot notices the fatal letter in the spill vase on the mantelpiece. The serving of food and drink is critical in both novels, as are beds and domestic heating. Shelter, warmth, and food are, for many of us, no longer about survival, as they were for Scott, whose words headed the chapter. All of these necessities are symbols and activities that are bound up with identity: a clean house, with tasteful décor and tasty food of good provenance. Warmth and light need no longer come from open fires, candles, and windows, yet the labor of cutting wood for stoves – and reading about it – is now a cult activity in Britain (Mytting 2015). So extreme is our reversal from treating houses as shelter, that woodburners and open fires add value to properties, just as woodcutting adds value to identities mired in the everyday of office work and sedentary screen-watching. Despite this effortful authenticity, the growing global demand for domestic power supplies means that the killing heat of Chernobyl is no antidote to the construction of more 'clean' energy nuclear power plants (Nuclear Energy Institute 2020). This idea of comfort, of warm, clean, light homes is cultural. And as a study of the history of American housing showed, while houses have been growing bigger since the post-war era, and the number of occupants smaller, happiness has not increased, and may even have declined (Lutz 2004). Has the sheer weight of stuff, of expectation, of judgement become too much? Those who are on the margins or altogether excluded from dominant circuits of taste through owning the 'wrong' stuff – or nothing except a few clothes and a rucksack – are treated as if they themselves were deficient as people (Skeggs and Wood 2009; Hurdley 2013).

A well-provisioned house, with perhaps more storage space off-site (Inside Self Storage International 2015; Greenbaum 2016) and display space for goods and possessions, is underpinned by cultural, economic, and social processes. But still, the unhoused individual, like Paul, is blamed, as being outside and unclean, in 'a state of moral disgrace' (Farrugia, Smyth, and Harrison 2016: 238). It is as if 'goods' and 'goodness' were connected: the person and the pantry. This prejudice against those who do not store up provision for the future is not purely economic (think of the fable of the ant and the grasshopper), but a moral economic judgement that admits neither compassion nor social explanations for individual difficulties. Has 'home' become too heavy with meanings, just as the house has become cluttered up with stuff, leading to the horrible irony that to become the sanctuary of collective Western nostalgia, all meaning and all that stuff must be emptied out, leaving a vacuum? To regain a meaning for home, must we become dispossessed?

CONCLUSION: MATTERS OF LIFE AND DEATH

> Far from the home becoming something as technical and impermanent as an appliance, the house has become an asset class, whose very permanence has allowed it in parts of the world to become a socially ruinous investment, as solid as ever, yet ever more melted into air. Instead of our being housed in bubbles, the monetary value of our housing continues to bubble ever more erratically. And instead of the modern human becoming a nomad, free to roam within their comfort shells, national walls appear to be growing higher again, with anti-immigrant politics on the rise in the wealthy nations and all the grim historical resonances that suggests.
>
> —Murphy 2016: 16

With the increasing popularity and cheapness of smartphones, more people can monitor their fitness, order groceries, and take 3D tours of houses while communicating through social media using a pocket-sized object (Ofcom 2015; Statista 2020). Mary Douglas's division between 'home' and 'hotel', made less than thirty years ago, is now blurring as Airbnb threatens conventional accommodation businesses in some cities (Bellafante 2016). The world, it seems, is on the move, as are everyday experiences of home, family, food, health, and leisure. The number of international migrants is growing annually, with 272 million in 2019 living in countries where they were not born (United Nations 2019). Through global communication and the web, diverse, multi-sited diasporic communities are connected in ways that no longer require physical proximity. Diasporic concepts such as the 'inter-domestic domain' and 'cosmonation' emphasize connectedness across distance (Werbner 1990; Faber and Nielsen 2016; Laguerre 2016).

However, forced migrations, with loss or destruction of property and possessions and social networks, accentuate how any displacement results in many different processes of adaptation, including ambivalent attitudes towards home and family in nations of origin (Crepeau et al. 2006). Losing a material house results in a sense of constant temporariness, ambiguity, and in-betweenness, producing a 'home' whose absent presence presses hard on the imaginations even of subsequent generations, something that has been called *'un/home'* (Chawla 2014: 10), a state that also defines the 'messy identities' South Asians feel 'at home and in the diaspora' (Singh, Iyer, and Gairola 2016: xiii). W.E.B. Du Bois' 'double-consciousness' is sensed still by people experiencing these changing identities ([1903] 2014: 7). Some encounter this tension who are already living in the (unfortunately termed) 'host' nations, whose citizens can feel threatened by perceived mass in-migrations, fearing the loss of identity and cultural values (Papademetriou 2012). The unprecedented exodus of Syrians from their devastated war-torn country, together with Iraqi and Afghan asylum-seekers and refugees is unsettling many Europeans (European Commission 2016; Newland 2016). The June 2016 EU Referendum in Britain demonstrated the frictions between different conceptions of nation, home, identity, belonging, and the pull between affinities for global, local, national, and ethnic identities. Global social inequalities prompting such migrations parallel social inequalities in developed nations; those seeking a new home are resisted by those seeking closure and certainty in their definitions of home and homeland.

Recalling Carol Kennicott's yearning, the desire to be comfortable at home in our own beds is powerful; it is where most of us want to die. The technologies that democratized penicillin, ice, convenience foods, personal transport, entertainment, and communication from the inter-war period onwards have become means by which older people in the West can live independently for longer in their own homes, as can those with special needs. Despite this, many older people feel lonely; the current piloting of 'care robots' is seen as 'another way of dying even more miserably' (Hanson 2016). Our ageing Western populations need young immigrants to make their homes with us, to care for us, to bring vigour into these old countries. Western elite democracies, whose political economies of the 1930s presented people with the 'progress' of electric refrigerators and cheap cars, now face popular cultural resistance to the 'progress' of globalization. Populist visceral distaste for sharing resources with strangers is an echo of Douglas's words that 'home starts by bringing some space under control' (1995: 269). Covid-19 is the latest challenge to our conceptions of home and away, kin and stranger. Perhaps this is our opportunity to stop making meaning through things, and the detritus trailing in their wake.

My two-year-old daughter loves a book called *The Three Little Wolves and the Big Bad Pig* (Trivizas and Oxenbury 1993). In a reversal of tradition, the sweet little wolves start by building a brick house. Their attempts to make their home and selves safe fail. The big bad pig explodes their penultimate house, a bastion made of reinforced concrete that is surrounded by barbed wire and further protected by a video surveillance system. Their last house, a fragile and 'very beautiful' home of flowers, smells so sweet that the pig, breathing in to huff and puff, starts dancing, and they all live together happily ever after. Homes of the future may not be the stuff of fairy tales, but questioning taken-for-granted meanings can change how and why they matter.

CHAPTER TWO

Family and Household: A Century of Bedrooms

ANNMARIE ADAMS

THE POSTWAR ERA (1950s–1970s)

In January 1953, 44 million people watched as actress Lucille Ball enacted the drama of pregnancy on television, following the birth of her son in real life.[1] This was a larger audience than watched the inauguration of President Dwight Eisenhower the next day (O'Dell 1997: 30). America applauded. Motherhood was first-rate entertainment. And not just on television. The titles of magazine articles also applauded motherhood. Examples include: 'Femininity Begins at Home', 'Don't be Afraid to Marry Young', and 'Have Babies While You are Young' (Friedan 1963: 92–93). Just as the writers of situation comedies and magazine editors glorified motherhood, so too did architects and developers, who shaped houses and neighbourhoods to accommodate expanded families.

In North America, thousands of suburbs sprung up on the edges of cities in order to accommodate the so-called baby boom. These houses featured picturesque front and back gardens, broad driveways and two-car garages, and inside, three to four bedrooms, playrooms, and kitchens decked out with the latest appliances. House styles ranged from nostalgic pitched-roof-and-shutters types (see Figure 2.1) to modernist houses that, to some contemporary eyes, looked like small factories. All these material details were in support of a post-war, middle-class lifestyle – the baby boom – that was surprisingly consistent in its endorsement of more people marrying, at a younger age, and rapidly having lots of children.

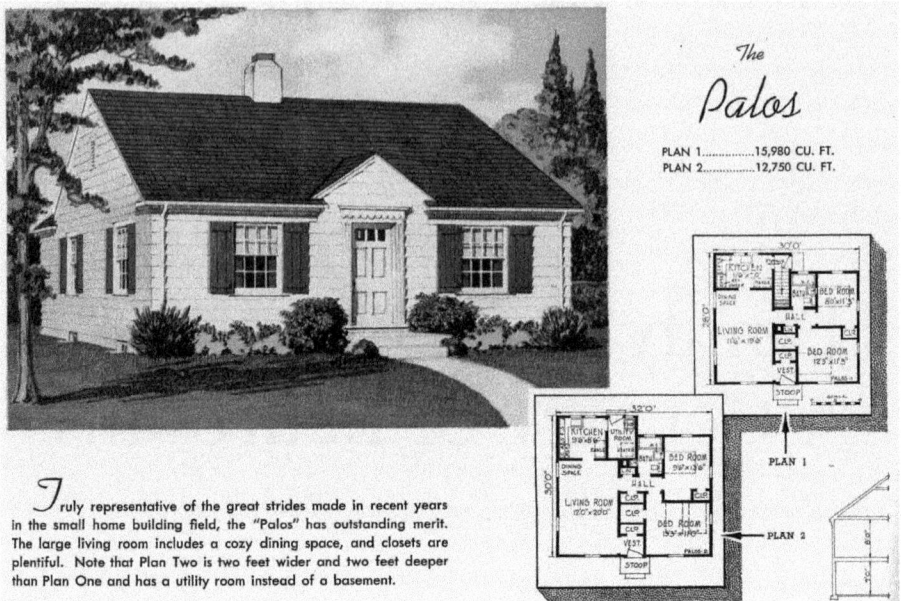

FIGURE 2.1: 'The Palos' house published in *Homes of Moderate Cost* brochure, 1941. National Plan Service, Inc., *Homes of Moderate Cost* [pattern book] (Chicago, IL: National Plan Service, 1941), 6.

This chapter explores nearly a century of family life – from 1920 to the present – through domestic spaces, especially bedrooms. The premise is that the design, location, and relationship of bedrooms to other rooms in the house reveal societal assumptions and priorities that may not be articulated in written or other sources. We begin in the middle of the century surveyed, the post-war decades roughly between 1950 and 1980, since marriage, reproduction, and childrearing were such strong themes during the so-called baby boom of this period. Domestic spaces of the inter-war period (1920s–1940s), by contrast, illustrate a time with less material emphasis on childhood and childrearing, and a less pronounced spatial hierarchy between adults and children.

Finally, the period since 1980, and especially the time since the development of the internet, sees the house linked to the world in previously unimaginable, technology-based ways. Additionally, children today see their bedrooms (and the electronic devices that bedrooms accommodate) as extensions of themselves, a concept that would have been inconceivable to a child of the 1920s, who was more likely to play in the streets or in a park. High-tech bedrooms for children, functioning as control centres for their busy lives, have now displaced playrooms. This shift is parallel to the rise of a new permeability in the family. New forms of family and household are simultaneously 'cocooned' by the home and connected to the world through the internet.

It is important to note that the examples cited here are from middle-class or wealthier families in North America. Architectural and material expressions of family are often expensive ambitions. As a consequence, working-class and poor families historically have had far fewer opportunities to express their care for children and family members in material ways. Another significant difference is that working-class families' private lives, their bedrooms for example, have been infrequently documented (Cohen 1986: 261–62). Certainly they did not appear in the widely circulated magazines, handbooks, and television shows that serve as the primary sources engaged for this chapter.

The history of domestic life that inspired this work draws on a broad definition of family. While most histories of domestic architecture presume a nuclear family, with two heterosexual parents and one or more children, this work sees families as fluid in terms of composition and roles. Unmarried adults, single-parent households, extended families, blended families, and same-sex marriage are major themes in the history of twentieth-century family life (May 1988; Comacchio 1999; Fass 2016; Mintz and Kellogg 1999). The spaces occupied by this expanded range of families and households, however these are defined, touch on themes of privacy, sexuality, reproduction, caregiving, health, sickness, recreation, labor, self-identity, and discretion.

The post-war, middle-class family has become something of a cliché. The husband and wife, so it goes, married soon after the end of the Second World War, gave birth to three to four children in quick succession, drove a station wagon, and had a dog (May 1988; Strong-Boag 1991; Owram 1997). The man of the family was the breadwinner and likely worked in a downtown corporation, some miles from home, and thus was absent from home for long days. The wife and mother stayed home, was the primary caregiver of children, cooked and cleaned, socialized with other mothers, transported children to music, sports, and other self-improvement programmes, and perhaps participated in community groups such as the Parent-Teacher Association (PTA). If we are to believe Betty Friedan, whose *Feminine Mystique* became a bestseller during this period, many stay-at-home mothers also took Valium to compensate for their feelings of isolation and discontent (1963: 76). Friedan's manifesto followed other critiques of post-war suburban blight. John Keats' *The Crack in the Picture Window* of 1957, for example, is a humorous and serious look at the social problems that emerged from this built environment.

Post-war, middle-class domestic architecture enabled this clichéd, child-filled home life. Playrooms, backyards, basement rec rooms, and specially furnished bedrooms are evidence that kids mattered and that houses served as architectural entertainment. In general, the house was divided into zones for day- and night-time use. Its layout tells us that women were the primary caregivers and were expected to care for children and do housework simultaneously (Adams 1995: 168; Lupton 1993: 7, 15; Harris 2013: 197–205; Strong-Boag 1991; Parr

1999). Key to maternal supervision in this period was the rise of the so-called 'family room' (Jacobs 2006: 71–72; Ogata 2008–9: 127-31), often located adjacent to the kitchen and where the television, what architectural historian Sandy Isenstadt calls the 'electronic hearth', replaced the fireplace as the focus of family togetherness (2007: 231). The 'convenience' of these adjacencies, spaces that had previously been carefully separated in earlier house plans, meant that the wife and mother could do everything at once. This 'opportunity' was noted in domestic magazines of the period:

> In a straightforward, thoroughly American way, however, the kitchen is the centre of the whole house. Its windows face in three directions. When its interior wall is pushed back out of sight, the woman of the house can keep tabs on almost any activity. She looks out on the deck where the children ride their tricycles: she can tune in on guest conversations while she's serving dinner: she even has a special lookout over one end of the sink counter to see who is at the door.
>
> —Brown 1962: 58

Simultaneously, in some parts of North America, a vibrant culture became the backdrop for older kids and teenagers, who sought a bit of distance between themselves and their parents, especially on weekends (Comacchio 2008). Previous to this time period, the basements of middle-class houses were often unfinished, service-oriented spaces that might accommodate the furnace of the house or extra storage. In the nineteenth century, house basements often contained servant spaces and/or summer kitchens. Certainly they would never have been considered appropriate spaces for children, due to their distant location, darkness, and underground humidity. Although seldom studied, post-war basements deserve scholarly attention, especially in their close links to the rise of domestic sound systems, special effects lighting, rock music culture (sound and graphic), fast food, cigarette smoking, recreational drug use, teen sex, and birth control. Sometimes parents (or maybe just husbands) carved out post-war basement space for themselves too, especially in the construction of home bars, complete with elevated counters, stools, and elaborate displays of alcohol, for the consumption of cocktails (these perhaps foreshadowed today's 'man caves', which feature more technology and less drinking).

A domestic space with a far less racy history, but no less important for studies of household and family, is the post-war suburban backyard (Colomina 1999: 149). Post-war suburbs were especially designed as continuous, romantic landscapes, including ornamental lawns and generous flower gardens, whereas suburbs of the 1920s tended to have small gardens (as opposed to spacious yards, with lawns intended for children's play) and might also have a separate garage in the rear (Jenkins 1994: 91). Typically surrounded by opaque fencing or hedges, backyards of the post-war period featured carefully tended lawns, play equipment, barbecues, and the all-important 'patio', which served as an extension of the house interior and was a significant site for outdoor dining, entertaining, and other expressions of class consciousness ('keeping up with the Joneses'). As architectural historian Dianne Harris has noted, the image of isolation was key. 'In the 1950s culture of containment, neighbours were to be kept at bay, on the other side of a fence that ensured family privacy and insularity, reinforcing the period cult of nuclear family togetherness and its counterpart, exclusion of outsiders', she explains (Harris 2007: 250). For wealthier families, backyard swimming pools were also part of this material expression of class conformity, reinforcing the idea of the home as a site of recreation and fun.

Master bedrooms

In the night-time zone and at the centre of baby-boom architecture was the private heart of the house, the so-called master bedroom. The master bedroom was the most exclusive room in the post-war house. Offset from children's bedrooms and part of a hotel-like suite with a relatively luxurious bathroom, the post-war master bedroom accommodated the parents' private life, symbolized their sex life, and provided some sanctuary to tired and anxious housewives. Apart from the kitchen, which is always associated with the stay-at-home wife and mother in this period, the master bedroom is the only room in the house where the woman head of the family could be alone, for example, to think or to rest (Tone 2008). As mentioned above, in plan, post-war family bedrooms occupy a separate, night-time zone, organized by a corridor or other circulation system, in the house with smaller children's rooms clustered somewhat apart from the parents' room (James 1996: 15). The master bedroom suite was always clearly identified in terms of architectural design, as it is larger, offset to have a superior view, and often has its own bathroom *en suite*. As Isenstadt has illustrated, landscape views came to dominate the literature on post-war housing (2007: 225–28). That master bedrooms had the best view from the house shows their pre-eminence in this period. Similarly, post-war master bathrooms were one notch up from the family bathroom down the hall, featuring decorator appliances, special textiles, and sometimes double sinks (James 1995: 109). While double sinks allowed couples to groom (hair, teeth, shaving, makeup) simultaneously, it also suggested that their shared, intimate lives extended into the bathroom, as up to this time most bathrooms were designed with single users in mind (Hoagland 2011).

Master bathrooms were for bathing and showering, allowing parents to prepare for bed and for their daily routines. Master bathrooms were also sometimes associated with dressing and undressing, which was a significant function, too, of master bedrooms. The master bedroom suite, in general, was

FIGURE 2.2: A couple conversing in the master bedroom of an Eichler house. The photograph appeared in a sales brochure for Eichler homes in San Mateo Highlands, California. Photograph by Ernest Braun.

the twentieth-century equivalent to the nineteenth-century boudoir, a place of primping and self-adoration (see Figure 2.2). Men and women in the post-war era, as the popular television show *Mad Men* has made abundantly clear, were expected to dress in particular ways for particular events. Knowing what to wear and when to wear it was part of the cultural capital of baby-boom parents. As a consequence, the master bedroom zone often included multiple and/or walk in closets, like in a hotel, which stored and showed the range of clothing both middle-class men and women were expected to own in this period (Beecher 2003). For women this might range from long, formal dresses for parties, as well as the shorter equivalent 'cocktail dresses', to 'house' dresses, loose-fitting, washable dresses intended for long days at home alone. Men in corporate and professional jobs, such as advertising executive Don Draper in *Mad Men*, wore business suits to express their high and shared social status; and would be expected to dress more casually on weekends, when men-only activities such as golf were popular (Rutherdale 1999). 'Golf shirts' and special shoes (and expensive memberships), of course, were prerequisites for golf culture. The suits, shirts, ties, and shoes required for men's work and recreational attire in the post-war period required ample storage spaces (Beecher 2003). Additionally, master bedroom suites often included multiple, large mirrors, reflecting (literally) this expectation to dress appropriately and be well groomed. Special lighting and storage for women's accessories such as cosmetics, handbags, and perfume were also quite common.

Needless to say, parents' bedrooms in this period comprised a private zone, with plenty of architectural cues designed to keep children out. Parents' bedrooms were offset from children's bedrooms, perhaps at the end of a hall or occupying a corner in the massing of the house. Parents' closets and those of other bedrooms were often configured to serve as buffer zones between spaces, adding acoustical privacy and a bit of distance between children and adults in the home (James 1995: 107). Some post-war houses even included separate wings for parents and children, granting parents extreme levels of privacy. A systematic survey of *House Beautiful* magazines in the post-war period shows several examples of this, including one home (see Figure 2.3) described as 'Two houses in one: A wing for the children and a wing for you' (Brown 1962: 55). According to architecture student Susan James, who studied master bedrooms through famous films, the idea of a master bedroom as an autonomous suite arose from this need to separate children and parents, in particular to provide parents a space in which to solve marital problems (1996: 16–17). The master bedroom was a togetherness space for parents, a spatial symbol of their intimate physical and social relationship. It was also a place, if films and novels are to be believed, where marital arguments might have taken place. In an era before divorce became a relatively 'easy' solution – which was not until the 1970s – parents stayed together and made it work. Whereas the American divorce rate was 26 percent in 1967, by 1975 it was up to 48 percent, meaning almost one in two marriages ended in divorce (Jones n.d.).

In addition, master bedrooms were fantasy spaces linked to parents' sexuality. The post-war decades saw a new openness around sexuality, heralded by studies such as those by Masters and Johnson (1966), which debunked long-held myths about female sexuality, underlining women's physical desire and sexual pleasure. Accordingly, as fantasy spaces, master bedrooms sometimes had double doors, or wider doors than adjoining bedrooms, giving the expectation of a special inner sanctum. Indeed, parents' bedrooms were often twice as big as children's rooms during this period. They accommodated a bed for two people, indicating that the social norm for the post-war family was a heterosexual couple, but also sometimes had seating furniture and television sets, material evidence that activities other than sleeping and dressing were accommodated in the room. 'With its own attached bathroom, telephone, and TV set', explains social historian Peter Ward, 'the "main suite" has assumed something of the character of a self-contained apartment' (1999: 87). In more expensive houses, master bedrooms might have fireplaces and be located directly over the living room, echoing its generous size and premium orientation. Indeed, in more expensive

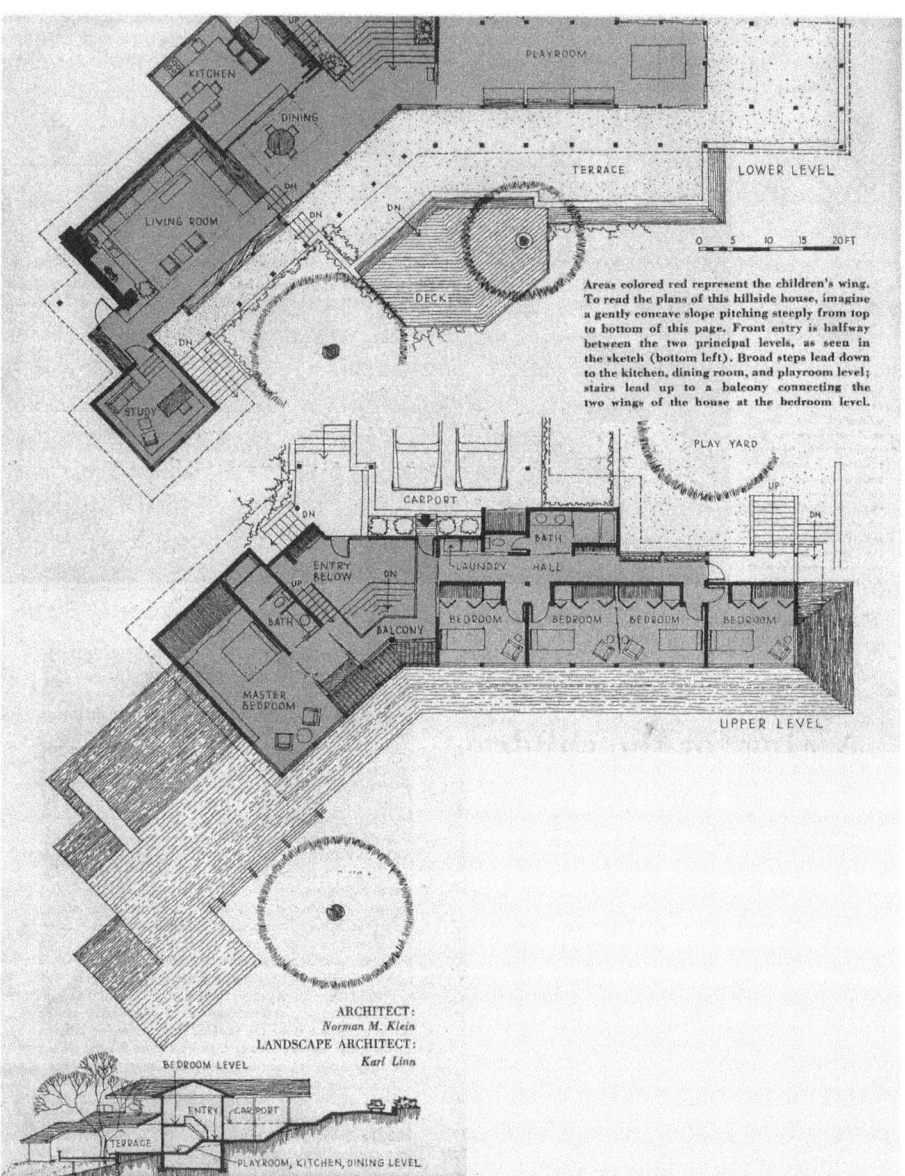

FIGURE 2.3: The post-war house separated parents and children. Architect Norman M. Klein kept the parents' and children's bedrooms far apart in this published house design (see bottom plan). 'Two Houses in One: A Wing for the Children and a Wing for You', *House Beautiful* (August 1962), 56. Courtesy Marilyn Klein.

houses, master bedroom suites resembled private apartments by accommodating daytime and night-time activities for parents, especially mothers, since fathers were presumably away at work all day. Bedroom furniture for couples often comprised matching dressers and matching bedside tables, all of which took up space and also meant that beds needed to occupy the geographic centre of rooms, rather than along a wall, as smaller beds were often placed. This furniture arrangement meant that marital beds appeared almost as islands, exposed and conspicuous in a sea of other 'matching' furniture. Also, master bedrooms were positioned in the house such that direct views of the bed itself were blocked, if possible, meaning being 'in bed' was doubly private.

As the site of parents' sexuality and subconscious togetherness, the bed itself was nearly sacred in the post-war era (Vollmer, Schulze, and Chebra 2005: 1). This special and even glamorous status was marked by expensive and sometimes symbolic bed coverings, such as linens, blankets, quilts, and bed spreads. Quilts, for example, were frequently passed down from mothers to daughters, especially if they were hand-made and/or had been used by several generations. Not coincidentally, such special bed coverings were often wedding gifts, linking the moment when the couple was married to the piece of furniture itself. The 'electric blanket', for example, was a popular wedding gift in the post-war decades. Although invented earlier (as a mattress heater), and advanced as heated clothing during the Second World War, electric blankets saw their golden age of use after the war and were a big part of the sensuality of the master bedroom, including the orange glow of controls on bedside tables and the 'click' these controls emitted in order to keep the bed a desired temperature (Coughlan 2009: 16, 64).

Whether passed down from parents or obtained as a high-tech wedding gift, such bed coverings were special. Not surprising, then, it was rare for parents or anyone else to lie or lounge on top of the bed (as we might do today), even to watch television or talk on the phone (two technologies often incorporated into master bedroom design). Certainly no outdoor shoes or clothing would ever purposefully touch the post-war parents' bed, perhaps because the bed should be kept clean and orderly (for example, respectable families 'made' their beds daily) and also because the bed was considered 'private' furniture. Special clothing – pyjamas – were always worn to bed; sensual or erotic night clothes were popular for women in the post-war period, marked by the rise in popularity of the French-inspired negligée. Notably, bed coverings of this period were often explicitly feminine – florals and light colours were particularly popular – expressing the bed and perhaps even entire bedroom as the 'territory' of the wife and mother and recalling the textiles of the parlour in the Victorian home. This link is significant, as the Victorian parlour was associated with the wife and mother, as was the post-war master bedroom. About 1950, in North America, the 'king size' bed became available, perhaps taking advantage of large master bedroom suites.

These material expectations for master bedrooms inspired much consumer activity. Advertisements in women's and domestic magazines of the period make a direct link from bedroom material culture to sexuality. While advertisements for kitchen and living room goods, for example, typically featured women as pure and innocent, ads for bedroom stuff showcased women as vamps, as erotic creatures who existed as aesthetic objects, to be consumed by the viewer. A good example is an advertisement (see Figure 2.4) for Utica sheets published in *Vogue* in January 1952. In this example, there is an explicit play on words engaging the brand name of Utica sheets: she lives in Atlanta, but she sleeps in Utica, suggesting a certain degree of unexpected mobility (perhaps including social mobility) but also the concept of 'sleeping' here and there. The woman in the centre of the ad,

FIGURE 2.4: As this 1952 advertisement for Utica sheets suggests, post-war adult bedrooms were erotically charged zones. 'She Lives in Atlanta . . . She Sleeps in UTICA', *Vogue* (January 1952), 119 (1): 52.

impossible to ignore, wears a low-cut purple cocktail gown and strappy 'sexy' shoes, long white gloves, and diamond earrings, as if attending a cocktail party. She sits on an iconic butterfly chair, one of the best known chairs of the twentieth century, designed in 1938 in Argentina by architects Antonio Bonet, Juan Kurchan, and Jorge Ferrari-Hardoy, but brought in to popular culture in North America through its acquisition by the Museum of Modern Art in New York and subsequent production by upscale furniture purveyor Knoll after 1947. With its easy mobility (it was inspired by so-called campaign chairs, seating furniture designed for military campaigns), the butterfly chair in the ad appears about to tip over under the model's shifting weight. This image of instability makes her seem intoxicated or 'on the move'. Women in such advertisements are projected as extensions of their things, here as an extension of the eroticized bed in the master bedroom, the power of which, in this case, stems from a simple set of sheets. The ad takes us, in a flash, from bedroom sheets to a drunk, dressed-up woman, 'available' for consumption.

Children's bedrooms

As design historian Amy Ogata writes, 'Whereas pre-war middle-class children were assigned nurseries in the attic or large upstairs bedrooms, post-war kids took their place at the center of the dwelling' (2008–9: 130). Children's bedrooms in the post-war house are very different from the parents' room. Although they, too, are part of the dedicated night-time zone in the post-war house, they are small, clustered together, and notably distinct in design from the larger master bedroom. Kids were separated by gender and age. Since many families had four children, for example, sisters would share a bedroom across the hall from their brothers. Even for working-class families, who occupied much smaller housing units, it was important to separate girls from boys. This was not new in the post-war period, but rather was a long tradition that separated sisters and brothers (Lauzon 2014). And even inside bedrooms, children were separated from each other. They often slept in single beds – called 'twin' beds perhaps because they so often came in pairs – and bedroom decoration was highly gendered. Because of the space crunch, it was not uncommon for small bedrooms to have bunk beds, especially for boys (Adams 2010a: 62–63). Bunk beds were common in military barracks and summer camps, and thus had connotations of rough-and-tough group living. Bunk beds or extra beds also meant kids could invite friends for sleepovers or slumber parties, a significant rite of separation from parents that was initiated in the baby-boom era, especially for girls (Mitchell and Reid-Walsh 2008: xxvii; Cromley 2008: 175). Experts were adamant, however, that children should occupy their own beds. They recommended removing infants almost immediately from both the parents' bedroom and their bed. Also to be avoided was sharing a bed with another child, of the same or opposite sex (Stearns, Rowland, and Giarnella 1996: 359). The prosperity of the post-war era, especially the opportunities for young couples to purchase multi-bedroom houses, meant that there was room for individual beds.

Children's beds were far less sacred than their parents' beds. Jumping on beds, often forbidden by worried parents, simulated play on trampolines. Adopting a child's perspective, a *House Beautiful* article stated: 'You think, because you are old and grown-up, that the function of a bedspread is to cover a bed decoratively and neatly. Bedspreads are for jumping and sprawling on, entertaining cats and dogs on, counting penny banks or dried frog collections on, and similar colourful enterprises too numerous to list' (Manners 1962: 64).

Like their parents, middle-class children in the post-war era kept their clothing and other belongings in built-in closets. Earlier houses also had built-in closets, but post-war closets tended to be larger and to extend horizontally along a wall, rather than occupy a corner of a room. Children's clothing did not have the wide range associated with parents' wardrobes at this time. Most kids would have 'play clothes' and 'school clothes', and one or two things for dressing up or 'Sunday best', for going to church in devout Christian families. The popularity of the department store at this time, and its wide reach through mail catalogues, meant that goods such as children's clothing could be delivered to the doorstep. This made a huge difference to families living in rural areas or in small towns, who had previously travelled to urban areas to shop for consumer goods (Belisle 2011).While girls' rooms would often have mirrors, boys were not expected to care so much about their appearances. Other common pieces of furniture in children's bedrooms in this era were bookshelves and small desks. These pieces enabled children to do homework, which was a major function of children's bedrooms in the post-war era, when homework was still a solitary activity, requiring quiet, good light, and few distractions.

A key function of the post-war child's bedroom was thus as a space where he or she could be alone. This focus on isolation was the result of a new understanding in the psychological needs of children. While being 'sent' to a bedroom was a common form of punishment during this time, being alone in general was part of a new understanding of the psychological depth of childhood (Gleason 1999). The post-war decades saw the rise of developmental psychology as a field that guided parents, especially mothers, outside the medical clinic. Bestselling books like Dr Spock's *Baby and Child Care* (1946) urged parents to treat their children as individuals. Reading, studying, playing, and thinking in quiet isolation, it was believed, was how children got to know themselves, and having their own space further allowed them to express their unique identities. Post-war television shows that featured large families, such as *The Brady Bunch* or *The Partridge Family*, portrayed kids' bedrooms as rooms where same-sex children shared secrets and provided support for each other. Television-show bedrooms also showed the importance of the room as a venue for 'display'. Walls might be decorated with artwork by kids, for example; sports trophies or team photos were commonly displayed in children's bedrooms. And the décor of bedrooms, frequently the responsibility of wives/mothers, was carefully chosen to accentuate what was understood as the child or children's budding personality (or more precisely, what parents wanted children to become).

Providing such a space for emotional growth was something middle-class parents were expected to do for their children as part of the nurturing process. Numerous articles in home magazines make this clear: 'Give your child a room for Christmas' urged Patricia Doherty in *House Beautiful* (1965: 155). Three years earlier, the author of a similar article asked 'What Makes a Good Room for a Child?' The author explained: 'A child's room is more than just a place to sleep. It can be his castle, his world, a place for living and growing' (Manners 1962: 63). Amy Ogata has noted the significant role of the post-war child's bedroom 'for its spatial and psychological potential as an incubator of the child's fragile ego and gender identity, and as a place where creative energy might originate' (2008–9: 139).

The story of teenagers' rooms is one of autonomy and goes hand-in-hand with the rise of youth culture, which historians date to the 1950s (Comacchio 2008; Adams 1997). As Jason Reid has noted, the autonomous teen bedroom came about as 'youthful demands for greater freedom and autonomy played themselves out within the home' (2012: 425). Inexpensive radios, record players, televisions, and specialty telephones, in particular, allowed teenagers to mark domestic territory in the post-war house by 'de-centring' leisure activities previously located only in the family room (Reid 2012: 427), foreshadowing the technology-rich bedroom that would emerge in the 1980s.

Counterexamples: bedrooms for diverse families and households

Several iconic modernist houses built in the mid-twentieth century offer a counterpoint to the role of bedrooms in the conventional post-war family home conceived around a heterosexual couple. Most famously, the house architect Philip Johnson built for himself in 1949 as a weekend retreat in New Canaan, Connecticut, the 'glass house', which contained the entire house in a single open, rectangular space. Only a brick cylinder containing the bathroom and fireplace separated the kitchen, living, and bedroom spaces. The house was thus completely transparent from the outside, and as architectural historian Alice Friedman (2006: 155) has shown, was complemented by an adjacent, closed brick guest house that contained two identical bedrooms with a sitting room and a bathroom. Friedman has argued that the glass house expresses the famous New York architect's gay identity, but also serves as a mask for it at a time when homosexual men kept their private lives private: with a 'theatricality of its own form and the life that was lived within its transparent glass walls' (2006: 152).

Homosexual acts were illegal at the time and, accordingly, gay relationships were shrouded in secrecy or purposeful ambivalence. What seems at first glance to be an exposed, open architecture, Friedman notes, is actually 'screened, distorted, and overtly denied visual access' (2006: 152) by virtue of its shielded position in a wooded landscape and the existence of the hidden guest house.

Before the publication of Friedman's article, Johnson's house was frequently touted as distantly related to Ludwig Mies van der Rohe's Farnsworth House, 1945–51, or other iconic inter-war glass buildings associated with the Bauhaus. The house was built in Plano, Illinois for Edith Farnsworth, a single, middle-aged woman and doctor. In designing for an unmarried woman, the architect assumed she would have no private or sex life to be contained by opaque walls. This view was generally held in the 1940s, when premarital sex was socially unacceptable. Such an assumption apparently gave him licence to build her a transparent glass house. Friedman asserts that the Johnson brick guest house, through which the architect created a space free from prying eyes, is not so much a 'metaphoric ruin' of the war as Peter Eisenman suggested (Johnson himself stated it was inspired by a burnt village) as evidence of the battle against traditional American family values. Together, the glass house and the guest house offer a two-fold domesticity whereby the guest house functions like a closet which 'turns its back on its surrounding' with an 'unequivocal drawing of the curtain' (Friedman 2006: 152, 154). It is significant, for Friedman's interpretation, that Johnson eventually used the opaque guest house as his bedroom, leaving the exposed glass house solely for entertainment. Nonetheless, Johnson posed on his bed in the glass house for a photograph, taken in 1966, that appeared in the *New York Daily News* (see Figure 2.5). Significantly, even in repose the architect's professional status is referenced – his leather brief case is in the lower left of the image – suggesting the relation of his demanding and lucrative city-based architectural practice to this ex-urban retreat. Also significant is the inclusion of a bedside telephone. As mentioned above, telephones were often accommodated and showcased on bedside tables, presumably in case of night-time or emergency calls but also because the bed could be a site for intimate telephone conversations. Iconic films such as 'Pillow Talk' of 1959, whose sexually titillating plot line revolved around a party line, have made this abundantly clear (James 1996: 62–73), though notably there would have been little or no acoustic privacy in Johnson's glass house. Thus, the public self that Johnson presented through this photograph of his glass house both suggests and denies sexual secrets.

Bedrooms in other houses designed for gay men, such as the Berkeley, California home of John Weston Havens, Jr., a philanthropist, similarly contained and subtly communicated the private lives of their inhabitants: 'brilliantly concealed within the publicity' (Adams 2010b: 93). As Friedman and I have noted independently, this duality of transparency and opacity in two mid-century, modernist houses is especially prominent in 'queer' architecture

FIGURE 2.5: Philip Johnson reading on the bed in the glass house, photograph by David McLane (June 1966), *New York Daily News*. Courtesy of Getty Images.

from this period. First, non-queer houses would never be fully open and transparent to the outside gaze (physically or in media images). Rather, they have opaque façades with carefully controlled doors and windows, protecting family life from the public realm of the street. Secondly, the private lives inside the idealized, heterosexual family houses that unfold in bedrooms are predictable, or contrived to appear predictable, in most houses. They have no social reason to conceal their existence, but equally no need to show them openly, since this private life and sexuality is already understood (like a taboo). However, in both the queer house and the non-queer house – notwithstanding Johnson's bed for show in the glass house – the actual sleeping areas are secluded. This shows the continuing belief that dark and quiet places are the best for sleeping, and equally that we are all (children and adults) particularly vulnerable when asleep.

The earlier Weston Havens house, built in 1939–41, illustrates some additional tenets of queer space in the mid-twentieth century. The house was built for a single man who loved architecture. Although he lived on his own, the home boasted three nearly identical bedrooms, each with access to a bathroom and without the spatial hierarchies of traditional homes, as discussed above. In the Havens house, we see no glamorization of the owner's bedroom as a 'master'. On the contrary, it is almost the same as the other bedrooms in size and location, all facing a courtyard. The bedrooms are carefully separated from one another, with closets and bathrooms serving as barriers, but a 'shared view unites them in purpose' (Adams 2010b: 87). Additionally, no other room in the house has a view on this courtyard. The courtyard thus functions almost as an ante-closet area (the space in front of the closet, as curator Henry Urbach uses the term [1996: 70]), serving as both a space and a non-space (Adams 2010b: 89). The Havens courtyard, as an ante-closet, has no specific domestic function, but rather it has ambiguous and multiple characters as a space freed from normative social codes.

Despite all the opacity and secrecy, and as part of a public campaign shaped by Havens himself (the building was featured in several design publications and the popular press while it was still under construction and afterwards), the ultra-private house became a 'public spectacle' (Adams 2010b: 91), gaining a well-known public image. This high visibility of the house in magazines also made it a destination for tourists, and its fame was enhanced by Havens himself, who commissioned a documentary film about the house. Ultimately, the renowned building became public property when Havens donated it to the University of California at Berkeley upon his death. In this way the house was both a highly visible stage – like Johnson's glass house – and an invisible backstage, like the opacity of the adjacent and little-known Johnson guest house. This two-sided domesticity marries an architectural image that is transparent, actually in the glass house and metaphorically in the Havens house, and one that is private and secret. Such houses served as public performances of their famous owners' ultra-private lives, telling the stories that society tried its best to suppress.

THE INTER-WAR ERA (1920s–1940s)

Family life in the 1920s was shaped by the past and inspired by the future. The end of the First World War meant chaos and crisis for many families in Europe and North America, but also a return to normalcy. The years following the First World War saw a new prosperity and a decidedly happier mood. The decade is known as the Roaring Twenties because of the decade's social and cultural dynamism, such as the rise of jazz and dancing. Many countries had recognized women's right to citizenship and granted them the right to vote. The so-called flapper was a liberated model for women, offering options (such as paid work) other than mandatory marriage. In the United States, family size was on the decline, thanks to inefficient but persistent recourse to birth control (Comacchio 1999; Tinkler and Warsh 2008).

Unsurprisingly, the ways families occupied dwellings followed a different spatial arrangement than in the post-war decades. The middle-class house of the 1920s was much more relaxed than its Victorian and Edwardian predecessors. Also significant is the fact that the middle-class house of the 1920s was the first servantless house. The major spatial impact of this massive social change is that the kitchen became part of the public zone of the house, as opposed to a separate space where servants were managed. Needless to say, this shift also saw the disappearance of servants' bedrooms or other spaces, and the 'back stairs' that symbolically and physically connected the work and living spaces of household servants. This architectural change that involved revolutionary transformations in the kitchen, as is well known from the work of architectural historians Gwendolyn Wright and Elizabeth Cromley, resulted in a much more open house plan (Wright 1980: 239; 1981: 169–72; Cromley 1996: 9). In terms of design history, the inter-war kitchen is thus much smaller and more integrated than its pre-First World War counterpart. Polychrome décor, too, marked the kitchen's new connection to other family spaces (Cromley 1996: 17).

A related aspect of this process of architectural relaxation was the inclusion of multi-purpose spaces, a hallmark of twentieth-century design that began about 1900. Whereas the Victorian house typically had highly specialized rooms clustered around the age and gender of the family members – the wife's parlour, the husband's library, the children's nursery, the servants' kitchen – the early twentieth century saw a collapse of such rigid divisions. By 1910, a single 'living room' sufficed for a middle-class family, while the house of 1880 would have boasted front and back parlours, a den, and a library. Why did houses get smaller? How did new household and family relations affect the house plan?

Family size and the middle-class house shrunk simultaneously, a process that began long before 1920. By about 1900, the birth rate in both Canada and the United States had dropped, from an estimated 626 children under five per 1000 women in 1850 to 474 in 1900 in the United States (Willcox 1911: 491). Whereas the average Canadian household recorded in the 1881 census included 5.76 persons, by 1901 the household was only 5.23 (Statistics Canada 2009). With fewer children and fewer servants, the twentieth-century house saw a revolutionary change in the design of the kitchen as domestic labor became the responsibility of the wife and mother. While Victorian-era kitchens were large spaces separated from other ground-floor rooms, such as the dining room, Progressive-era kitchens were more modest and often linked to the dining space. Nineteenth-century kitchens had boasted extensive pantries for food storage (Cromley 1996: 13). A generation later, however, kitchen cupboards replaced the room that once held a season's worth of pickling and preserves.

These changes in house planning mirrored larger shifts in beliefs concerning health and hygiene, as well as in the role of the mother. The germ theory of disease had been articulated about 1870, but it was not until the first decade of the new century that scientific or post-germ theory preventive medicine was practised at home (Tomes 1998: 135–56). Bathrooms were included in houses designed and built in the early twentieth century (replacing the water closets in the Victorian home), which had a large impact on the plan. Plumbing was clustered or stacked; two-storey houses even included a bathroom upstairs, near the bedrooms (but never *in* the bedrooms, as in the post-war era).

Downstairs the kitchen and laundry were often adjacent (Lupton and Miller 1992: 27; Lupton 1993: 15, 23).

Family health and domestic hygiene were the responsibility of mothers, who took care of sick family members and also interfaced with family doctors. The cleanliness of houses and the regulation of fresh air through the house were also part of maternal responsibilities. In the late nineteenth century, mothers even tested their drains using household products such as peppermint oil (Adams 1996: 82–83). These expectations came from a long-standing belief that domestic health was an innately feminine concern. Women were seen as healers because they bore children. Because women were seen as tender and caring, sick-nursing fell to wives and mothers. The rise of the modern profession of nursing as a female-dominated profession is an outcome of this cultural norm (Adams 1996: 81).

This urge for healthy homes shaped bedroom spaces. Compared to the Victorian/Edwardian house, where kids and parents were separated thanks to the inclusion of live-in servants, the inter-war house saw a new integration of the bedrooms of parents and children. Unlike the post-Second World War house, which saw a measurable difference in size and luxury between the parents' and children's bedrooms, a typical house of the inter-war years had an array of bedrooms that were almost identical in size. The parents' bedroom might be slightly larger, or have a larger closet, but this dissimilarity was subtle (see Figure 2.6). This is a marked difference between the inter-war and post-war family, where after the Second World War the master bedroom expresses a clearer hierarchy between parents and children. Inter-war bathrooms were shared among parents and children and accessible from a single circulation space, often a corridor. As we know from Regina Lee Blaszczyk, coloured kitchen and bathroom fixtures flourished after 1926 thanks to R.H. Macy & Company's promotion 'Color in the Kitchen' and the popularity of Kohler Color Ware in bathrooms (2012: 256).

Same-sex couples sharing a house in the early twentieth century were rarely documented, because homosexuality was illegal and shunned as morally deviant by large segments of society. For same-sex couples, one way to disguise the relationship was to live in houses which also included workspaces, such as a doctors' office. In 1915, for example, physicians Clara Williams and Elsie Mitchell lived together in a house in Berkeley, California designed by Julia Morgan. Their shared doctors' office hid the stairway down to their shared bedroom, shielding their private lives from patients, and couching their partnership as professional. As Henry Urbach has noted, gay couples had continued into the late twentieth century to use this strategy in the creation of their domestic spaces, as if they could be together only for the sake of a business relationship (1992: 39).

The accommodation of illness as well as its prevention in the 1920s was another important difference from the post-Second World War house. In the

FIGURE 2.6: Parents' bedrooms of the inter-war period were slightly larger than children's bedrooms. Mr Hadrill's house, Montreal, 1924. Courtesy of McCord Museum, Montreal, VIEW-21064.1.

nineteenth century and up to the mid-twentieth century, sick family members were cared for at home, rather than in the hospital. While wealthier families could afford hospital stays for serious illnesses, it was common for working- and middle-class families to treat illnesses at home, often but not always advised by family physicians who would make 'house calls'. Indeed, one of the important roles of hospitals in this period was to remove seriously ill people from their usual environments, providing allegedly superior food and surroundings in order to speed recovery and offset contagion (Adams 2008: 35).

Preventing the spread of disease, in this period, meant plenty of fresh air and light, mostly through large, open windows and the use of natural materials in the house. Before the widespread availability of penicillin after the Second World War, infant and child mortality rates were extremely high. While a child with tuberculosis might be removed to a specialty hospital in the 1920s or 1930s, in order to protect family members, one with pneumonia or rheumatic fever would have been treated at home, secluded in a bedroom (see Figure 2.7). Meals would be brought into the bedroom for the patient, where visitors might also be received. Consequently, home was also the place where most family members died, and bodies were ritualistically laid out in parlours in anticipation of visitors and as the focus of wakes before the Second World War.

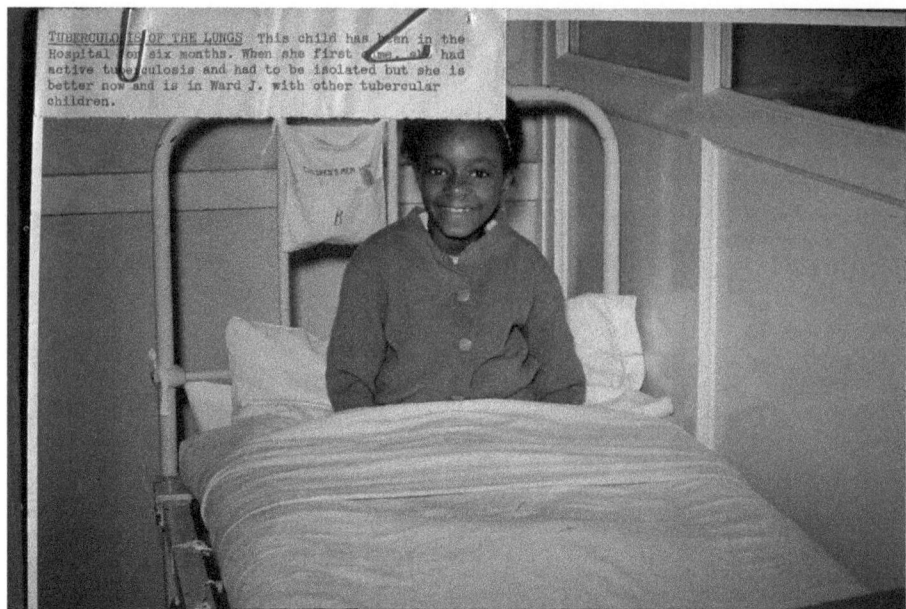

FIGURE 2.7: Children with tuberculosis were often hospitalized for long periods. Children's Memorial Hospital, Montreal. Courtesy of RBC Art and Heritage Centre of the McGill University Health Centre.

Other life rituals we associate now with hospital visits or stays, such as childbirth, also took place at home (Adams 1996: 103–28; Mitchinson 2002). Babies of the 1920s were delivered in kitchens or bedrooms, with family members banished from the room during the event. Mother and child would then recover for up to a month – a period known as 'lying-in' – in a dedicated bedroom. By the 1920s, middle-class patients went to hospitals for surgery. They might return home to recover, however, spending several months isolated in bedrooms, including for meals and visiting. A significant function of the middle-class home of the 1920s and 1930s, then, was to facilitate family and health milestones – birth, sickness, and death – foreshadowing the mandate of hospitals and funeral homes in the late twentieth century.

THE POSTMODERN ERA: 1980s–PRESENT

The era commonly referred to as postmodern, from roughly 1980 to the present, is characterized by affluence, globalization, multiculturalism, and high technology, particularly the rise of the internet. Not surprisingly, then, middle-class children's bedrooms after about 1980 have become luxurious worlds of their own with a pronounced separation from their parents' room. A survey of magazines over the past forty years tells us that houses after 1980 are quite different from those designed in both the inter-war and post-war eras. Although North American households and families have become smaller, their houses have become bigger. For example, in Canada the average family size has gone from 3.9 in 1961, to 2.9 fifty years later (Statistics Canada 2015). At the same time, the average house size has gone from 800 square feet in 1950 to 2,250 square feet in 1999 (Hayden 2003: 190). A derogatory term for oversized family houses, especially those considered ostentatious and lacking in architectural 'taste' is the McMansion. Luxury living for children derives from these larger quarters, but also from bedrooms that function as 'electronic cocoons' (Denhez 1994: 217–26). Children living in houses from the 1980s and 1990s might even have their own bathrooms, depending on the income of the family.

While houses were growing in size, families were not only getting smaller, but also fracturing. By the 1980s, divorce rates in North America were much higher than in the previous decades: for example, in the United States, divorce numbers increased from 400,000 in the 1950s to 1.2 million in the 1980s (National Center for Health Statistics 1991), due to better access to divorce and women's increased autonomy. As a result, many households have come to be headed by single parents, especially women. In Canada, for example, access to divorce was liberalized in 1968, a year that also saw the decriminalization of homosexuality and contraception. 'There's no place for the state in the bedrooms of the nation', declared Justice Minister Pierre Trudeau in 1967 (CBC Digital Archives 1967).

In 1984, then-Prime Minister Trudeau divorced his wife, Margaret Sinclair, and raised his three young sons in the Montreal home architect Ernest Cormier had designed for himself in 1930. The occupation of bedrooms is a key aspect of how the all-male Trudeau family lived in the famous Art Deco house in the 1980s, as the Trudeau boys inhabited rooms Cormier had designed for his model and live-in lover, Clorinthe Perron. The inward-turning house, which spills down a steep site, allowed Trudeau to retreat from the public eye, while simultaneously focusing on single-fatherhood long before such arrangements were common. 'Domestic masculinity', as we call it in a study of sequential occupation of the house, illuminates how architecture, space, and artefacts strengthened vulnerable masculinities that emerged through new relationships with the home in the late twentieth century. Domestic masculinity foreshadows subsequent, twenty-first-century gender roles, including the expectations today that men are strong and sensitive. We argue that Cormier's non-traditional family life at 1418 Pine Avenue set the stage for the Trudeaus' way of life (Adams and Macdonell 2016).

Introversion is an apt way to describe late-twentieth-century bedrooms. Some major differences in contemporary children's rooms include their occupants' aesthetic control over the space, the affluence and consumption culture that children and teenagers have become a part of, and the new technologies incorporated into the bedroom space. First, the spaces are arranged by their occupants, especially if they are teenagers. In the 1980s, teens' bedrooms 'were no longer expected to be decorated with handsome, mother-approved *objet d'art*, as earlier design experts had urged, but were now expected to house a vast array of cultural detritus, much of which reflected their teen occupants' various consumer loyalties and could be arranged in a seemingly anarchic manner' (Reid 2010: 122). While children emerged as consumers in the post-war era, in the affluent 1980s this reached a new peak. The goods that kids purchased were conspicuously centred around home electronics (Reid 2012: 425). The cheap radios and record players of the 1960s enabled post-war kids to demarcate space and may have even driven away parents. But the technologies of the internet era interactively transport users to alternative places/sites and allow open communication with anybody else on the internet. This transformation of children's rooms into communications centres began with the rise of video games and has exploded in the cell phone era.

Because of such communication technologies, spaces that were once conceived to be protective in their isolation – from other rooms and from the outside world – are now 'accessible' to strangers via the internet. While post-war parents might have delighted in their children spending time alone in their rooms, contemporary parents might worry that their kids alone in their rooms could be conversing with a paedophile, planning a school shooting, or reading pornography, thanks to the World Wide Web. At the same time, the rise of social media has had other effects for children, including making friends across the globe. In material terms, kids now use bedroom design as an expression of self. Instagram and Facebook sites are filled with images of teen bedrooms (see Figure 2.8). A bedroom setting, for example, is a common backdrop for a 'selfie', a photographic self-portrait taken at close range with a cell phone.

A kid's bedroom today is a site of self-expression for its young inhabitant, who personalizes the space to the extent that parents are sometimes forbidden to enter. The bedroom is often the only place in the family home where kids socialize with their friends. Perhaps because social media has made bedrooms more public, gone are the prohibitions on socializing with friends of the opposite sex in one's bedroom, so prominent in the post-war decades. By the 1990s, sleepovers including both girls and boys became acceptable in many families (Annin 1996: 57).

This notion of the family and household as a richer mix of members extends beyond the bedroom. The parents of children today are less likely to be a married, heterosexual couple, as less traditional households and families are more broadly accepted and widespread. Whereas *I Love Lucy* reflected the typical post-war couple – young, married, and keen to have children – the television show *Modern Family*, one of ABC's top-rated series, is a good mirror of today's myriad of family types. The show's plot revolves around three types

FIGURE 2.8: 'Selfie' photograph of Lindsay Mazliach, 16, in her Montreal bedroom, shared on Instagram. @lindsaymazliach (September 2016) [Instagram post].

of families: a nuclear family, blended families (through divorce and re-marriage), and a family with same-sex parents and an adopted child. Its popularity also reflects how these diverse family portraits are now the new realities for millions.

As we have seen, domestic architecture and material culture serve as powerful evidence in the evolution of households and families. The three eras we have examined – the post-war decades, the inter-war era, and the postmodern period – represent distinct periods in the history of houses. The post-war house, designed with children in mind, provided separate spaces for parents and children; it also served as an appliance-based command centre, with the wife and mother at its helm. Master bedroom suites were erotic and near-sacred spaces for young married couples. The house of the 1920s, by contrast, emphasized family togetherness and the maintenance of health, with fewer distinctions between parents and children. Finally, in the houses of the recent past and present, children and teenagers occupy their rooms as 'total environments', finding little use for other spaces in the house. Handheld devices, cell phones, video games, and social media connect these electronic nests to a virtual universe, where home and home life is curated for strangers. How domestic architecture, including bedrooms, may change in the future is unknown. By moving away from a long-held idea of the nuclear, heterosexual family, unimagined architectural paradigms may appear, inspired by changing households and families.

CHAPTER THREE

The House: The Global Age of Housing

KENNY CUPERS

During the twentieth century, the world's population increased more than in any other period in history, from about 1.6 billion in 1900 to over six billion in 2000.[1] The number of new dwellings needed to accommodate this increase is almost impossible to fathom. The sheer variety of dwelling types and styles across the world parallels the diversity of contemporary ways of life. What history accounts for the myriad social practices and materialities of dwelling that emerged in this period? To begin answering this question, this chapter will focus on the major kinds of housing that accommodated the past century's unprecedented population growth and that, in doing so, shaped the vast expansion of our urbanized world.

A first paradigmatic case is the suburban house. Often though not always speculatively built, privately owned, and grouped in subdivisions, the single-family house continues to be a widespread ideal for middle- and working-class families. Its sprawling reality from California to Brazil or Australia, however, is far more diverse than Hollywood films tend to suggest. A second typical category consists of slabs and blocks of flats, often though not always aggregated in state-subsidized and/or publicly owned estates. In France, Russia, or Singapore, inhabitants have celebrated these prevalent housing forms as achievements in modern comfort and public provision, while also denouncing them as traps of relegation and exclusion. A third, perhaps the most characteristic, category of housing in the twentieth century is the shantytown. From Istanbul to Mumbai and Lima, shack dwellings on squatted or pirated land have become a dominant mode of contemporary urbanization.

Even if they are far from exhaustive and do not represent the wide range of dwelling forms globally, these three categories – subdivisions, slabs, and shantytowns – reveal the major changes and forces that shaped dwelling in the last century. In this period, dwelling was no longer just a matter of individual needs, local traditions, or national law; it also became a product and an engine of our increasingly global political economy. Although this evolution is integral to a much longer and deeper history of modernization, it is especially in the twentieth century that housing coagulated into a globally interconnected economic, social, and epistemological complex.

In everyday lived experience, the house still fulfils the basic functions it has for thousands of years. Houses provide shelter and comfort, as well as a sense of self and of community. They organize both a material world of objects and an imaginary landscape of belonging (see, for example, Meier 2018). They are places of labor and leisure as much as they are sites of social reproduction. And they tend to be deeply intertwined with our personal histories and aspirations. Yet, even if the house still organizes our individual world in this sense, over the past two centuries house construction and development have also become thoroughly enmeshed with entirely different forces: industrialization and the national economy. Elites have employed the house as a technique to build nations and to categorize classes and races. Particularly in the West, the material and cultural forms of dwelling have increasingly been regarded as a reflection of national identity and social structure. This is a quintessentially modern vision, one that has served not only to describe but to actively shape how humanity lives. Whether as a guarantor of freedom and political participation through homeownership or to improve the conditions of the working class, dwelling became an instrument in a system for organizing society at large. In most urban societies, the house became a key concern of social reformers and the state, even if private individuals and market institutions often remained central to financing, planning, and building it. In this development, houses – in many places but not everywhere – became housing, an integral part of the process of moulding social and economic relations. Subdivisions offered one way of doing so, slabs another, while the shantytown can be understood as the failure of both, even as it constitutes a system in itself.

SUBDIVISIONS: DOMINIONS OF THE SINGLE-FAMILY HOUSE

The single-family house on its own lot is so commonplace in much of the world that to describe it as an invention, let alone one that is tied to the twentieth century, almost seems foolish. And yet, even if families and kinship communities have long built separate dwelling structures and cultivated the surrounding land as gardens, the production and meaning of these dwelling environments has differed so vastly across time and space that the idea that they pertain to a single type seems untenable. To talk about the single-family home as a twentieth-century phenomenon is to talk, then, about an ideal type. That type tends to be widespread in societies characterized by private landownership, the morality of the nuclear family, and a (post-industrial) division of labor, even if the separation between work and home is often fluid and contested. In this sense, the single-family home can be understood as a more specific product of modernity rather than a timeless manifestation of human dwelling.

Just as the house stands in a larger environment, so it is tied not only to the fashioning of self and family but to the organization of society at large. Individual, exclusive ownership of land presumes a doctrine of individual rights and the rise of the modern bureaucratic state as the guarantor of such rights (MacPherson 1978). This is what allows land, and the dwellings on it, to be bought and sold as a commodity on a market. Even though private land- and homeownership took many guises throughout the previous centuries, their typical form today is the suburban subdivision (Linklater 2013). Spurred by industrial capitalism and its concomitant forms of urbanization, the bourgeois migration to the suburbs was most clearly manifested in nineteenth-century Britain and subsequently in the United States (Archer 2008).

In this context, the pre-industrial farmhouse and the elite villa retreat served as templates for the development of middle-class domestic architecture. These suburban houses, which mushroomed in the outskirts of the fast-growing industrial city, were occasionally designed by architects but were more often part of speculative projects undertaken by private developers. Indeed, the main actors in the history of the suburban house are homeowners and developers rather than architects or the state. Contrary to conventional understanding, suburban homeownership was never just limited to the elite. Nineteenth-century suburbanization also included poor, working-class, and middle-class settlements and eventually shaped the massive decentralization of the industrial metropolis (Binford 1985; Harris 1996; von Hoffmann 1996). Spurred by the construction of street cars and other technological inventions, real-estate developers not only speculated on subdividing peripheral land but also, directly or indirectly, fostered new, often socially homogeneous, middle-class lifestyles (Nicolaides and Wiese 2006).

In essence, the suburban house was a particularly productive way to cope with industrialization and was therefore arguably a product of the West. Nevertheless, just as industrialization required resource and labor networks spanning all continents, the suburban house was not culturally inscribed within the boundaries of Europe or the United States. When twentieth-century Anglo-American suburbanites called their homes 'bungalows', they emphasized an aspiration for middle-class comfort, family morality, informal sociability, and contact with nature. But the very term *bungalow* – derived from *banggalo*, a Bengali peasant dwelling – reveals the global provenance of this domestic ideal (King 1995). British colonists had first encountered such peasant dwellings during their colonization of the South Asian subcontinent. Appreciating how these dwellings adapted to the tropical climate, they appropriated the type as a dwelling for European colonists. Bungalows consequently appeared in other colonies and in the metropole, taking on new forms and meanings as they spread across continents. In Africa, the bungalow made its first appearance in the late nineteenth century as a racially defined dwelling type that suited the health needs of Europeans in the tropics. In this context, the single-family house – from prefabricated cottages to villas with verandas – was a 'tool of empire' for colonial administrators, allowing them to control larger territorial domains than would otherwise have been possible (Headrick 1981). The low-density compounds of bungalows in colonial Africa thus differed fundamentally from the suburban homes that middle-class Americans also called 'bungalows'.

This ambivalence – the single-family house as both an instrument of selfhood and of social organization and governance – is what architects inherited and further articulated as they developed a new formal language for the house. Nineteenth-century reformers such as Catherine Beecher and designers such as William Morris already understood the home as a site for the construction of a new society, not just of the self or the family (Hayden 1981). Nevertheless, Frank Lloyd Wright's 'Prairie Style' house designs still affirmed the dominant norms of Victorian domesticity with their central hearths and parapet walls that protected the family from prying eyes while providing the inhabitants with views of the surrounding landscape (Upton 1998).[2] After the First World War, avant-garde artists and architects developed innovations in house design as part of a modernist project that was both formal and social in nature. Even though their focus was increasingly on the design of collective housing, modernist architects in this period did not neglect the single-family home. Le Corbusier's Villa Savoye, for example, is both an architectural revolution in single-family dwelling and an affirmation of dominant bourgeois values (Benton 1987). An abstracted 'machine for dwelling', the Villa Savoye celebrates the sanctity of private homeownership, the nuclear family, industrial culture, and the suburban commute. Its modernist aesthetics, such as the strip window and the roof deck, were inspired by a new machine aesthetics but also by the traditional architecture and dwelling culture of the Mediterranean and Balkan regions, in the spirit of an older, orientalist, and colonial tradition (Çelik 1997; Crane 2010).

Yet, the formal development of the single-family house as a paragon of twentieth-century modernity was spurred not only by Eurocentric appropriation of the colonized other but by a more general process of transculturation in which the primary movers were not necessarily European or architects. In the first decades of the twentieth century, for example, the Kemalist regime in Turkey attracted German architects and planners in order to align itself politically with Europe. Turkish political elites adapted German concepts of modern dwelling, such as the functionalist kitchen, to their own cultural and political context (Akcan 2012). The house became central to the modernization of everyday life for Turkish working- and middle-class citizens. This process also took place in other countries across the globe, albeit in distinctly different ways. In rapidly modernizing Japan, for example, the house lost its traditional role in shaping stable family community and social status and gained new meanings as middle-class citizens conceived of the act of dwelling increasingly in terms of cosmopolitan consumption and personal expression. In this context, Japanese architects and designers adopted new ideas from Europe and the United States (Sand 2005).

Despite the efforts of such self-conscious modernizers, real estate developers, homebuilders, homeowners, and homebuyers undoubtedly constituted the most important modernizing force in suburbia. In the first decades of the twentieth century, particularly in the United States, rapid suburbanization was accompanied by often rapidly changing styles and forms of architecture responding to modern consumer taste. 'Catalog' homes, such as those offered by Sears, Roebuck, and Co., featured not just the latest modern conveniences and technological inventions but an eclectic mix of styles, from the stately symmetry of English neoclassical revival to the gambrel roofs and dormers inspired by the Dutch colonial barn. Commercial homebuilders were finely attuned to homebuyers' changing tastes, adapting not only style and decoration but also the layout and organization of kitchens and bathrooms (Schweitzer and Davis 1990).

Even if the modern single-family house is an artefact of creative imagination, cultural translation, and commercial pragmatism, its forms have nonetheless been shaped by national law, finance, politics, and geography. In Belgium, for example, Catholic anti-urban housing and labor policies focused on working-class homeownership. In this context, a dense network of regional and local railways and tramways coupled with inexpensive tickets spurred the distribution of the working class over the traditional countryside (Seebohm-Rowntree 1910; De Meulder et al. 1999).[3] This prompted the development of a new suburban house type. Working-class, self-built houses were adapted from the urban row house to fit narrow but deep lots along countryside roads. With a front room reserved for official purposes, such as visits by the local priest or notary, these brick houses made modest allusions to bourgeois domesticity. At the same time, everyday life took place in the back of the house, and its self-built additions – workshop, washing room, or chicken coop – accommodated

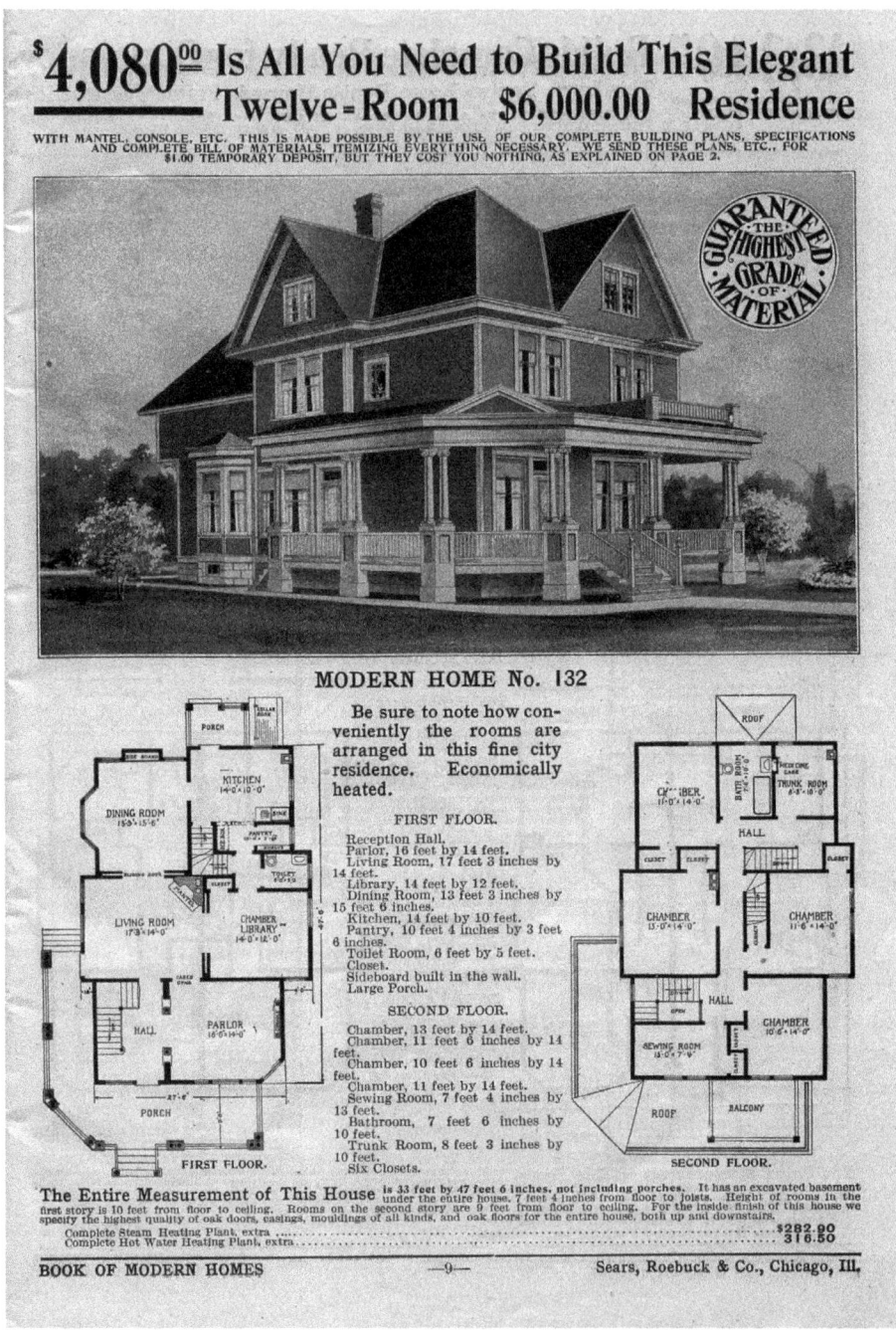

FIGURE 3.1: An early twentieth-century catalogue home from Sears, Roebuck, and Co. From the Sears Holdings Collection.

FIGURE 3.2: A detached house in Belgium, typical of the country's suburbanization in the first half of the twentieth century, as it appears in 2016. © Kenny Cupers.

inhabitants' rural lifestyles, as subsistence gardening often complemented wage income. The modernity of this house type was thus an ambivalent one.

In the first half of the twentieth century, suburbanization and the ideal of single-family homeownership were thus not exclusively limited to the middle or upper-middle classes. Even in the United States, where private real estate developers reigned supreme, land was not solely subdivided for planned neighbourhoods with ready-built homes. Some subdivisions were the product of the labor and vision of working-class and African American families, who understood homeownership as a guarantor of economic and family security (Nicolaides 2002; Wiese 2004; Harris 2012). Since the mid-nineteenth century, European social reformers had promoted working-class homeownership as the solution to labor unrest, but only in the first half of the twentieth century did suburban subdivisions expand rapidly across Europe. The post-First World War housing crisis led to the proliferation of self-built cottages on peripherally located allotments, in particular around Paris and Berlin, often without access to basic utilities or paved roads. Even though their inhabitants were isolated and cut off from the city and its amenities, they realized the petit-bourgeois ideal of private homeownership (Fourcaut 2000). The *lotissements défectueux* (defective subdivisions), as officials termed them, informed the social stigmatization of the suburban single-family home that would shape French housing policy in the post-war decades.

The Second World War accelerated the globalization of the suburban house, spurring technical inventions and reorganizing the construction industry and the role of developers, homebuilders, governments, architects, and other professionals in the process. From the microwave oven to prefabricated building techniques, the aftermath of war was the predominance of a new, technologically advanced domesticity in which the United States took a leading role (Colomina 2007). To address the housing shortage that had existed since the Great Depression and been deepened by the post-war return of veterans and the baby boom, the US government privileged individual, suburban homeownership. This was both an ideological project and a pragmatically driven economic strategy. Post-war America became a suburban nation, with Levittown, built by Levitt and Sons for returning veterans, as the paradigmatic example of a new reality of large-scale subdivisions with assembly-line houses. With a transportation policy serving the automobile and the indirect support of government-backed mortgages, but without direct subsidies and little involvement of architects or planners, large-scale homebuilders developed standardized house types in traditional forms and styles, from which customers could choose.[4] The owners of these 'Cape Cod' and ranch-style houses often drastically redesigned them to conform to their tastes and needs. This large-scale modernization of dwelling was the work of both builders and buyers who wanted houses that would improve the lives of their children and that espoused a modern, democratic way of life. In this way, these houses differed not only from European modernist models but also from older forms of American domestic architecture (Kelly 1993; Lane 2015).

Subdivision or tract houses, a typical product of post-war America, helped reshape class, race, and gender relations. To their white homeowners, they were a vehicle of upward social mobility; to African Americans and other minorities, a barrier of segregation (Harris 2012). Furthermore, suburban subdivisions reflected the dominant ideology of the period; namely, mass consumerism. In the world of the suburban subdivision, the housewife was the expert consumer, removed from the 'male' world of production and the city (Cohen 2003). In these multiple ways, the post-war single-family home structured both the nuclear family and society at large, while rising family incomes and a government-backed mortgage system set in motion the transformation of housing into a financial instrument in subsequent decades. In doing so, it made the single-family home both the unquestioned norm of middle-class living and a cog in an economic system that continues to shape horizons of materialist aspiration as well as social structures of inequality (Immergluck 2015).

Even though quintessentially American, the dream of the single-family home travelled across the networks of the Cold War – whether via kitchen appliances, prefabrication companies, or architects' journals. Yet its global predominance was not a matter of simple transfer.[5] In Belgium, arguably continental Europe's premier suburban nation, the government was equally encouraging of private homeownership through a new mortgage system. At the same time, few large-scale homebuilding ventures took hold, and much of the country's suburbia is still semi-self-built or custom designed rather than speculatively planned (Van Herck and Avermaete 2006; Heynen 2010). In France, the government turned towards single-family homeownership as an alternative to mass collective housing and developed a corresponding mortgage system only in the mid-1960s (Cupers 2014). At this time, Levitt and Sons set up shop in France, but the company had to develop a significantly different product in response to state regulation and thus targeted a more affluent middle-class audience (Gournay 2002). Surprisingly, many French suburban houses are built by the same large-scale construction companies responsible for the country's much-reviled mass housing projects. In West Germany, private homebuilders also spurred suburban development, typically in the form of flat-roofed, single-storey, brick or concrete houses called 'bungalows'. They nevertheless differed in both material and shape from the low-pitch-roof houses Americans called 'bungalows' at this time, although they were inspired by modernist American designs such as those of the Case Study Houses, post-war experiments organized by *Arts & Architecture* magazine (Ebert 2012).

Although the American single-family home has changed somewhat as an object of design and as a material technology since the 1950s, many of its core features remained consistent throughout the second half of the century. Architects, standing at the side-line, have tended to dismiss the suburban single-family home as they have traditionally dismissed suburbia altogether. In their study of Levittown, however, postmodern architects Denise Scott Brown and Robert Venturi (1970) legitimized suburban architecture by exploring its everyday meanings. In contrast, the designers of the New Urbanism in the 1980s and 1990s launched another attempt at reform. Following older critiques of suburbia as monotonous and isolating (see Archer 2008), they emphasized the need for walkable neighbourhoods, multi-family housing, social control, and community building without questioning other basic assumptions of suburbia. In fact, with their emphasis on homogeneous design as lifestyle branding, they accentuated the value of the house as a commodity in a late-capitalist real estate market (Ross 1999). Meanwhile, a far more significant transformation of suburbia has taken place with the growing presence of Asian and Latino immigrants in the American housing market in the last decades (Myers and Liu 2006). The emergence of 'ethnoburbs' in California, for example, illustrates how both lower-class and upper-class immigrants appropriate the single-family home by creating new styles, uses, and forms (Rojas 1991; Li 2006).

But suburbia is transcultural in regions of the world other than just the United States. Since the economic reforms of the 1980s in China, global geographies and architectural motifs, from Mediterranean or Tudor to Orange County and Australian beach, have informed the design and marketing of new housing developments. Despite the role of Western celebrity architects in high-profile projects in China, this development is not simply an import or a mirror of the West. Even if the speed of China's state-capitalist development might recall the industrialization of the nineteenth-century Western world, the country's process of modernization is fundamentally different. Some of its housing developments look at first glance like McMansion-type developments and many are branded using Western lifestyle motifs and architectural styles (Campanella 2008). Yet the design of Chinese villa complexes builds on a long history of national housing models and planning practices that are averse to suburban subdivisions. Moreover, the driving force behind new housing developments are not Western architects but Chinese expats who bring design ideas back to China.[6] The 'international' stylistic packaging is what Chinese modernity looks like for its growing middle classes. In many post-independence African countries, single-family homes in enclosed suburban divisions are also a sign of desired middle-class identity. They are often seen as a product of Westernization even though they are more specifically the aftereffect of colonization. In fast-growing Nigerian cities, for example, the suburban bungalow has become the new norm for nuclear families, contrasting with the colonial-era tenement housing for singles and the traditional compound for larger kinship groups. The African middle class in this context has appropriated a European colonial heritage – the bungalows once built for European administrators – and transformed it into an elite aesthetic and form (Chokor 2005).

The most recent subdivision developments in cities globally have not gone without diversification and transformation. Suburban developments in Europe as well as in the United States over the past few decades have also featured gradually higher densities, including experiments with multi-family housing such as townhouses and condos, which aim to reproduce the advantages of suburban living in more-compact forms (Leinberger 2008; Lasner 2009). Another recent trend is the adaptation of suburban developments to meet rising expectations for privacy, and developers are building gated communities not just in the United States but across the Americas, South Asia, and Africa (Caldeira 1996).

Instead of conceptualizing the history of the single-family house as one of linear transfer or influence, we might instead consider its development as part of a history of globalization that transcends the centre/periphery binary. The single-family house represents a world revolution in kinship and property, underway since the advent of modern capitalism in the later eighteenth century but fully realized only in the twentieth century. The house – as a cultural form, a commodity, or a technology – was central to the modernization of peasant cultures and the making of industrial societies. As such it is a primary element of the suburbanization of large swaths of what has in the process become a thoroughly globalized world. The house is also part of a history of expanding homeownership characteristic of the vast majority of capitalist states in the twentieth century (Aalbers and Christophers 2014). Even though it is global in the sense of being a worldwide phenomenon, the house is not universal, as the history of collective housing demonstrates.

SLABS: EXPERIMENTS IN COLLECTIVE DWELLING

The slabs, blocks, and towers dotting metropolitan horizons from Paris to Moscow and from Singapore to São Paulo appear as the antithesis of the single-family house in its subdivision: high instead of low, urban instead of suburban, collective instead of individual, concrete instead of green. Collective housing differs not just in terms of landownership structures – built as it often is on public or cooperatively owned land – but also in terms of its mode of production, with local or central governments rather than private builders or developers often taking the lead. Yet the history of modernist mass housing – a dominant form of urbanization in much of the world during the twentieth century – belies such a duality.[7]

This history is inextricably linked to the history of social reform under industrial capitalism. Since the studies of Edwin Chadwick and Friedrich Engels in the 1840s, the squalid living conditions of the working poor in the rapidly growing industrial cities of nineteenth-century Europe and America became central to social and political debates. To ameliorate these conditions – and prevent working-class uprisings – social reformers suggested a variety of solutions, dominant among which was the idea of building better housing for workers. In his *The Housing Question*, Engels ([1872] 1988) dismissed the idea that the housing problem can be resolved within the existing condition of capitalism and argued that any such solutions ultimately mean conservative class politics. Early on, progressive reformers and philanthropists provided housing for the working classes. So did industrial capitalists, who built at times rather luxurious and stately housing complexes for their workers, from Jean-Baptiste André Godin's Familistère in Guise to the community of Pullman in Chicago. Only later did the state become involved. Thus, before it became a technosocial government enterprise that would come to shape dwelling culture and urbanization throughout the century, modern mass housing emerged within, not just in reaction to, nineteenth-century liberal capitalism.[8]

Surprisingly, modern collective housing grew in part out of initiatives based on anti-urban ideals that were not too different from those undergirding the single-family home subdivision. Chief among these was Ebenezer Howard's turn-of-the-century Garden City, a reformist proposal to counter uncontrolled urbanization by building new settlements in the English countryside. Inspired by cultural reform movements and the cooperative ideas of Peter Kropotkin, Howard proposed collective landownership and amenities based on voluntary cooperation. But the form these took was suburban (Fishman 1982). In Germany as well, the garden city movement, closely linked to the land reform movement, was often informed by pastoral ideals – close contact with nature, safe haven at a distance from the city yet dependent on it. These ideas influenced the first mass housing estates in the 1920s.

In material and technical terms as well, collective housing came out of experiments with single-family dwelling. Industrialized construction and prefabrication techniques, which would become indispensable to massive production of housing slabs and blocks in the post-war period, appeared first in the colonial world and then in the United States and Europe. The prefabricated cottages for colonists that British, French, German, and other colonial officers shipped to their colonies were predominantly in wood or in metal, although at least one French company developed hollowed concrete panels (Junghanns 1994; Bergdoll and Christensen 2008).

In the first decades of the twentieth century, architects such as the California-based Irving Gill advanced such techniques for domestic housing construction. Inspired by scientific management and Henry Ford's factory assembly line, Gill poured concrete into flat slabs that were then hoisted vertically into place to serve as outer walls (Hines 2000). Yet beyond Rudolph Schindler or Grosvenor Atterbury, the concrete tilt-slab construction method had no large-scale influence in the United States. In Europe, however, architects who experimented with concrete prefabrication enjoyed much greater influence. With his Maison Domino project of 1915, for example, Le Corbusier proposed a standard dwelling module that could be mass-produced and configured in a variety of ways, as a large-scale solution to the wartime housing crisis (Cohen 2013).

Experiments in mass housing were also spurred by wartime emergencies, which often exacerbated long-standing housing shortages, overcrowding, and lack of sanitation. In the wake of the First World War, mass collective housing became a key site of social and political experimentation for European public authorities. But mass housing schemes were not just a result of ideological consensus about government intervention and the failure of liberal capitalism to provide decent housing. In many cases, they were also led by pragmatic needs and economic strategy. For example, after the territorial reorganizations of the Treaty of Versailles, Vienna had a population out of proportion with the city's resources, and could survive only by restricting wages and low rents, which in turn allowed for the development of a huge housing construction programme (Benevolo 1977). Government intervention in housing across Europe took two main routes, either directly (public bodies to oversee construction of housing, as in England) or indirectly (with credit given to private associations or cooperatives, as in Sweden). Aiming to civilize workers by imitating middle-class dwelling, architects and housing associations transformed an older social reform agenda into a massive construction programme that changed the face of the city. In Amsterdam, for instance, the new housing projects boasted expressionist façades that celebrated uniqueness and monumentality, while the units behind them, designed independently, were increasingly standardized (Stieber 1998). This ambiguity constituted a key moment in the development of housing, from a cultural artefact into a governmental system. Architecture and social policy became directly intertwined, first at the municipal and then at the national level.

The mass housing schemes in 1920s Germany were generally based on earlier garden city ideas, often leading to low-rise, suburban schemes with private allotments and gardens. These layouts were as much a hygienic reaction to the dense fabric of the nineteenth-century city and its lack of light, air, and space as they were a negation of this city's bourgeois structures of private landownership. For Das Neue Frankfurt, the housing construction programme that changed the face of Frankfurt from 1925 to 1930, Ernst May and his team, including Grete Schütte-Lihotzky, who was responsible for the kitchen design, developed a comprehensive standardized construction system. May's collaborators were the first to use prefabricated concrete panels on a large scale, a technique that lent itself more to the creation of strips of multi-family blocks than to single-family homes (Henderson 2013). In contrast to these suburban solutions was the housing programme of Red Vienna. In an otherwise conservative Austria, Vienna's municipal socialist government launched a massive building programme within the existing city boundaries, leading to resolutely urban, dense, and often monumental housing forms. Reminiscent of nineteenth-century bourgeois architecture, the architecture of Red Vienna manipulated the traditional perimeter block and fostered new collective spaces and uses, suggesting a gradual transformation of the city into socialism (Blau 1999). In post-revolutionary Russia, the housing crisis led to more radical architectural experiments, but they remained small in scale until the 1930s. The Narkomfin Communal House in Moscow was designed by Moisei Ginzburg in 1928 as a transition between the traditional organization of private flats and the new type of total communal living. In addition to a mix of dwelling units, it contained a variety of communal spaces, including a kitchen and canteen, library, day nursery, roof terrace, and laundry rooms. The underlying assumption was of architecture as a social condenser – that architecture had the ability to shape social behaviour and thus provoke the new socialist way of life (Buchli 1999).

These housing designs were not conceived in isolation from one another. The Narkomfin's strip windows and roof terrace, like Le Corbusier's Villa Savoye, resulted less from isolated geniuses than from the circulation of ideas among an international avant-garde of architects, artists, and designers. They were brought together in institutions such as the Bauhaus and associations such as the International Congresses of Modern Architecture (CIAM). The latter was in fact crucial to debates about the 'minimum dwelling' (*Existenzminimum*), designed according to objective standards of light, space, and air, and the growing consensus among international modernists in the late 1920s that collective rather than individual housing was most suited to modern needs, at least in metropolitan areas. The association's 1933 Athens Charter posited both the idea of high-rise mass housing and the reorganization of landownership by the state as starting points for planning – assumptions that would become dominant in the post-war period.

What the Second World War did for the single-family home in terms of technological acceleration, it also did for the development of collective housing. Even though the standardization of construction elements had first developed in the early 1900s in the United States, followed by Germany during the First World War, and even though standardization was a crucial part of architectural discourse in the 1920s, only during the 1930s and 1940s did it become a broader development in housing. Ernst Neufert, an architect associated with the Bauhaus who subsequently worked for the Nazi regime, developed a 'building design method' (*Bauentwurfslehre*) as a standardization of the design process itself, rather than of only its material components. But the war served as a catalyst in many other ways: it legitimized a strong interventionist state, prompted the modernization of the construction industry, and, particularly in France, led to the emergence of large corporate firms focused on concrete prefabrication techniques – all of which were preconditions to the development of mass housing estates in the post-war period (Cupers 2014).

Different regimes of collective housing production developed in Europe as part of national reconstruction programmes and within particular frameworks of economic planning – from Keynesian to Soviet-style. In the eyes of many architects at the time, the key prototype for mass housing was Le Corbusier's Unité d'habitation, built in Marseille from 1947 to 1952. The building, a high-rise containing housing as well as collective amenities in a sea of green space, was a symbol of modernity, conceived as the perfect opposite of the suburban sprawl of single-family homes. Yet architects were not the only shapers of housing production in the post-war period: government officials, housing organizations or developers, social science experts, and, at times, resident associations were also powerful. The increase in production signalled a fundamental shift in approaches to mass housing (Cupers 2014). First, this change represented not just the dissemination of inter-war modernist ideas and planning practices but a qualitative transformation in the relationship between modern architecture and society. Second, it was a shift in the logic of welfare, which expanded beyond working-class reform to rational and efficient provisioning, whether of socialist subjects or citizen-consumers.

In France, the construction of mass collective housing estates or *grands ensembles* on the urban outskirts was, though supported by leftist municipalities, essentially guided by the centralized, technocratic state. In this context, architectural standardization made social normalization sensible in the form of identical apartments with identical windows. The state aimed to build quickly and economically for a broad range of constituents. But this did not mean socialism or social equality. While mass housing fostered upward mobility for white working- and middle-class nuclear families, it excluded many others, in particular the growing number of immigrant construction workers who rarely had the opportunity to live in the new apartments and often lived in the shantytowns next to them (Cupers 2014). In Great Britain, large-scale housing construction was afforded by a similar modernization of the construction industry but was organized by municipal councils rather than national authorities. Furthermore, rental 'council housing' was often coupled with slum clearance and thus situated in more central urban locations, where slums were typically located (Bullock 2002; Finnimore 1989; Glendinning and Muthesius 1994). In Sweden, a strong functionalist discourse reshaped the politics and aesthetics of housing production from the 1930s onward (Mattsson and Wallenstein 2010). Even though housing production in European welfare states was technocratically guided by experts and the state, it was not always the product of top-down imposition. In the Netherlands, housing was shaped by clear mechanisms of mediation between state and citizen, in the form of civil-society organizations (Bervoets 2010). Most important, against the dominant perception of monotony, the housing schemes of this era were not one-off schemes that were repeated everywhere in the same fashion. In fact, the production of mass housing from the end of the Second World War until the oil crises of the mid-1970s was varied and evolving, with experiments in high-, medium-, and low-rise housing types, sometimes with the crucial input of sociologists or landscape designers.[9]

The divergences – and convergences – of mass housing types become even clearer when we look beyond Western Europe. In the Soviet bloc, mass collective housing was rigorously planned from above, especially in the USSR, but it was also caught in a Cold War competition of models – one in which Berlin served as the world's showcase (Harris 2013; Berlinische Galerie 2015). Even though the Eastern bloc's doctrines – in particular the economically prompted shift from neoclassical to functionalist architecture in 1954 – were largely Soviet inspired, mass housing models were shaped by varieties of Second World socialism. In Czechoslovakia, for example, mass housing, including its prefabrication techniques, developed less from Soviet doctrine than from the region's modernist functionalism of the 1930s (Zarecor 2010). In China in the 1950s, mass housing policies were promoted by the new Communist regime with a primary focus on controlling rural-urban migration (Zhang 1997). Even though Chinese designers worked with colleagues from the Soviet Union to develop low-cost standardized designs with great uniformity, housing was organized around the Chinese concept of *danwei*, an independent live-work compound that included high-rise housing and all necessary collective amenities (Lu 2006).

In technological terms, mass collective housing was not a product of either the First or the Second World. Techniques for the production and assembly of large prefabricated concrete panels came from post-Second World War France and Sweden as much as from Czechoslovakia, Yugoslavia, and the USSR, and both engineering expertise and architectural ideas consistently crossed Cold War boundaries. The East German *plattenbauten* construction technique, for instance, seems to have been derived from the Camus system in France rather than from the USSR, as officially declared (Hannemann 2005). The Soviet Union exported their panel systems as far as Cuba and Chile (Alonso and Palmarola 2009), while the Yugoslav skeletal concrete prefab system went as far as Angola and the Philippines (Kulić, Mrduljaš, and Thaler 2012). At times, the housing forms were exported without the corresponding construction techniques. For the new socialist regime in Zanzibar, for instance, East German architects and planners built slab-type housing but without system-building methods (Wimmelbücker 2012).

FIGURE 3.3: Mass housing in Michanzani, Zanzibar, constructed from 1970 to 1973, as it appeared in 2014. © Kenny Cupers.

If modern collective housing in the form of blocks and slabs was one of the quintessential products of Cold War globalization, the 1970s were a key turning point in this development. In much of Western Europe as well as in the United States, where it was more occasionally deployed for low-income families, publicly funded collective housing fell disastrously from grace in this decade, even if critical voices had sounded much earlier. Critics cite the demolition of Pruitt-Igoe in 1972 as the end of public housing in the United States, and with it, the end of modern architecture more generally (Bristol 1991).[10] In France, the 1970s signalled a shift from the *grands ensembles* serving as icons of modernization to becoming suburban sites of relegation for a post-colonial underclass. Housing policies in many countries shifted from brick-and-mortar subsidies to indirect support through vouchers or the non-profit sector and, in some cases, from an emphasis on redistribution to a preoccupation with privacy, security, and criminality (Scanlon and Whitehead 2008). Indeed, the gradual withdrawal of the state in direct housing provision during this period is seen as exemplary of neoliberalization, the process of economic restructuring during the 1970s away from direct government regulation and welfare spending. A more precise category to analyse the changes in housing form and policy, however, is privatization (Cupers 2017). The increase in owner-occupation during the previous decades squeezed the rental housing sector, both quantitatively and ideologically (Kemeny 1995). Paradigmatic of this shift is Margaret Thatcher's 'Right to Buy' scheme of 1980, which allowed tenants to buy their homes and was extraordinarily successful in the selling off of British council housing, effectively privatizing the country's substantial public housing stock (Jones and Murie 2006).

Yet the shift away from publicly funded high-rise housing was not a global one. Despite being almost universally contested in North America and Western Europe, public housing programmes continued to flourish in Hong Kong, South Korea (Gelézeau 2004), and Singapore, where they still constitute the bulk of current housing stock, albeit in ways unrecognizable to the West. Their mass housing programmes are not associated with welfare-state social democracy or Soviet socialism but with authoritarian free-enterprise capitalism. At the same time, these housing programmes are not historically unrelated to their European counterparts. Housing programmes in both Hong Kong and Singapore, British colonial city-state ports, were developed through long-established administrative and political mechanisms of British colonialism and the processes of decolonization (Glendinning 2015). Hong Kong experienced massive urban growth in the post-war period, and public housing was first geared to resettling refugees from China. The initially basic housing models – H-shape six-storey blocks without elevators or electricity – evolved towards public housing estates in the mid-1960s (Castells et al. 1988). After Singapore became independent in the early 1960s, the government also focused on low-cost emergency housing,

FIGURE 3.4: King Ming Estate, Hong Kong, public rental housing by the Hong Kong Housing Authority, completed in 2003. Baycrest Photography Service.

gradually shifting its focus to a more general policy of homeownership through state-led housing production (Castells et al. 1988).

High-rise housing production following the European welfare-state model of public financing and mass renting has become exceptional today, but high-rise housing is in fact booming globally, and governments have played a role in its success. Across the BRIC countries (Brazil, Russia, India, and China) and beyond, new, often gated, communities of luxury housing towers are being built for the new middle classes (Pow 2009). Since its economic reforms in the 1980s, China has been experiencing unparalleled urbanization and a shift in mass housing. Even though suburban townhouses have also emerged, the common type of suburbanization in post-reform China is in the form of mid- and high-rise housing compounds. Modelled after the socialist *danwei* production unit as well as the modernist concept of the neighbourhood unit, these gated complexes feature themed gardens and a great array of amenities such as kindergartens, clinics, restaurants, convenience shops, and sports facilities. They are marketed as lifestyle choices and often branded with English-sounding names to emphasize the sophisticated cosmopolitan outlook of homebuyers (Chen, Wang, and Kundu 2009; Shen and Wu 2011). In Mumbai, two types of modern housing represent starkly different sides of a single coin: the government builds drab concrete housing slabs to house the poor and remove them from high-value land, which is then developed to build high-rise condominium housing for the global elite (Chalana 2010).

Rather than a shift from high-rise to low-rise, or from state to private provision, mass housing production in recent decades has undergone a general convergence of state provision with market-led models. Even if, historically, high-rise housing was largely a product of the state as the suburban house was a product of the market, the relationship between political economy and built form was never absolute. Moreover, suburban development, garden cities, and council estates initially shared basic ideas, subsequently diverging as both state and market production were in full force by mid-century. The rise of market-rate apartment living, then, can be understood as a re-convergence of social and market models, of subdivisions and slabs, both physically and in terms of ownership.[11] Indeed, both the US market-led model and the Singaporean mass housing model rely on fungible individual ownership, embraced by private builders and by government nearly everywhere – West, BRIC, and beyond.[12]

State-aided high-rise housing cannot simply be written off as part of Cold War history: it is as much a product of authoritarian capitalism as it is a bygone product of the Communist or Social Democratic welfare state. Some scholars nevertheless argue that public or any form of non-market housing is historically abnormal – that recourse is made to state-funded, 'de-commodified' housing only when the capitalist market is unable to provide housing (Harloe 1995). Such an argument rests on the assumption that housing is and always has been a commodity, an object bought and sold on a market. This is not only a partial view of reality but a historically blind one. The market is a complex historical construction, market values do not preclude social meaning, and the interrelations between the private rental market, owner-occupation, and the public rental sector are always shaped by the specific fabric and forces of social life (Kemeny 1995). Most pertinent in this respect is the contemporary legacy of social housing: the post-socialist transformation of collective land- and homeownership, and commons of all kinds, into private property has caused huge waves of displacement that are still felt in neighbourhoods and cities today (Ghertner 2015).

SHANTYTOWNS: FROM EXCEPTION TO RULE

Despite the popularity of the single-family home and the vast production of high-rise housing, the twentieth century was perhaps first and foremost the century of the shantytown. The proliferation of informal settlements of self-built shacks continues to define the rapidly urbanizing regions of the Global South. Built by squatters on public or private land without official permission and public infrastructure such as roads, water, or electricity, such settlements seem to defy both the role of government and the laws of private landownership. Nevertheless, state governance, albeit in an unconventional guise, is rarely absent, and neither is private homeownership, which is often the focus of a complex social struggle. Self-built huts may look timelessly backward, but the shantytown is a quintessentially modern phenomenon. Even though informal settlements are often discursively dismissed as the antithesis of the modern, they are by-products of twentieth-century modernization – just like the nineteenth-century slum was a direct consequence of industrial capitalism.[13]

A history of squatter settlements might begin in Paris or Berlin just as well as in Rio de Janeiro. In the beginning of the twentieth century, the 'zone non ædificandi' of the old fortifications around Paris became a zone for squatters, ragpickers, and beggars. Coming from the impoverished countryside or pushed out of the city by real estate speculation in the wake of Haussmannization, these very poor 'zonards', as they were called, built a circle of shantytowns around the City of Light (Le Hallé 1986). More squatter settlements emerged across Europe as a result of the catastrophic conditions during and after the First World War. The citizens of Vienna and Berlin, among other cities, took it upon themselves to find a solution to the severe housing and food crisis by building makeshift shelters on public land and planting subsistence gardens on

FIGURE 3.5: The 'Zone' of Paris, as photographed by Eugène Atget, 1913. Library of Congress, Prints and Photographs Division, Washington, DC.

the urban outskirts. In Vienna, this 'wild settlement movement' encompassed more than 100,000 people by 1918 and set in motion the city's mass housing programme the following decade (Blau 1999). Squatter settlements were thus a feature of European urbanization before they prevailed in the Global South.

Turn-of-the-twentieth-century Rio de Janeiro was perhaps the first place outside Europe where squatter settlements emerged. The city's first favela was founded by soldiers who, returning from war and not provided the housing they were promised, occupied the hills close to the city centre. The settlement grew quickly after engineer Pereira Passos's hygienist urban renewal programme, inspired by Baron Haussmann, led to the demolition of poor neighbourhoods, forcing the inhabitants to squat in the hills. The term *favela* derives from the name of the plant covering these hills, which was popularly known as 'Morro da Favela', and soon came to be used to describe other shantytowns in Brazil (de Almeida Abreu 1994).

Only in the second half of the twentieth century, however, did the shantytown become the dominant form of urbanization, in particular in the Global South. Squatting began to spike in Africa, Latin America, the Middle East, and Southeast Asia during the 1960s and 1970s (Davis 2006). In contrast to the growth of industrial cities in nineteenth-century Europe and North America, this recent urbanization was 'radically decoupled from industrialization, even from development per se' (Davis 2006: 13). Even without the pull factor of formal employment, cities of the South have grown exponentially, and the majority of this growth is in the form of shantytowns (Davis 2006). Even using UN-HABITAT's restrictive definition of what constitutes a slum, the number of slum dwellers had exceeded one billion by 2005 and continues to grow every year. Some have estimated that formal housing stock in these cities amounts to no more than 20 percent, leaving the majority of citizens to house themselves illegally or informally (Davis 2006). Africa's shantytowns are growing no less than twice as fast as its rapidly growing cities (Davis 2006).[14]

This extreme proliferation of shantytowns is driven by the various forces that push people out of the countryside, whether environmental catastrophe, military and ethnic conflict, or agricultural policy. Perhaps the most crucial factor, however, has been the legacy of colonialism. Many colonial government policies were anti-urban, focused on territorial control and agricultural modernization, and rural people were often excluded from urban citizenship (Davis 2006).[15] The South African apartheid system criminalized urban migration and segregated Blacks in exurban townships (Ginsburg 2011). At the same time, colonialism unsettled traditional countrysides and set in motion the migration of peasants to the city. Not surprisingly, then, decolonization coincided with explosive urbanization. In the process of Algeria's violent decolonization, for example, Algiers became acutely urbanized with *bidonvilles*, shack settlements built with found materials such as corrugated metal sheets and oil barrels (Descloitres,

Reverdy, and Descloitres 1961). A French term for shantytown, *bidonville* was first coined in the late 1920s to describe an area on the outskirts of Casablanca where recent rural migrants to the city had built shack dwellings without the colonial regime's authorization (Crane 2013). But *bidonvilles* emerged not just in the colonies at this time; they also appeared in the metropole. Mid-1960s Paris had no less than 119 *bidonvilles*, home to about 47,000 people from Italy, Portugal, and Africa (Gastaut 2004). Despite the key importance of colonialism, however, restrictions on rural-to-urban movement were not just limited to colonial contexts, as the impact of the *propiska* system in the Soviet Union and *hukou* system in China illustrate.[16] In both regions, shantytowns are currently a dominant feature of urban development.

Fundamental to slum dynamics are ecological precariousness, toxicity, and impending disaster – from landslides to the health consequences of living on a garbage dump (Davis 2006). The slum system itself is characterized by deep poverty and inequality, structural violence, grey areas of ownership, and weak systems of governance. Slums and shantytowns, such as Rio de Janeiro's favelas, are certainly shaped by a politics of destitution, and known as places of extreme violence perpetrated both by drug traffickers and the police. At the same time, how such spectacular violence is mediated tends to hide the ways the poor continue to be marginalized (Robb Larkins 2015). Slums, shantytowns, and even camps are not just spaces of exception. To their inhabitants, they are also the spaces of everyday life, with homes that fulfil, albeit in often extremely precarious conditions, roles similar to those fulfilled by houses elsewhere: providing a sense of self, of community and belonging, of personal histories and family aspirations.

Throughout much of the past century, the dominant government response to shantytowns was removal and forced eviction. From the emergence of the first favelas in Rio through the end of the Brazilian dictatorship in 1985, the dominant policy was to 'cut out the cancer' from the city. Elites and officials perceived shantytowns as a health, moral, and political threat, akin to the nineteenth-century slum. By the middle of the century, however, favelas had become the principal form of housing for the poor in cities such as Rio. Despite a struggling industrial sector, Rio grew exponentially, leading to an informal local economy in which many of the favela inhabitants found work in construction and as domestic servants, forming a 'subproletariat' of sorts (Pino 1998). Although shantytowns were being cleared earlier, clearance projects dramatically picked up pace during the dictatorship period from 1964 to 1985, and favela inhabitants, despite their resistance, were usually resettled in distant housing projects (Perlman 2010; McCann 2014). Squatter settlements also shaped the urbanization of Turkey in the post-war decades, a period of industrial modernization in that nation. After an initial period of uncontrolled squatting, which mostly occurred on public land in large Turkish cities, the state adopted repressive measures (Balaban 2011). Squatter settlements were often constructed overnight (hence the name *gecekondu*, literally 'built overnight'), torn down by police, then rebuilt and torn down again, until the authorities tired of the cycle.

Even though state intervention focused on shantytown clearance, from midcentury onward the shantytown also represented hope, even inspiring architects and designers to rethink their housing solutions. Instead of seeing this type of environment simply as an obstacle to progress and modernization, they studied the shantytown as an inspiration for future dwelling. In 1953, Algiers-based architects associated with CIAM pursued detailed architectural studies of la Mahieddine, then the city's largest *bidonville*. Unlike the Egyptian architect Hassan Fathy, who adopted traditional dwelling forms and ornaments in his government-led resettlement project of New Gourna around the same time, these architects translated the lessons from everyday life in the *bidonville* into resolutely modernist housing designs. Despite their rhetoric of emancipation and anthropological interest in everyday life, the Algiers group's attempt to learn from the shantytown was situated within France's colonial project and its (implicitly) racist gathering of knowledge for colonial control (Crane 2013).

The approach inspired numerous housing experiments in subsequent decades, transcending European colonialist purviews. A key example is the Proyecto Experimental de Vivienda (PREVI) neighbourhood in Peru, which was launched in 1965 with the support of the United Nations by Peruvian president Fernando Belaúnde Terry, who was also an architect and urban theorist. As a strategy to regulate the explosive growth of informal migrant settlements around Lima in particular, the project adopted a threefold approach: the construction of a new

FIGURE 3.6: PREVI housing project, with architecture by Charles Correa, c. 1976. © José Orrego and Sharif Kahatt.

neighbourhood of 1,500 low-cost housing units, a neighbourhood rehabilitation project, and a strategy for 'rationalizing' 'spontaneous' housing settlements. Designed by a collection of local and international architects, including Candilis-Josic-Woods and Christopher Alexander, the new neighbourhood was directly inspired by the shantytown. In contrast to conventional housing that could not accommodate the rapid stream of migrants, the neighbourhood would grow and develop with its inhabitants ('PREVI/Lima' 1970).

This project represented a new neighbourhood model. The next steps were to upgrade and improve existing shantytowns, which entailed a sea change, not just in design but in global economic policy. Key to the broader shift was the English architect John F.C. Turner, who spent his formative period in the squatter settlements or *barriadas* of Lima from 1957 to 1965 and was also involved with PREVI (Bromley 2003). As a self-proclaimed anarchist, his central thesis was that housing needed to be built and managed by people themselves. Turner criticized anti-squatter governments, arguing that self-building would prove more efficient and beneficial than any government housing provision (Turner 1976). Like the Algiers group and many other modernist architects, he was fascinated by the creativity and resourcefulness he saw at work in squatter housing. Instead of shantytown eradication, he proposed improvement. People should be given the 'freedom to build' and should control both the finance and management of housing (Turner and Fichter 1972).

Turner spoke out at the right time. Although he was not the only one to argue for self-help housing, he would have considerable influence in global policy-making. The United Nations held its first HABITAT conference around the time when Turner's *Housing by People* came out in 1976, and these conferences further galvanized Turner's ideas. The shift from shantytown clearance to upgrading was also part of a larger economic restructuring that was the result of the growing influence of global institutions such as the World Bank and the IMF (Davis 2006). On the one hand, these institutions' neoliberal economic policies informed market deregulation of agricultural products, thus fostering deagrarianization, which pushed peasants out of the countryside and multiplied the world's shantytowns (Bryceson 2000). On the other hand, they proposed to 'regularize' or legalize squatter settlements – either by the accrual of property rights over time or through official actions of infrastructural upgrading, such as the cable car in Cazucá, Colombia (Bocarejo, José, and Rivadulla 2014). The economist Hernando de Soto gained enormous influence in this shift to regularization. He argued that unlocking the potential of the global poor required the removal of obstacles to the ownership of property. Despite many limitations, de Soto's doctrine spurred a variety of so-called regularization programmes, including in his home country of Peru, involving the legalization of squatters' tenure through titling.

In the last decades of the twentieth century, many countries adopted policies, sometimes with unintended or even unfavourable consequences, to provide legal title to land held under a wide range of illegal or extra-legal forms, such as squatting, collective ownership, cooperatives, and other forms of commons (Bromley 2004). Since the 1980s, Turkey has given land titles to squatters, who have subsequently become the petit bourgeois landlords for newly arriving migrants. This has resulted in a de facto 'enclosure' of urban space: the privatization of common land, comparable to the English enclosure movement of the eighteenth century (Balaban 2011). The movement for self-help in Turkey has thus become a major mechanism in the commodification of urban space, at the expense of the poor. Elsewhere, these policies have had equally ambiguous outcomes. From 1996 to 2006, Peru issued over 1.5 million freehold titles, but studies indicate that this has had little impact on alleviating poverty (Fernandes 2011). In Brazil, regularization programmes combined legal titling with the upgrading of public services, job creation, and community support structures. These more costly programmes have had mixed success and, what is more significant, have been unable to keep up with the sheer growth of new shantytowns (Fernandes 2011). Despite important exceptions, such as Nigeria, the privatization of squatting – giving residents a legal or de facto title to their plot – has now become the dominant mode of dealing with shantytown urbanization (Mamman 2015). Despite Turner's own critiques of World Bank policies, his anarchist ideas continue, ironically, to unofficially guide the neoliberal policies of shantytown regularization (Harms 1982; Harris 1998, 2003).

Shantytowns are one of the world's major housing challenges for the future. The majority of all housing associated with the projected population growth on the planet in the coming decades is predicted to be in the form of shantytowns and squatter settlements in the Global South (United Nations Population Fund 2007). Squatting can be understood as an act of self-determination by rural-to-urban migrants. By squatting, these migrants create a place in the city for themselves and, in so doing, assert their right to urban citizenship (Berner 1998; Holston 2009). But squatting is not simply 'free', nor is it always emancipatory. Squatters are subjected to structural violence and bribery by politicians and gangsters. In addition, squatter settlements have their own class structure and their own internally structured housing markets, often with exorbitant rents for extremely low-quality shelter (Gulyani and Talukdar 2008). With or without an actual legal title to the land, homes are bought, sold, and rented (Fernandes and Varley 1998; Davis 2006). We still know little about what shantytowns mean to those who inhabit them. How can we begin to know this world of the global urban poor, beyond simply recognizing that they are extremely creative and resourceful in organizing their livelihoods, even in the most precarious of conditions? (Boonyabancha 2011). Can shantytown removal or upgrading be more than a way for elites, in collaboration with the state, to suppress and benefit from the poor? In some cases, shantytown residents themselves facilitate, resist, subvert, or transform the top-down projects of eradication to their own ends (Doshi 2013; Patel 2013). In the end, what is perhaps most important to recognize is that shantytowns are not just abject states of exception but also spaces of everyday life, shaped by those who use and inhabit them, just like the world's cities and suburbs at large.

CONCLUSION

As the histories of subdivisions, slabs, and shantytowns reveal, dwelling is fundamentally shaped by political-economic modes of production and regimes of land tenure. Even though these three housing types have their internal dynamics of production and function as systems in this sense, they are also fundamentally and intricately interconnected as global cultural artefacts. Subdivisions, slabs, and shantytowns did not emerge naturally nor from a singular design. Nor do they spring from a singular political economic system. Bengali cottages and Dutch farm houses inspired the American suburb, even if real estate developers now build bungalows and McMansions across the globe. Concrete panel housing was invented by American and European modernist architects in the early 1900s, but only after the Second World War reshaped the construction industry and the interventionist state did this new technology change the face of socialist countries such as Czechoslovakia as much as capitalist ones such as France and Singapore. Shantytowns, in many cases an indirect product of colonialism, entered into the purview of governance when they emerged on the outskirts of Paris and the hills of Rio de Janeiro, before defining the urbanization of the Global South at large.

Because the perception persists that the single-family home belongs to the First World, mass collective housing to the Second, and squatter settlements to the Third, a history of our global age must address not only the colonial and transnational circulation of each of these forms but also the geopolitics in which they participate. A so-called global history should not just examine the diffusion of housing types and forms across the world but how these types and forms participate in the making of what we understand as the world system today. To cast the modern housing estate as historic proof of the failure of state intervention is not only to ignore the ongoing success of such dwelling forms; it is to reduce housing to a commodity in the capitalist housing market. Such a view ignores the fact that the market is itself a (fallible) product of history. Similarly, to cast the welfare state as the only beneficial alternative to the evils of capitalism is to ignore an entire history of diverse housing types and forms. It goes without saying that to divide the world into three dominant housing types is itself reductionist. What threatens to escape such a historical outline is a rich account of the everyday realities of domesticity, of attachment and belonging. Yet, that does not mean that these do not matter. My limited aim has been to show how the everyday reality of the house is reframed as part of the technopolitical system we call 'housing'.

During the last century, the house became a primary tool of political economy and, as such, a crucible of its global wealth inequalities (Martin, Moore, and Schindler 2015). Houses, as the primary stuff of the real estate market, are a store of private wealth and a tool for making profit. The materiality of housing is essential to the circulation of capital, regulated and/or fostered by the state (Aalbers and Christophers 2014). In the last decades, moreover, housing has increasingly served as a tool of financial capitalism: houses have been subjected to risk-limiting secondary-market speculation or securitization (Aalbers 2008). The central importance of housing to today's globally interconnected economy is regularly demonstrated in our era's housing bubbles and busts. Despite being entangled in our increasingly globalized political economy, however, the forms and meanings of dwelling are not just shadows of an economic logic or contained within the institutions that produce housing. If housing systems are the dominant worldview according to which housing is 'produced' and 'consumed', a critical history should also convey how dwellings are built and lived. To understand how the material culture of dwelling became a global housing system requires sidestepping the very way of seeing that identifies housing as a simple reflection of political-economic forces. Instead, therefore, I have approached dwelling forms as emerging from a transnational process of cultural invention. This perspective allows us to see the house as more than a static commodity – dwelling as reduced to economic relations between people and things – and instead to understand housing as world-making. Because the house, ultimately, is a world we make ourselves, individually and collectively.

CHAPTER FOUR

Furniture and Furnishings: Material Culture and Making the Modern

PAULINE GARVEY

In studies of the home, furniture and furnishings are often neglected. Distinct from architectural structures, these mobile elements of domestic construction – tables and chairs, china and glassware – often rate as minor in significance when compared to broader global forces, such as religion or economics, that shape our experience of home. Why should we prioritize the seemingly trivial, the rudiments that we pick up in the course of our lives? One might assume that furniture represents the flotsam of everyday life, at best a series of conveniences that keep us comfortable, at worst the siren-call of a consumer culture to which we are enthralled. And yet, scholars from diverse disciplines turn their attention to the home and its material culture in order to understand the scaffolding on which we build social bonds.

Writing to his fiancée Martha Bernays on an August night in 1882, Sigmund Freud hinted at the deeper significance of everyday things when he portrayed their coming married life, when they would live blissfully under one roof, as a cherished collection of objects and possessions:

> Tables and chairs, beds, mirrors, a clock to remind the happy couple of the passage of time, an armchair for an hour's pleasant daydreaming, carpets to help the housewife keep the floors clean, linen tied with pretty ribbons in the cupboard and dresses of the latest fashion and hats with artificial flowers,

pictures on the wall, glasses for everyday and others for wine and festive occasions ... Are we to hang our hearts on such little things? Yes, and without hesitation.

—Freud 1992: 27

As journalist Lauren Collins (2011), referring to the letter, suggests, 'We are attached to our belongings because they are vessels for our memories and for our aspirations'. For the individual, possessions are inextricably linked to identity – both to our remembered past and to our imagined future. Home, then, is where we house those possessions: in Freud's terms, where we house the little things on which we 'hang our hearts', or in Collins', the collective vessel of our many vessels.

At first glance, domestic space may appear to be a bastion of privacy – a place for cultivating personal relationships and familial identity, removed from social pressures and perhaps even a bulwark against them – from another perspective, the home is as public as it is private. Home perpetuates idealized perceptions of domesticity and concretizes myriad relationships. It represents a primary locus for imagining large-scale social formations; it is a centre for political strategy and class consolidation; a cornerstone for the state/citizen contract, and a canvas for group identity formation (Blunt and Dowling 2006; Buchli 1999, 2013; Cieraad 1999; Clarke 2001; Drazin 2001; Miller 2001; Schuldenfrei 2012). Emotional investment in loved ones is materialized through domestic practices such as everyday shopping and provisioning (Miller 1998), but in addition to love and care, the home is a source of contradiction, anxiety, and violence (Chapman and Hockey 1999; Das, Ellen, and Leonard 2008). Moreover, furniture is particularly salient in individual understandings of home because it is mobile (Reimer and Leslie 2004: 193). Often the house or the apartment may not conform to individual choices, but furniture is more easily negotiated with and manipulated to allow multiple individuals within a shared space to identify with it.

This chapter revisits selected moments in furniture and interior design from the past century. Focused on pivotal developments in Europe and the United States associated with the Modern Movement in architecture, it investigates how modernist design altered the arrangement of the domestic interior and relates this alteration to broader cultural trends. More than to simply provide an overview of design 'classics', the chapter serves to amplify the hum of shifting social and political resonances that form the background of modern domestic life.

DESIGNING THE MODERN MOVEMENT

If one movement dominated twentieth-century European and North American design culture, it was modernism. Rooted in the reformist impulses of the Arts and Crafts movements that emerged in England and Germany in the late nineteenth century, modernism in architecture and design emerged following the widespread trauma of the First World War, when a variety of practitioners from multiple countries began creating work that shared similar aesthetic qualities, ideological positions, or utopian ambitions. The influence of this work – from the scale of the city to the building to the room and even the individual object – eventually spread beyond national borders and today continues to be felt globally. Indeed, because of its ubiquity, we often fail to recognize just how profoundly modernism changed our world.

One of the earliest and oft-cited articulations of the modernist sensibility in design dates from 1910 (Long 2009: 204–5). At a lecture in Vienna, Austrian architect Adolf Loos delivered an impassioned attack on the decorative excesses of Victorian-period design. In particular, he vehemently criticized the application of surface ornament on furniture and other decorative objects, which he claimed was used to hide flaws in manufacture and also perpetuated nineteenth-century social hierarchies embedded in its labor and production processes. The rejection of ornament was for Loos the measure of civilization: what was acceptable in less developed countries he deemed wasteful – or debased – in developed ones: 'The Papuan tattoos his skin, his boat, his paddles, in short everything he can lay hands on. He is not a criminal. The modern man who tattoos himself is either a criminal or a degenerate' (Loos [1913] 1970: 19). Published in 1913 under the title 'Ornament and Crime' (Long 2009: 215), Loos's rejection of the overwrought, late-nineteenth-century interior would become a basic premise of modernist design thinking.

Tracts like Loos's, written by other architects, artists, and social reformers of the time, similarly examined the material realities of people's lives and emphasized the ability of 'good' art and architecture to transform that reality. Rejecting cultural traditions and established social hierarchies, these polemicists framed civilization as a progressive march forwards, in which design helped metamorphosize society and create model citizens. As much an ideological movement as an aesthetic one, early modernist design dedicated itself to a kind of mass cultural reprogramming. By producing artefacts fit for an age of social, cultural, and material progress, modernist designers would help reinvent the world from the ground up.

The act of stripping away the extraneous ornament of earlier styles, while perhaps the most obvious change befalling early-twentieth-century design, was not the only one. Modernist designers also shared a commitment to exercising the power of the machine and industrial technology. The mass production of objects, materials, and design components would ensure that good and inexpensive design reached the masses, while also lightening the load of laborers. Design would be grounded in function.

In addition to this emphasis on function or purpose as the main determinant of form, other generally accepted principles of modernist design included the simplification of construction, the direct expression of materials, an experimentation with new materials (especially lighter ones, more transparent ones, ones that were easier to keep clean or that allowed for more light and air to enter), and a preference for layouts that allow for physical interaction and movement (such as open floor plans) supporting a new conception of the dynamic modern body in movement. By following these general directives, proponents of the modern movement believed that architecture in general, and modern furniture in particular, would advance the health and well-being of all in a society characterized by greater equality and freedom.

Modernist design surfaced most visibly within a relatively small number of industrialized nations and among a professional minority in these places. Indeed, modernism was not a homogeneous movement: diverse emphases developed across different regional and national spaces (Woodham 2004; Betts 2004; Fallan and Lees-Maffei 2016; Attfield 2007). Although architects active in Germany and Holland during the 1920s and 1930s are arguably best known today, designers in Britain, France, Italy, Poland, Scandinavia, the USSR, and the United States also embraced modernist principles of design in the years before the Second World War. Variation in expression emerged throughout the 1920s, 1930s, and 1940s, motivated at turns by forces both internal and external to architecture and design proper (not only materials availability, craftsmanship, and building construction tradition but also climatic conditions, social outlook, and political ideology). Expressionism vied for influence with functionalism; subjectivity with objective rationalism. Nonetheless, these different currents were united in the desire to reinvent the world from scratch, through actual living environments.

FURNISHING THE MODERN INTERIOR

Although domestic interiors had traditionally been the purview of women, male modernist architects asserted their hegemony over this realm. They did so not only by denigrating the impact of housewives in furnishing the home, but also by seeking to undercut the influence of female designers emerging after the turn of the twentieth century. Architectural historian Despina Stratigakos has explored these gendered battles as they played out in the German Werkbund, an organization of designers and industrialists founded in Munich in 1907 that was highly influential in the development of modernist ideas in Germany. Werkbund spokesmen such as Karl Scheffler, an architectural critic, pitched the struggle for aesthetic renewal in gendered terms, describing it as 'a campaign to achieve a new masculine reason' (Stratigakos 2003: 491). He and others seeking to limit women's involvement derided so-called feminine influences in domestic interiors – identified as an excess of display and ornamentation – as a backward relic in a modern world, much like Loos's perception of the tattooed Papuan.

Modernist architects thus conceived of their influence extending over all aspects of domestic design in the creation of a total, integrated environment. In early-twentieth-century Vienna, the concept of the *Gesamtkunstwerk* – a work that united all arts into the creation of a harmonious whole – had previously been explored by the Wiener Werkstätte (Vienna Workshops), a collective of progressive artists and craftsmen who produced exquisite modern buildings, such as the Stoclet Palace in Brussels, for a largely wealthy clientele (Fahr-Becker 2008). In Germany, the Werkbund shifted the search for modern, integrated environments from handicraft to industrial processes, arguing for integrating good design with mass production and standardization (Schwartz 1996). After the First World War, their efforts were taken up and further developed by the Bauhaus.

The fragile social democracy that emerged in Germany after its defeat, commonly known as the Weimar Republic, gave hope to artists who had fought in the trenches and imagined a better world to come (White 1985). The Bauhaus, a residential art school established in the small town of Weimar in 1919, harnessed those utopian impulses. In keeping with the interdisciplinary idea of the *Gesamtkunstwerk*, the school sought to unite (and level the distinction between) fine and applied arts under the framework of building. The open spaces and clean lines that would emerge from the combined efforts of the school's various workshops, and that would come to define the school's signature 'look', signified not only a new approach to design, but, more fundamentally, a new optimistic culture of dwelling that would overcome old social hierarchies.

The residents and way of life at the Bauhaus were an important part of that challenge. In keeping with the new equality guaranteed to women in the Weimar Constitution, women as well as men were admitted to the school, although this progressive stance was somewhat undercut by restricting female students to the weaving workshop (Droste 1998). Moreover, teaching staff and students all ate together in the canteen and occupied the same seating area in the Bauhaus theatre. Walter Gropius, its founding director, envisioned the Bauhaus as much more than a school: it would be a vibrant community, in which 'the mobile, living creative spirit' would challenge 'bourgeois pigheadedness, soppy sentimentality and fictional existence' (Gropius 1918/19, cited in Blume 2015: 37). Creative muses were to be found in a variety of performative genres, including fancy-dress parties, poetry, music, and theatre, and Bauhaus learning, like its architecture, encompassed all aspects of life.

Although founded with the slogan 'Art and Craft: A New Unity', the Bauhaus took a new direction in 1923 when Gropius changed the motto to 'Art and Technology: A New Unity'. Wanting to put the school, which relied on state subsidies, on more solid financial footing, Gropius advocated a design agenda that would foster partnerships with industry. The Bauhaus furniture workshop seems to have been among the first to accept the need for standardization in shifting from craft to machine production, and its earliest effort took the form of a chair (Droste 1998: 82).

MODERN CHAIRS AS ALLEGORIES

Given its relatively small scale, household furniture represented an attractive design project for modernist architects. Experimentation with style, shape, structure, and material could be accomplished more easily than at the scale of an entire building. Furniture thus provided a vehicle for testing and expressing the ambitions of modern architecture. Chairs, in particular, offered an important opportunity. As architectural historian Charlotte Benton notes, 'Virtually every architect of note felt the need to design at least one "modern chair" during the formative years of the Modern Movement' (1990: 103). In addition to the advantages of scale, chairs were economically expedient. During the impoverished inter-war period, luxuries were in short supply and many traditional household items were forsaken. The chair, however, remained essential – a fundamental necessity in every Western home.

Beyond the pragmatic, experimenting with the design of chairs also held another appeal for architects. Chairs are corporeal in a way that other pieces of furniture are not. Unlike objects such as lamps or tables, a chair must be occupied to be appreciated. Its design speaks to the body as well as the mind, and when it works well, a chair can provide a unique feeling of physical relief. Both ordinary and extraordinary, 'the design of the modern chair thus became a kind of exemplary allegory of modernism' (Benton 1990: 104) – an important 'vehicle for arguing [its] case' (Wilk 2006: 226).

At the Bauhaus furniture workshop, in 1922 Marcel Breuer, then a journeyman, created a simple wood-slat chair as a prototype for mass production. It was presented as the functional outcome of an analysis of sitting. A few years later, Breuer laid out the requirements needed to achieve a comfortable chair with a simple design: an elastic seat and backrest, free of dust-collecting textiles or cushions, to support the body; and a carefully angled seat to bear the full length of the upper leg and to support the upper half of the body without putting pressure on the spine (Droste 1998: 82). Significantly, Breuer's focus here was not on aesthetics, but rather on health. In the effort to convince men and women to accept industrially produced furnishing, Breuer and others at the Bauhaus made the claim that it was good for you.

In 1925, the Bauhaus relocated to Dessau, where the school's masters intensified their focus on designing for an emerging mass market. Breuer, now himself a teacher, produced two chairs – the Wassily or B3 (1925) and the Cesca or B64 (1928) – exemplifying that commitment. Both chairs used nickel-plated tubular steel that Breuer claimed was inspired by bicycle-handle design, bringing industrial materials indoors. Both chairs also attempted to minimize the structure

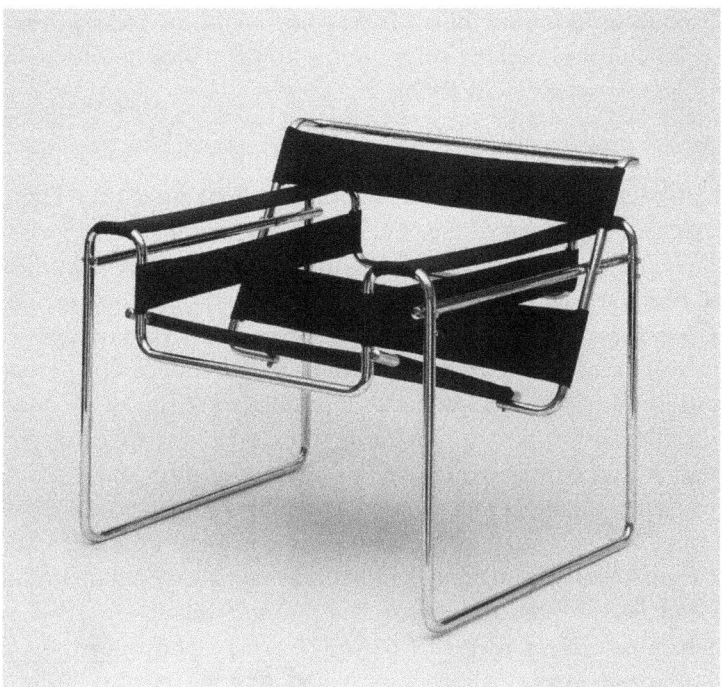

FIGURE 4.1: The B3 Chair by Marcel Breuer. Breuer designed several variations of this tubular chair, the first dating from 1925. The design illustrated here, from the collection of the Museum of Modern Art in New York, was manufactured in 1927–28 for the Standard Möbel in Berlin, Germany, a company that Breuer himself co-founded. Digital Image © The Museum of Modern Art / Licensed by SCALA / Art Resource, NY.

of the chair as much as possible to foster the sense of sitting on air (Wilk 2006), either by using strips of suspended fabric for seating (B3) or a cantilevered principle of support (B64). This gave the chairs a sense of dynamism and innovation, making them seem like a technological feat. The openness of the chair also enhanced, rather than interrupted, the sense of the flow of space around it. This was an important consideration to modernist designers, who created furniture to fit the new uncluttered and transparent architectural interiors.

Not everyone approved of metal furniture. In his 1930 review of a Werkbund exhibition in Paris that featured designs by Breuer and Gropius, writer and philosopher Aldous Huxley complained about 'the aseptic, hospital style of furnishing' on view. Picking up on modernists' arguments about health, but giving them a negative slant, he compared metal domestic furniture to the dentist's chair or a surgeon's operating table, and argued that it would hardly represent, for him, 'domestic bliss'. It was not metal furniture *per se* that he objected to, so much as metal furniture in the home, which he and many others considered inappropriate (Wilk 2006: 233).

Nonetheless, by the mid-1930s, metal furniture had begun to sell, if mostly to commercial and institutional clients (Wilk 2006: 229). Although Breuer's tubular chairs were mass produced by the furniture manufacturer Thonet, they remained expensive and out of the reach of most consumers. The pursuit at the Bauhaus and elsewhere of good design for the masses through cheap mass production remained frustratingly elusive. Even so, demand for such products began to grow. Especially among younger people, exposed to modernist design in cinemas, restaurants, and in rapidly proliferating modern design magazines, the desire to live a modern life in modern settings took root. Like Martha and Sigmund decades earlier, young couples in pre-war Europe envisioned a marital dwelling that would express a new shared identity, and for many that meant a visible break with their parents' homes. If young couples could not afford a Bauhaus chair, perhaps they could manage a cheaper variation, such as the bentwood chairs also produced by Thonet and favoured by many modernists. Thus, we can look at the modernist chair – and the many other types of modernist furniture created in this period – as an opportunity not only for architects to experiment, but also for customers to imagine their modern domestic selves, even in the absence (for the designer and the consumer) of the ideal of a totally designed environment.

EFFICIENT KITCHENS AND HOUSEWIVES

Because modernist furniture was designed as much to foster new lifestyles as to create new products, household activities were at the heart of the design process. This is perhaps most apparent in the planning of kitchens. In the early years of the twentieth century, the kitchen received far more attention than it had previously, while the parlour received somewhat less. For the middle classes, kitchens were to become the housewife's workplace rather than the servants' and maids' alone. The rise in the numbers of kitchen exhibits in this period testifies to the increasing interest in this domestic space, as well as to the efforts by modernist designers to shift perceptions of what constituted a modern house.

In 1923, the Bauhaus organized its first exhibition in Weimar, at which Gropius proclaimed the school's new industrial orientation. The show centred on the experimental, functional housing prototype Haus am Horn designed by Adolf Meyer and Georg Muche. The interior furniture, fittings, and equipment were produced by the school's workshops as prototypes for industry. These were especially evident in the kitchen, a collaboration between Ernst Gebhardt and Benita Otte, a weaving teacher at the Bauhaus who, in keeping with the school's

MATERIAL CULTURE AND MAKING THE MODERN 99

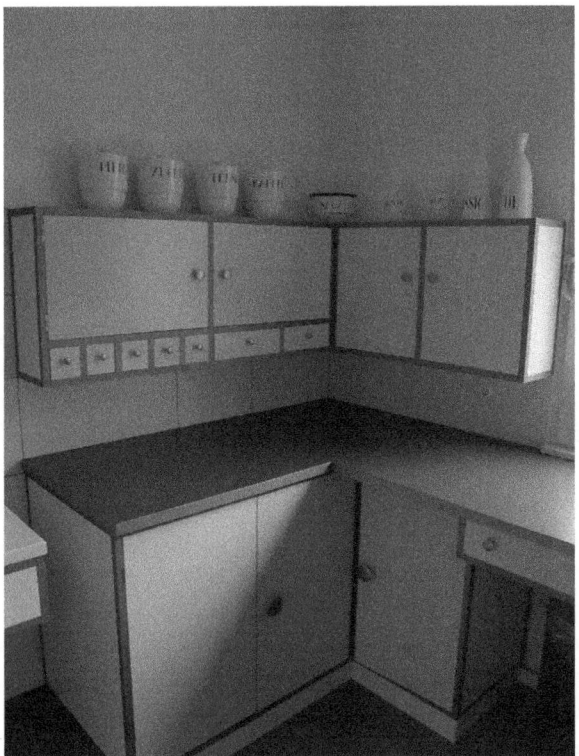

FIGURE 4.2: Contemporary view of cabinets and earthenware containers in the kitchen of the Haus am Horn in Weimar, Germany, built in 1923. sailko via Wikimedia.org.

gendered notions of creativity, had been brought on to lend a '"woman's view" in the male arena of industrial design' (Woodham 1997: 40). The exhibit identified the kitchen as a place just for cooking, departing from older German traditions of the *Wohnküche*, a room typically used for cooking, eating, housework, and informal family socializing. The Haus am Horn kitchen was thus made smaller, and its design – featuring standardized built-in cabinets and mass-produced earthenware containers – carefully coordinated to the housewife's activities.

The Haus am Horn kitchen attracted immense architectural interest, and although Germany continued to lead the race to rationalize domestic work, similar initiatives emerged throughout Europe. The Viennese architect Margarete Schütte-Lihotzky, seeking to improve on the Haus am Horn's labor-saving design, used time-and-motion studies to produce her tiny, fully rationalized Frankfurt Kitchen of 1926, which was intended for the city's state-sponsored housing projects (see Figure 6.4). In 1930, in anticipation of the first modernist housing exhibition to be held in Switzerland, the Swiss Werkbund (founded in 1913) commissioned Hans Richter, a German artist with close ties to modernist designers, to produce a film, *Die Neue Wohnung* (The New Dwelling), to demonstrate the advantages of these new smaller kitchens over the older *Wohnküche*, as well as how to use their rationalized design features – suggesting how radical (and perhaps even bewildering) these must have seemed when they first appeared (Janser 2001: 16). Ultimately, however, the designs themselves were meant to instruct the housewife. Belgian architects also conceived the rational kitchen as a pedagogical tool to teach the housewife efficient work methods, thereby freeing her to focus on other family-centred and socially oriented tasks. Like their German colleagues, they focused their efforts on designing a kitchen that facilitated diverse activities with a minimum of movement as the housewife proceeded from one task to another. Louis-Herman De Koninck, a leading Belgian architect, argued that his colleagues should be well versed in the 'art of housekeeping' and especially kitchen equipment in order to cater to the requirements of modern living. Based on his inspection of the Frankfurt Kitchen, he believed that its equipment was not sufficiently standardized and he thus developed the CUBEX cupboards, which consisted of four cupboard types that could be arranged in many different ways, allowing families to compose their own ideal kitchen (Van Caudenberg and Heynen 2004: 27).

The Frankfurt Kitchen and CUBEX cupboards are among the biggest commercial successes of pre-war modernism, and their designs undoubtedly modified women's housework habits. As Richter's film *Die Neue Wohnung* makes clear, modernist designers saw in such transformations the basis for profound social changes. Richter's film compares old and new forms of dwelling. In the former, an exhausted housewife lashes out at her children. Precious domestic space is wasted because the woman clings to the prestige of a company-only parlour, where the many bibelots gathering dust create more work for her. In one scene, these 'useless' objects, taking on a sinister tone, attack the occupants, forcing them to flee. By contrast, in the new dwelling, design engenders not only new efficiencies, but also 'better' behaviours and attitudes. Her labor lightened, a housewife is shown relaxing, enjoying her family, and playing with her toddler in the sunny outdoors. In the minds of modernist designers, then, a cupboard was not just a cupboard; it was a portal into a better world.

EXHIBITING MODERNISM

Beyond educating users, museum exhibitions in the twentieth century also served to elevate design as inherently valuable and worthy of serious consideration. Anthropologist Daniel Miller argues that museums and galleries act like frames, defining the products of human creativity, and ensuring that we privilege certain things more than others. When placed in institutions such as galleries, furniture and household objects are similarly framed and legitimized as noteworthy, valuable designed artefacts (Miller 2005: 5).

Established in 1929, the Museum of Modern Art (MoMA) in New York played a pivotal role in establishing a modernist canon, underscoring design historian Jonathan Woodham's contention that such institutions 'have been powerful conditioning agents in the establishment of cultural hierarchies' (1997: 30). In 1932, the museum opened the world's first curatorial department devoted to architecture and design, with Philip Johnson as its director (see Figure 2.5). The same year, he and Henry-Russell Hitchcock organized the 'Modern Architecture: International Exhibition', which introduced the sleek machine aesthetics of the Bauhaus to American audiences. The exhibition catalogue described the architectural and design projects presented as characteristic of the new 'International Style' (Hitchcock and Johnson [1932] 1995). The choice of the word 'style', aligning the work with modern art, indicates the curators' emphasis on form divorced from its political and social roots. Moreover, the insistence on a global phenomenon served to minimize differences among designers and schools.

With the rise of fascism in Europe, the socially progressive aspirations that had driven modernist experimentation in the 1920s evolved in complex and unexpected ways. National Socialists, opposed to the 'Jewish' and 'Bolshevik' internationalism of the school, closed the Bauhaus in 1933, forcing many of its students and teachers to immigrate. The refugees brought their skills to new countries across the globe, most notably to Britain and the United States (Powers 2019). Although this diaspora served to disseminate modernist ideas, they also changed in the voyage. By the outbreak of war in 1939, the 'international' context that MoMA had defined seven years earlier had vastly changed.

If the museum and art gallery have represented powerful institutional framing devices that have shaped how designed furniture is popularly received, government support (or lack of) also exerted a strong influence. Some governments were highly effective in guiding tastes towards the modern. These efforts were more overtly political, using design to legitimize policy-based values and bolster the political agendas of the sponsor (Tigerman 2015: 280).

In Britain, a utilitarian version of modern furniture was not only financially supported by the national government, but the state was also active in the proscription of both the design and the materials employed in the production of what was called the Utility furniture scheme (see Figure 7.2). In the early 1940s, designer Gordon Russell was instrumental in the production of Utility pieces under the auspices of the British Board of Trade. Catering to newlyweds setting up home and victims of wartime bombing, the production of furniture was limited by both shortages of skilled labor and restricted supplies of raw materials. Because of the war effort, the Board of Trade was active in limiting the materials used in making everyday goods, and the furniture industry had to adhere to statutory designs determined by the State Advisory Committee. The result was the Utility Furniture Catalogue of 1943, which divided the house into five units – living room, bedroom, kitchen, nursery, and miscellaneous (such as bookshelves) – and offered minimal but sturdy oak or mahogany furnishings for each room. Strict control of designs and materials is evident, right down to the minutiae of construction methods: the use of wooden handles was specified because metals were needed for the war, veneered hardboard replaced plywood, and although metal screws were used, items of furniture were often held together with mortise and pegged joints.

The resulting basic forms were valorised for their simplicity, agreeableness, and solidity, and admired in government documents not only for their cost-efficiency with scarce timber resources but also because they carried the potential to eliminate the 'frills and fancies' associated with the 'lower end' of the British furniture industry (Reimer and Pinch 2013: 103; Attfield 1992; Raizman 2004). A Board of Trade memorandum noted the silver lining in these war-enforced conditions – the opportunity to improve British furniture design and popular tastes for the long-term: 'there is a chance here, during our period of greatest economy, of influencing popular taste towards good construction in simple, agreeable design to the benefit of our after-the-war homes' (Reimer and Pinch 2013: 103).

In Germany, as noted above, economic necessity and the desire to provide good design to the masses had similarly driven modernist reform. But in the absence of the vast coordinated government effort represented by the Utility schemes, innovative furniture designers at the Bauhaus struggled to bring affordable, mass-produced furnishings to market (the Frankfurt Kitchen, by contrast, was state-sponsored). The economies of scale achieved through standardization and coordination of production, meant that the British state, as geographers Suzanne Reimer and Philip Pinch point out, acted as a proto-Ikea, 'closely specifying designs with the intent of controlling costs and efficiency' (2013: 105). The scheme continued for a few years after the war, officially coming to an end in 1952.

MODERNISM AS A NORDIC MOVEMENT

In the immediate post-war period, Scandinavian furniture quickly made an impact on the international furniture trade. International exhibitions represented Scandinavian design as an alternative to the austere forms and radical politics of earlier modernist movements, framing its principles as humanist and democratic. As the Cold War heated up in Europe, this image was deeply appealing and strategic for the purposes of trade and marketing (Kristoffersson 2014: 62). At the same time, the key convictions of modernist utopianism that circulated in Sweden in this period built on an established tradition that had already foregrounded furniture in social reform. The argument for a unified taste founded on simplicity and accessibility and mediated by everyday things was advanced by key leaders in the Svenska Slöjdföreningen (Swedish Society of Craft and Industrial Design), the world's first design organization, founded in 1845. The society was originally created in reaction to the perceived threats posed by modern industrial methods but soon came to focus more exclusively on the benefits of mass production.

In 1919, art historian Gregor Paulsson published Svenska Slöjdföreningen's manifesto under the title *Vackare Vardagsvara* (More Beautiful Everyday Things), arguing that the Swedish design industry should focus its purpose squarely on the creation of functional, affordable, and beautiful objects. Paulsson's interest developed while living in Germany, where he was exposed to the design ideals of the German Werkbund. As Svenska Slöjdföreningen's director, Paulsson also played a pivotal role in the landmark Stockholm Exhibition of 1930, the slogan of which was acceptera! (accept!), which aimed to introduce the Swedish general

FIGURE 4.3: A bedroom interior on display at the 1930 Stockholm Exhibition. The room was designed by architect Sven Markelius, a pivotal player in the introduction of international modernism to a broad Swedish audience. Photographer: Okänd. © Nordiska Museet.

public to the new design trends, technological innovations, and spirit of social utopianism that characterized Swedish design at the time (Mattsson and Wallenstein 2010; Murphy 2015; Garvey 2018). *Funkis*, the Nordic name for Functionalism, was presented as the harbinger of a new era that would inspire through light interiors, the relinquishment of former social pretences, and the development of ideal common forms or types (Creagh, Kåberg, and Lane 2008: 223). Affordable, quality homes and furniture were primarily showcased, but also on display were gardens, transportation, and burial grounds. In short, *funkis* was shown to span the life cycle, from cradle to grave.

In Nordic countries the starker, industrial look of modernist furniture associated with Bauhaus designs was soon replaced with a 'softer' aesthetic that derived from craft traditions but that nonetheless allowed for the mass production and standardization of furniture. Scandinavian design also departed from its European counterparts in incorporating pale woods such as pine, spruce, and birch, and natural materials including ox-hide, jute, or linen-based fabrics (Howe 1999). The use of laminated woods and organic forms was pioneered in the 1930s by designer Bruno Mathsson, who replaced both the solid wood and

FIGURE 4.4: Alvar Aalto's Armchair 400, designed in 1936, here from the collection of the Museum of Modern Art in New York. Digital Image © The Museum of Modern Art / Licensed by SCALA / Art Resource, NY.

tubular steel popular at the Bauhaus. Mathsson, together with designers Carl Malmsten and Josef Frank, were leaders in defining and disseminating Swedish versions of modern design. They embraced the idea of 'furniture architecture' and espoused the benefits of light and humanistic design, which garnered broad popular appeal in the mid-twentieth century (see Robach 2002; Selkurt 2003; Sörlin 2002).

The folded plywood chairs that Finnish designer Alvar Aalto developed in the 1930s exemplify what came to be known as 'Scandinavian Modern'. Influenced by the tubular steel of Breuer chairs but in keeping with Scandinavian trends, Aalto opted for the use of birch, which is native to Finland, while also adopting the cantilever principle to develop a series of chairs that could support the weight of the human body. The use of wood softened the austere look of Breuer's steel prototypes. In his lecture 'Rationalism and Man', delivered at the Swedish Craft Society in Stockholm on 9 May 1935, Aalto made the case for wood because it avoided the 'excessive glare from light reflection' and did not have the disadvantage of conducting sound in the manner of tubular steel. In this way, Aalto's wooden cantilevered chairs translated Breuer's industrial aesthetic into a material whose qualities contributed, according to the designer, to 'the mystical concept of "cozy"' (Pallasmaa 1984: 116). Scandinavian furniture of the post-war period tended to be 'slight and slender', lacking heavy sprung and webbed upholstery. The form was designed to provide comfort in itself or lend itself to the addition of cushions, therefore encouraging the use of fabric and textiles as accessories (Howe 1999). This feature tended to characterize Scandinavian furnishing as modern but 'homely', more 'human' and less radical than the chrome and tubular steel designs of Central Europe. Aalto embraced a rich palette of materials, which promoted tactility. In his design of the Villa Mairea, for example, he integrated views of the Finnish forest and rippled sunlight through large glazed windows with the aim of enhancing experiential qualities in the architectural structure (Miller 1990). But as well as the tactile and experiential qualities afforded by diverse materials, colours, and styles, Scandinavian design tended to be associated with the unassuming quality, the delightful ordinariness, of the Scandinavian home. In a 1961 study of Scandinavian design, Ulf Hård af Segerstad claimed that functionalism never fully took root in Nordic interiors. Instead, 'the Scandinavian home is a little place where one quite naturally employs unpretentious means to bring comfort and warmth into the confining circle of the evening lamp' (Hård af Segerstad 1961: 13).

Associations between Scandinavia as a geo-political entity and 'democratic design' were strengthened through exhibitions and model-home expositions. Design historian Kjetil Fallan has noted that the moniker Scandinavian Design was devised for a series of exhibitions in the 1950s that promoted objects from Nordic countries to an international audience. The label was applied to a

FIGURE 4.5: In the 1940s, a number of Swedish organizations (both state-funded and commercial) offered classes to young couples on how to decorate their homes effectively. Here we see a man and woman discussing a model of a furnished apartment on display at the Bride and Home Exhibition, held at Nordiska Kompaniet, an upscale department store, in Stockholm in 1944. Photographer: Erik Holmén. © Nordiska Museet.

limited cluster of objects rather than representing the full variety of design works in Nordic countries, and carefully selected items chosen for showcasing were 'almost exclusively objects for the home conforming to a modernist notion of aesthetic quality' (Fallan 2012: 3).

The post-war launch of Scandinavian design on the American market promoted the region's democratic credentials and simultaneously distinguished it from the stark minimalism popularly associated with the International Style. The 'Design in Scandinavia' exhibition that toured the United States from 1954 to 1957 therefore did not advocate strict minimal living spaces but instead presented a pleasing alternative: beautiful displays of possessions in uncluttered household settings. The exhibition was organized around the themes of 'Good Articles for Everyday Use' (inexpensive household goods, like cutlery), 'Living Tradition' (contemporary handicrafts), 'Form and Material' (ceramics, glass, and metalwork), and 'Scandinavia at Home' (furniture and textiles). The exhibition began with huge photographs of landscapes, thus creating in the visitor's mind a connection between the objects on display and Nordic nature (Guldberg 2011: 43).

The initiative for the exhibition is attributed to Elizabeth Gordon, then editor-in-chief of the magazine *House Beautiful*, and it successfully toured twenty-four locations in the United States and Canada over a three-year period. Gotthard Johansson, then president of Svenska Slöjdföreningen, wrote the introduction for the exhibition catalogue, which was meant to provide viewers with background information on the displayed objects from Denmark, Finland, Norway, and Sweden. Johansson focused on people rather than things, thus fostering the myth of a pan-Nordic identity. Wanting to appeal to American audiences, Johansson presented Nordic values as unity (the closeness of the four countries), a blend of tradition and modernity, a democratic outlook, and a human interest in ordinary, everyday things (Guldberg 2011: 48ff.).

Although 'Scandinavian Design' was an identity constructed for international audiences, similar design principles were touted in exhibitions that took place within Scandinavia. In the summer of 1955, the international exhibition H55, organized by the Swedish Society of Industrial Design, opened in Helsingborg. As much trade fair as cultural show, it set out to demonstrate how modern design could be integrated into everyday commercial products that used new technologies and materials, thus democratizing quality. The show included the Swedish architect Nils Strinning's String shelves, created in 1949. This lightweight and adjustable shelving unit, supported by thin, string-like metal side panels, epitomized the quiet, humble simplicity of Swedish design for the home as well as its commercial potential.

The full significance of these developments can only be understood, however, within the context of housing standardization then in the process of being implemented. In 1954, the Swedish National Housing Board (Bostadsstyrelsen) published the book *God Bostad* (Good Housing), which established the norms that came to dominate twentieth-century housing in Sweden. *God Bostad* specified the regulations for minimum living space and outlined in detail the requirements for every part of a dwelling: bedroom, living room, utility room, kitchen, hall, and so on. Exact measurements resulted from observations of household activities, such as washing-up or preparing food, which led to requirements as to the height or width of kitchen worktops, and the distance between stove and kitchen sink. The architectural norms published in *God Bostad* were not only endorsed by the state but were also obligatory in cases where the building industry wanted to procure municipal funding. Such efforts aimed to manage domestic spaces, to standardize the size and shape of rooms, and to facilitate the storage of personal possessions. A subsequent edition of *God Bostad*, published in 1964, coincided with a government announcement that one million homes would be constructed in the coming decade.

BEYOND SCANDINAVIA: THE POST-WAR ERA AND CONTESTED MODERNISMS

Although domestic consumption was formative in the consolidation of the social democratic welfare state in Sweden, design historian David Crowley reminds us that the home also emerged at the centre of international debates about the reconstruction of war-torn Europe following the end of the Second World War. Within these debates, modern design was 'conscripted' for architectural reconstruction and social healing. As an affluent society took shape in the 1950s, 'North American and Western European industry turned to modernist designers to provide the blueprints for chic modern furniture and electronic consumer goods' (Crowley 2012: 277). Eastern European states favoured a modernist aesthetic in mass housing, and Western European governments similarly endorsed modernist-block architecture as appropriate for social housing, schools, hospitals, and prisons. In Britain, the early 1960s witnessed the large-scale construction of high-rise blocks in metropolitan centres that were subsidized by local government and built in large numbers. Modernist architect and designers could claim in the 1960s that the style had shaped the world (Crowley 2012: 277), but by the 1970s the aesthetics and tenets of the Modern Movement were deemed a catastrophic failure. Criticisms of the sterility of modern design and its unsuitability for everyday living abounded (Crowley 2012; Morley 2000). In the UK, the faceless homogeneity and unalterable façade of the concrete block associated with modernist design became a symbol of governmental control, and those settled in council housing often felt alienated from their own living environments: here, the egalitarian aspirations of early modernist polemicists were paradoxically transformed into tools of authority. High modernism was lambasted for destroying the fabric of the traditional city centres and associated social networks, while some saw in its monumentalism an expression of elitism and authority (Jameson 1991).

In furniture design, a range of new products emerged in the European and American furnishings markets that eschewed the modernist principle of 'form follows function'. They were informed by a wide variety of sources, including historical allusion, symbolic form, and sleek design principles that hid their inner workings. The purity of geometric principles and direct expression of materials were rejected in the face of a preference for hybridity and playfulness. Designers who had once advocated the International Style, such as Aldo Rossi in Italy, Philippe Starck in France, and Michael Graves and Charles Moore in the United States, rejected modernism's functionalist doctrine and began new, 'postmodern' experiments in design. The latter group includes Philip Johnson, who as a young curator in the early 1930s, had introduced America to the Bauhaus; fifty years later, he himself designed a postmodern skyscraper (the AT&T Building in New York, completed in 1984) that looked like a Chippendale highboy.

DEATH AND RESURRECTION: IKEA

Since the 1990s, there has been a visible return to the aesthetics of modernism in furniture design (Leslie and Reimer 2003). A major contemporary retailer of modernist furniture design is the transnational furniture retailer Ikea. Ikea has been described as a contemporary form of the International Style, perpetuating (as critics of modernism once argued) homogeneous domestic environments on a global scale (Hartman 2007: 492). The Ikea corporation has capitalized on the history of Scandinavian Modern to great effect and extols the benefits of cheap modern furniture and furnishings to people of modest means. We find this claim in the founder Ingvar Kamprad's slogan 'to create a better everyday life for the many people', declaring a commitment to provide consumer goods for the purchasing masses and implying a non-elitist ethos (Kamprad 1976: 2).

Ikea has largely succeeded in presenting itself as a contemporary form of benign modernism and in avoiding the stigma of extreme corporate greed that attaches to comparable transnational corporations. Although critiques of the corporation do exist, they are more muted and have developed less momentum than the popular activism that surrounds other global products. Instead, Ikea manages to purvey a cultural package made up of tantalizing images of wholesome Swedish domesticity. Moreover, in addition to the humanistic and gentler versions of modernism that are associated with Scandinavian design, the company closely aligns its branding with that of Sweden. From the building's blue and yellow exteriors to imported Swedish meatballs in its café, the marketing image of the store links common icons of 'Swedishness' with a non-elitist modern solution for the purchasing masses (Garvey 2018: 18). Design historian Sara Kristoffersson traces the history of Ikea branding throughout the twentieth century and finds that images of Sweden feature in Ikea advertisements to the degree that Sweden and Ikea are 'co-branded' (2014: 84). In other words, the image of one supports and feeds into the international perception of the other. Since the turn of the twenty-first century, such branding has gathered momentum, driven in part by the Swedish Institute, a state agency tasked with promoting Sweden abroad. The Institute's web page makes explicit the entanglement of national profile and corporate brand: 'To visit IKEA is to visit Sweden: IKEA fits very well onto the official brand platform of Sweden . . . The brand of the company could very well be described in the same terms as the platform for Sweden' (Kristoffersson 2014: 84).

Not surprising, then – and as an echo of the modern movement that emerged one hundred years ago – Ikea is shot through with its own series of contradictions. The Ikea 'vision' as promoted by the marketing arm of the corporation may be experienced as contradictory by the householder who witnesses a vision of Swedish modern living on the one hand and corporate rationalization and unsustainable mass production on the other. The intimate resonances of its slogan 'Home is the most important place in the world' may be contrasted with its transnational reach. Moreover, the idiom of democratic design or design for the many, as Ikea's design philosophy, is pitched as an egalitarian solution for the purchasing masses, but the map of Ikea's centres of production and consumption presents us with a cartography of worldwide poverty and affluence (Hartman 2007; Garvey 2018).

In view of these contradictory elements in the design production, dissemination, and consumption of furniture – which recall contradictions seen in modernist enterprises a century ago – it is perhaps fitting that we find a reference to Ikea when we return full circle to the centre of modernist design in Dessau. Here, the Bauhaus foundation today offers tours of the Gropius-designed Törten housing estate. The Törten estate was designed from 1926 to 1928 as a prototype of modern living and arose from a shortage of reasonably priced housing after the First World War. Under the slogan of 'light, air, and sun', Gropius intended to build affordable housing for the masses. Today, a visitor to the exhibition in the Konsum building – which holds the estate's tourism office – finds an unexpected reference to Ikea. Included on a wall that chronicles the historical evolution of modernist housing from the early twentieth century to the present is an image of Ikea's new prefabricated housing in Scandinavia. In 1997, Ikea ventured into the market of offering 'affordable homes for ordinary people' by selling whole residences, not just objects, that cater to an Ikea style of living (Nenonen and Storbacka 2018: 65–66). In Dessau, Ikea is thus presented as a contemporary avatar of pioneering modernist housing movements. Associations between Scandinavia as a geo-political entity and democratic design continue to exert influence.

CONCLUSION: SLIPPERY MEANINGS

Citing philosopher and sociologist George Herbert Mead's remark that 'The chair is what it is in terms of its invitation to sit down' (1934: 279, in Keane 2003: 418), anthropologist Webb Keane reminds us that the significance of material things is always open to change or negotiation. Objects instigate action and invite particular practices, but they do not determine them. We tend to view ordinary things such as furniture as the 'natural' outcome of needs, rather than as the material manifestations of cultural conceptions. To emphasize design icons risks, therefore, relying too heavily on the sign-like value of an object, which in turn obscures the many actors and practices that intervene in its social reception. In museums and galleries, the limelight gathers around famous works rather than on objects used, appropriated, and lived within everyday situations (see Fallan 2012; Attfield 2000). The label 'design icon' suggests that the object is a sign, a symbol of its age, but icons in the abstract are relatively meaningless, Keane asserts, because their semiotic potential must be recognized, one meaning may be realized, and another masked (2003: 418–

19). Hence, social frames such as exhibitions, as noted above, are important in defining design classics or 'iconic' works.

But Keane's point goes further in unpacking how certain materials, shapes, colours, or forms may also be foregrounded as the defining quality of an object. A wall may be described as light, but only if one recognizes and privileges the white colour of the paint over the heaviness of the plaster. The lightness of birch might be stressed in a celebration of its colour and form, but only to neglect the dead weight of the table. Keane refers to the quality of lightness of 'canoes, garden plots, decorations, bodies and so forth' (2003: 414), but within this chapter, we have encountered the quality of 'lightness' as referring variously to tubular steel or wooden furniture, to fresh air or glass. Signs, therefore, are not fixed but are sites of unrealized potential, and their sensuous qualities are materialized and foregrounded on an on-going basis (Keane 2003, 2005; Garvey 2013). In other words, beyond being an abstract sign, the sensuous qualities of a chair, such as its colour, material, and shape, are perceived and appreciated within socio-historically grounded ways.

With this perspective we can return to Adolf Loos's condemnation of ornament not merely as an aversion to decoration as defiling pure form but as illustrative of his deep suspicions regarding the superficiality of the surface and the immorality of the exterior compared to the purity of the interior. This widespread belief features in nineteenth-century Protestant doctrine and entailed a distrust of elaborate surfaces, which were perceived as dishonest (Keane 2005). Early-twentieth-century theorists were not necessarily pioneering in espousing the moral benefits of minimal interiors and light-flooded rooms: European colonial actors had already aligned metaphors of modernity with visuality, 'shedding light' on the colonies and unmasking perceived superstitious beliefs (Rowlands 2005). But the belief of the superiority and morality of clear surfaces infiltrated twentieth-century architecture, design, and commentary as found in Loos's thundering critique of ornament, or in Le Corbusier's designation that 'Trash is always abundantly decorated; the luxury object is well made, neat and clean, pure and healthy, and its bareness reveals the quality of its manufacture' (Le Corbusier [1925] 1987: 87). Thus, perceived morality – ideas concerning the right way of doing things – was objectified in the materials and arrangements of furniture, in the spaces between objects, as well as in the practices that surrounded these pieces.

Unlike Loos, who believed utterly in the fundamental truths of things, Sigmund Freud, a fellow Viennese, understood the elusive meaning of domestic objects in their shifting contexts. In 1938, the famous psychoanalyst, by then an old man, and his wife Martha, were forced to flee their home in Nazi-occupied Austria under harrowing conditions for the security of London. They brought with them all their furniture and household effects – those 'little things' on which they had hung their hearts as newlyweds – and tried to recreate a sense of home in an alien land. The objects were a comfort, and Freud arranged his study exactly as it had been in Vienna. Nonetheless, even surrounded by these familiar things – the very same objects that had furnished his Viennese house – Freud was surprised by the nostalgia he experienced for 'the prison from which I have been released' (Young-Bruehl 2008: 235). Freud's household objects had come with him to London, but home remained in Vienna.

CHAPTER FIVE

Home and Work: Household Labour and the Making of Inequalities

ROSIE COX

INTRODUCTION

On a Tired Housewife:
Here lies a poor woman who always was tired,
She lived in a house where help wasn't hired.
Her last words on earth were: 'Dear friends, I am going
To where there's no cooking, or washing, or sewing.
For everything there is exact to my wishes,
For where they don't eat there's no washing of dishes.
Don't mourn for me now, don't mourn for me never,
I am going to do nothing for ever and ever.[1]

Home and work do not exist in opposition to each other. A huge amount of work goes into making homes and the work which is done at home profoundly affects the work which happens outside the home: who does that work, how it is organized, and what the possibilities are for changing that organization. A 2011 report found that in the twenty-six member countries of the Organization for Economic Co-operation and Development or OECD (the most economically advanced countries in the world), between one-third and one-half of all valuable economic activity was unpaid work not accounted for through traditional measures. The majority of this work is what we would think of as 'housework': cooking, cleaning, and caring for others. The average person in the OECD spends 3.4 hours a day (14 percent of their time) doing these tasks, compared to 19 percent of their time in paid work or education (Miranda 2011). The work of home is significant.

There is a division of labor inside the home just as there is outside, most often on the basis of gender; the same OECD report found that on average women spend 2.5 hours more per day than men doing unpaid work and that the more unpaid work they did, the fewer hours they did of paid work. Domestic work can also be organized along divisions of age and by class and race/ethnicity when people from outside the family are paid to take on that work. The work done in homes creates inequalities, it does not just reflect those which already exist in the wider world. This work matters to women and to men, it affects economic opportunities, shapes identities, and has also influenced widespread and enduring political movements.

This chapter is organized into three sections, which look at work on and in the home in the period from around 1920 to the present day. The first section examines the changing relationship between home, work, and housework, showing how the separation of 'home' and 'work' arose through the process of industrialization and urbanization producing the figure of the 'housewife' as the normative role for women. The section outlines how heavy the burden of labor was for working-class women in the pre-war period and then shows how women's responsibility for housework underpinned 'first-wave' and 'second-wave' feminist movements. Women involved in these movements strove to understand the relationship between gender, work, and home and to challenge it. The last part of this section examines how work at home affects opportunities for work outside the home and the extent of women's segregation in relatively low-waged feminized work.

The second section explores the growth, decline, and resurgence of paid domestic labor. It examines how trends in the employment of domestic workers relate to broader economic trends and to global-scale relationships through international migration. Paid domestic work was once the most common form of employment for women but it declined after the 1930s so rapidly that many commentators thought it was gone for good. However, in recent years the numbers of paid domestic workers in Western countries have been growing again and now workers are drawn from all around the world. The home provides an unusual workplace, which as well as potentially providing care, can be a site of extreme exploitation and abuse. Domestic workers routinely suffer low pay and long working hours and are rarely protected by legislation to the same extent as other workers because the home is not recognized as a workplace and household tasks are not recognized as work.

The last section takes a slightly different angle in its consideration of home and work and delves into the work which is done to more literally make homes, particularly the work of 'do-it-yourself' (DIY). This focus allows for consideration to be given to one way in which gendered expectations of men produce work in the home for them. The section looks at the examples of the United States in the first half of the twentieth century and New Zealand from around 1920 to the present, to show that in some places and at some times the demand for work on the home is extensive as people not only repair, renovate, and improve existing dwellings but also build their own homes from scratch. Undertaking home maintenance and improvements was celebrated as morally uplifting and as evidence of responsible citizenship, reflecting the strong link between homeownership and belonging in the nation in both these countries. As a result, those who are excluded from owning their homes are also marginalized within the nation. Throughout, the chapter shows that rather than being juxtaposed, home and work intertwine to define each other, the people involved in them, and the social world at large.

HOME, WORK, HOUSEWORK, AND HOUSEWIVES

The contemporary relationship between home and work is historically specific rather than natural or inevitable. The process of industrialization profoundly affected the organization of work and home, by separating out paid, 'productive' labor from unpaid work in the home. This, in turn, produced the modern understanding of home and housework and the housewife as the person who should do this work. As Ann Oakley ([1974] 1976: 32) succinctly puts it:

> The most important and enduring consequence of industrialization for women has been the emergence of the modern role of housewife as 'the dominant mature feminine role.' Industrialization affected the roles of men as well as the roles of women. But while for men it enlarged the world outside the home, chiefly by expanding the range of occupations available to them, for women it has meant an involution of the world into the space of the home.

In pre-industrial societies, the role of the 'housewife' as we think of it today did not exist. Women were responsible for the majority of reproductive work but the tasks involved were not separated from the 'productive' work of the family unit, either in space or in terms of their organization (Hall [1973] 1995). A woman might spin wool while watching her children, and that wool might be used in domestic production of cloth or sold to be woven elsewhere. She might prepare meals for apprentices or laborers who were part of her household alongside providing food for family members. The process of industrialization, and with it urbanization, separated home from 'work' for men and in popular imaginings of what 'work' meant. It is not the case that women were not engaged in paid 'productive' work, but that the work of home fell to them whatever their other responsibilities were and that the separation of 'work' and 'home' defined women's participation in life outside home.

Hard labor at home

For most women, what it meant to be a housewife in the twentieth century was to be involved in long hours of heavy labor. In the early inter-war period, most working-class families were living in conditions that made women's work particularly strenuous. Few working-class homes had direct running water, so water would have to be carried up from a basement to a flat or apartment on a higher floor, or from a shared tap to a house up the street. Cooking would have to be done on an open fire or coal-fired stove and fuel would also need to be carried to feed this (Spring Rice [1939] 1995). Men's work patterns, such as shift work, could increase women's domestic labor as the men would need meals at different times of day from children, or from each other if there was more than one man in the house working and women would need to be up to produce food for the time it was needed:

FIGURE 5.1: Woman outdoors washing clothes in a copper, Melbourne, Victoria, c. 1935. In homes without running water or electricity, housework, particularly laundry, was hard physical work. F. Oswald Barnett Collection, State Library of Victoria, Australia.

'I go to bed only on Saturday nights,' said a miner's wife; 'my husband and our three sons are all on different shifts, and one or other of them is leaving or entering the house and requiring a meal every three hours of the twenty four'.

—Webb 1921, quoted in Massey 1994: 194

Women's work in the home contributed to men's work outside, enabling them to work the long hours often demanded of them and to do the hard physical labor involved in jobs such as mining. During this period, for example, there were no pit-head showers or company provision of clothing, and miners' wives would also be responsible for washing their husband's work clothes and heating the water needed for baths to clean off coal dust after a shift in the pit.

Women's domestic burden was increased by relatively large families and limited control of their fertility. Children increased the amount of work that needed to be done, tied women to the home, and threatened their health. One mother interviewed by Margery Spring Rice in the 1930s explained what this was like for her:

My life for many years consisted of being penned in a kitchen nine feet square, every fourteen months a baby, as I have had five babies in five years at first, until what with the struggle to live and no leisure I used to feel I was just a machine, until I had my first breakdown, and as dark as it was and as hard as it was it gave me the freedom and privilege of having an hour's fresh air.

—[1939] 1995: 74

For working-class women like this, home was a place to labor in both senses of the word – a place to work and a place to give birth. Large families increased the work women had to do and reduced the space available to do that work, making the burden heavier still.

As with many other aspects of life, the Second World War marked a watershed in the organization and understanding of housework and housewifery, underpinning both the post-war apogee of the housewife role and the conditions for it to be challenged. The war drew large numbers of women into paid work, and governments temporarily eased some of the burden of reproductive work through the increased provision of nurseries, subsidized or free foods for infants, and collective facilities such as the British Restaurants – government-run, subsidized cafeterias which were originally set up to help people who had been bombed out of their homes but which were widely used, particularly in urban areas. After the war women were encouraged, or forced, through policies such as 'marriage bans' which kept women out of many jobs, back into the home to free up jobs for returning men. The 1950s marked a low point in the numbers of women employed outside the home and a high point in the cult of

FIGURE 5.2: 'The more WOMEN at work, the sooner we WIN!' A Second World War recruitment poster to encourage women to take up 'war jobs' outside the domestic sphere. World War II Posters, United States National Archives, Identifier 513676.

the housewife. This was particularly marked in the United States and Australia where average incomes at this time were high and new housing in suburbs was being built at a rapid rate (Friedan 1963; Johnson and Lloyd 2004). However, as Johnson and Lloyd (2004) argue, it was the strength of the post-war political and cultural emphasis on women's role as homemakers that enabled the birth of the women's movement. In their role as housewives, women were given, for the first time, a shared identity based on gender rather than one based on their class.

Housework and feminism

The roots of second-wave feminism are based in women's struggles around their responsibility for reproductive labor and the implications of the housewife role. In 1963, Betty Friedan published *The Feminine Mystique*, a book which is credited with kick-starting second-wave feminism (Bowlby 1987) and 'upend[ing] Western women's vision of what constitutes the good life' (Shriver 2010: vii). Friedan argued that American housewives were unhappy, trapped, and wasted. The book opens:

> The problem laid buried, unspoken, for many years in the minds of American women. It was a strange stirring, a sense of dissatisfaction, a yearning that women suffered in the middle of the twentieth century in the United States. Each suburban housewife struggled with it alone. As she made the beds, shopped for groceries, matched slipcover material, ate peanut butter sandwiches with her children, chauffeured Cub Scouts and Brownies, lay beside her husband at night, she was afraid to ask even of herself the silent question – 'Is this all?'
>
> —Friedan 1963: 15

Friedan calls this 'the problem with no name'. It is the general dissatisfaction, and sometimes great misery, that women feel when their only role is try to make perfect homes and be perfect women. She identifies the routine drudgery of housework as problematic but she also strongly links 'the problem' to women's role as consumers. She sees women as manipulated by the media, primarily women's magazines and advertisers, into believing that buying things will give them the purpose, identity, creativity, and self-respect they lack in their lives (Bowlby 1987). The endless round of consumption and display to create the perfect home drains women's lives of meaning (think Betty in the television series *Mad Men* [Shriver 2010]). Friedan is clear that her analysis focuses on educated, middle-class, suburban housewives. A group of women for whom, because of their relative wealth, consumption was central to their daily lives. Learning how to be good consumers had become the work of these women.

FIGURE 5.3: From the 1950s, housewives were increasingly expected to be good consumers, and the image of the housewife was bound up with new forms of mass consumption. Vintage illustration via Pixabay (Creative Commons).

Other texts from the period focused on the labor involved in housekeeping as a way to have women's contributions in their homes recognized as work. Oakley ([1974] 1976) compared the activities of housewives to those of factory workers and showed how housework made similar demands on both mind and body to routine factory work. This desire to have housework recognized as work was part of the 'domestic labor debate' (Malos [1980] 1995), a debate within the feminist movement to try to both understand how to value women's work and to communicate its value in ways that would be taken seriously.

The second-wave feminists were not the first activists to highlight the problems for women caused by their isolation in the home. The first-wave feminists, such as Mary Livermore and Charlotte Perkins Gilman, had identified women's isolation in the home and confinement to domestic life as the basic cause of their unequal position in society in the late nineteenth century. Their ideology of 'material feminism' focused on the way that women's work was organized within the home and they developed designs for more rational housing, for example with public kitchens and shared dining rooms, and broader plans for urban design (Hayden 1981). Rather than campaigning to support individual women to move away from the work of the home, they campaigned to move 'housework' out of individual homes. Whereas more recent feminist movements have focused on improving women's rights at work or women's bodily autonomy, early feminists identified women's responsibility for work at home as a key arena for their struggles.

Women, housework, and work outside the home

Women's responsibility for work inside the home has never meant that they are not also involved in paid work outside the home, or in other people's houses. However, this responsibility for reproductive work, and particularly the social construction of women as the appropriate people to do cleaning and caring labor, has had a profound effect on the types of paid work that women tend to do. This is most obvious in the large proportion of women employed as paid domestic workers, considered in detail in the next section, and it is also true of the tasks that women do in non-domestic settings. Women are much more likely than men to be involved in paid work which involves tasks similar to housework: cleaning, caring, cooking. Sociologists Jennifer Jarman, Robert Blackburn, and Girts Racko (2012) carried out research in thirty industrialized countries and found that in all of them women were concentrated in traditional 'female' roles. For example, in the United States in 2009, 97.8 percent of all pre-kindergarten and kindergarten teachers and 92 percent of all registered nurses were female, whereas only 1.6 percent of all carpenters and 2.2 percent of all electricians were female (Hegewisch et al. 2010: 2). Ariane Hegewisch and her colleagues (2010) also found that occupational segregation fell between 1972 and 1996 in the United States but has hardly changed since then. Women with the lowest levels of education are most likely to be in gender-segregated jobs.

Occupational segregation matters not only because it means that women and men may be funnelled into work which is less than ideal for them as individuals but also because a significant share of the gender wage gap is accounted for by the differences in men's and women's occupations. There is a negative relationship between the proportion of women in an occupation and the average earnings of the occupation – that is, the more women there are in a job, the more likely it is that the job will be poorly paid. There are many reasons for this but it has been argued that when women do cleaning and caring tasks, the skill or difficulty of those tasks is overlooked. Women's traditional responsibility for reproductive roles in the home means that the ability to carry out care work and similar jobs is seen as a 'natural' aptitude rather than an acquired skill.

WHO DOES THE WORK OF HOME?: PAID DOMESTIC WORK

While the responsibility for unpaid reproductive labor in the home has been defining of gender inequalities and a catalyst for the women's liberation movement, gender is not the only axis of social inequality which organizes who does what around the house. In the first part of this section, I examine the phenomenon of paid domestic labor; a type of work which was modal for women in many Western countries until the 1930s and which is booming again today after a period of almost total decline in the late twentieth century. The recent growth in paid domestic employment is very largely dependent on the work of migrant women and the question of who does the washing up is connected to global scale inequalities and labor flows. In this section, I examine trends in domestic employment in the twentieth and twenty-first centuries, using the example of the growth in the number of paid domestic workers in the Nordic countries. The recent growth in numbers of paid domestic workers is socially significant for a number of reasons. First, the employment of domestic workers is strongly correlated to income inequality and growth in this form of employment indicates increasing inequality in societies more broadly. Secondly, the organization of domestic work is fundamental to gender roles and changes in the way domestic labor is organized both reflect and produce gender relations. Lastly, paid domestic workers tend to work in very poor conditions, for low wages, and without adequate protections or recognition of their work.

In 1973, Frank Victor Dawes wrote 'The days when butlers, footmen, cooks, nurses, governesses, housemaids and nannies were in plentiful supply have gone forever' ([1973] 1989: 15). Dawes was not alone in seeing the decline of domestic service in the 1960s and 1970s as a permanent change (Milkman,

Reese, and Roth 1998). By the 1970s, domestic employment appeared to be outmoded; superseded by both new domestic technologies and 'modern' social attitudes which sat uncomfortably with 'upstairs–downstairs' divisions. Yet an article in *The Times* in December 2015 reveals that such assumptions were misplaced:

> Something terrible is about to happen in my little area of north London. In the next few days all the cleaners and ironing ladies, housekeepers and au pairs we hire to keep ourselves sane, our marriages together and our children in clean pants will go home for Christmas . . . It's never nice to be left high and dry by the extra pair of hands you depend on to keep your domestic 'bliss' just about ticking over, but being left holding the Marigolds at Christmas is another nightmare altogether.
>
> —Walker 2015

The twenty-first century has seen a substantial resurgence in the numbers of domestic workers employed in many advanced industrial economies and a realignment of social attitudes towards this way of organizing housework. What had been seen as backwards and undemocratic is increasingly recast as necessary to a stress-free, middle-class life.

Historical trends in paid domestic work

Although the precise histories of paid domestic work in each country are different, there is a shared pattern in most of Europe, North America, and Australasia of high levels of domestic employment in the late nineteenth century and decline during the twentieth century, particularly after 1940 (Higman 2002: 25). In the UK, for example, numbers peaked in the 1890s, declined slightly in first decades of the twentieth century, and then grew again during the depression of the late 1920s. Nearly 1.5 million people (1,333,224 women and 74,489 men) were recorded as domestic servants in the 1931 census (Dawes [1973] 1989: 165; Todd 2014). There was a similar pattern in the United States, with peaks in the numbers of domestic workers as a proportion of the population around 1890 and 1930 and a rapid decline thereafter (Higman 2002).

In the Great Depression, high levels of unemployment held the wages of domestic workers down, making them affordable to households who did have work, and high levels of male unemployment meant that more women took on whatever work was available (Higman 2002; Todd 2014). By the 1930s, most salaried professionals could afford household gadgets such as vacuum cleaners, fridges, and cookers but they preferred, in the words of Winifred Foley, who entered service at the age of fourteen, 'a creature that would run on very little fuel and would not question her lot'. Servants, therefore, had to cost less than

FIGURE 5.4: Class at the Household Workers Training Project in San Jose, California, c. 1940. In the 1930s, high levels of unemployment led to a growth in the number of women entering domestic service. Governments supported this trend, and the Works Projects Administration (WPA) in the United States trained women to be domestic workers. Records of the Work Projects Administration, United States National Archive, National Archives Identifier 296101.

the time and money a middle-class woman would have to invest in domestic appliances. The result was that middle-class households employed a 'maid-of-all-work' who was paid a pittance (quoted in Todd 2014: 43; see also Delap 2011).

The decline in domestic service from the 1940s is generally explained by the improvement in alternative employment opportunities for women, in factories, shops, and offices. The Second World War accelerated the process as women were encouraged to leave domestic service to join the forces or take over jobs vacated by men. The war also changed attitudes towards class and 'knowing one's place'. Fewer people were prepared to behave in a subservient way even if the pay and conditions in domestic work were ostensibly better than many of the other jobs available to women (Dawes [1973] 1989). In the UK, the establishment of the National Health Service and the welfare state meant that fewer people were forced into service through dire need and that more egalitarian attitudes prevailed, undermining the assumption that some people should serve while others should be served (Todd 2014).

The decline in the availability of servants signalled a reorganization of work within the home for middle-class and upper-class families and the cementing of the housewife role as the 'right' thing for women. For a small number of wealthy families, the decline in domestic service meant a substantial change in their way of life. Dawes ([1973] 1989) gives the example of the Marquis of Bath who was born in 1905 into a household with forty-three indoor servants, including his own valet. By 1973, the Marquis lived in a much smaller establishment with only two servants and his grand stately home was opened as a public attraction. However, most servants had worked as 'maids-of-all-work' in quite modest middle-class houses (Delap 2011) and the work they had done was either taken on by household members or not done at all. Numerous magazines, self-help books, and advertisements advised on how to cope in a 'servantless' household and coached women to become housewives rather than mistresses. In the post-war era, the role of housewife became the normative status for adult women in North America, most of Europe, and Australasia. Housework tasks were organized by gender rather than by class for all but the wealthiest households. As a result, a shared identity developed, uniting women from very different backgrounds, which provided a foundation for second-wave feminism as outlined above (Johnson and Lloyd 2004).

Paid domestic work in the twenty-first century

Then, in the late 1980s and 1990s, the trends in the employment of paid domestic workers in the most industrialized countries changed, and after five decades of decline they started to rise again. The contours of this resurgence are geographically specific, affected by migration regimes, welfare state policies, and demographics – and the numbers of domestic workers employed are hard to glean, as many workers are employed informally. In the United States there has been notable growth in the numbers of housekeepers and nannies (see, for example, Hondagneu-Sotelo 2001; Macdonald 2010; Romero 2002); in the UK, au pairs, nannies, and cleaners seem to be most numerous (Cox 2006). In Southern Europe, domestic workers are concentrated in care for the elderly (see, for example, Bastia 2015; Marchetti and Venturini 2014). The International Labor Organization (ILO) estimates that there are 67 million paid domestic workers in the world (ILO 2020a).

In many countries, paid domestic work is now largely undertaken by migrant women, often women who lack citizenship rights and are discriminated against on the basis of their race/ethnicity (see, for example, chapters in Lutz 2008). The work of home is now organized at a global scale and segregated by class, gender, and ethnicity (Labadie-Jackson 2008). Migration for domestic work is often fuelled because the economies of sending countries, such as the Philippines and Sri Lanka, have been restructured and these governments encourage women to migrate as domestic workers in order to earn foreign exchange through remittances (Parreñas 2001; Stenum 2015).

One area of the world in which research on paid domestic labor has been flourishing recently and which exemplifies the way in which housework is increasingly organized by gender and nationality is the 'woman-friendly' Nordic countries: Denmark, Finland, Norway, and Sweden. These countries are often looked to as ideals of social equality and social welfare support, particularly for their generous state childcare provision and support for women's work outside the home. However, the numbers of paid domestic workers in these countries has been increasing relatively rapidly in recent years, albeit from a very low base, and researchers have shown how the generous Nordic welfare policies actually facilitate the employment of paid domestic workers (Isaksen 2010). Gender equality has been conceptualized within Nordic welfare regimes as the ability of middle-class women to compete in the labor market on equal terms with men and this has been supported through schemes such as direct payments to subsidize the cost of domestic workers (Platzer 2010) and migration rules which facilitate the movement of workers to undertake low-waged domestic work (Stenum 2010, 2015).

One notable way in which migration for domestic work has been facilitated in the Nordic countries is through the expansion of au pair schemes. Au pairs are ostensibly involved in cultural exchange rather than domestic work and their employment is more socially acceptable in the Nordic countries than the employment of someone called a 'domestic worker' would be. However, questions have been raised about au pairs' working conditions and rates of pay (see, for example, Bikova 2010; Calleman 2010; Stenum 2010; Løvdal 2015). The largest single group of au pairs in these countries is from the Philippines, and for many years the Philippine government refused to issue exit visas for nationals to take up au pair posts in Norway or Denmark because of their concerns about the poor working conditions (Stenum 2010). The employment of paid domestic workers, the overwhelming majority of whom are women from poorer countries, highlights that the 'woman friendliness' of the Nordic states is not a universal value. As Helle Stenum puts it, 'Gender equality is made irrelevant to the life of the au pairs – it is only relevant for the career women for whom the au pair is essential everyday support' (2010: 41).

We now see an increasingly similar pattern of growth in the numbers of paid domestic workers across the globe as even nations which have traditionally shunned private solutions and invested in state support for childcare, such as the Nordic countries (Isaksen 2010), are moving towards increased use of paid domestic workers. In the Global South, the middle classes are becoming more urban and more women are working outside the home. There have long been very large numbers of domestic workers employed by the wealthy in the South (Ray and Qayum 2009). At the same time, the former state-socialist countries of Eastern Europe and the former Soviet Union have reduced investment in public childcare facilities and allowed the market to take over provision, while at the same time promoting women's continued commitment to paid work and the adult worker society (Lutz and Palenga-Möllenbeck 2012). We now see flows of migrant domestic workers to and from these countries, which, until the late 1980s, could be assured of both plentiful childcare and universal employment. As Lutz and Palenga-Möllenbeck put it, 'at the end of the twentieth century Eastern Europe and Western and Southern Europe – despite their very different histories – arrived at a nexus in which labor market participation was seen as an adult citizen's duty, while states were not or no longer prepared to deliver the necessary support for the balance of waged and care work' (2012: 19). To this constellation of European states we could add that North America and many parts of the rapidly developing economies of the Global South were moving in a very similar direction.

The home as a workplace?

The home is also not just another workplace for domestic workers. Its strong association with women's unpaid reproductive labor for family members has meant that it is conceptualized differently from other workspaces by both workers and employers and by regulatory authorities, and domestic workers generally have fewer protections than people working in other settings. Domestic labor in the home in many countries is excluded from key employment protections such as maximum working hours or minimum wages, and immigration schemes which are designed to facilitate the movement of migrant domestic workers generally offer fewer rights than those for other groups of workers (for an overview, see Cox 2012). This is a practical manifestation of imagining 'home' and 'work' as separate and of tasks done within the home as the 'natural' duty of women, rather than an important form of paid work. One outcome of this is that research on domestic workers often reports the very poor pay and working conditions they face and the relatively high levels of abuse that these workers are subject to (see, for example, Anderson 1993, 2000). In 2011, the International Labor Organization (ILO) introduced Convention 189 to try to guarantee minimum rights for domestic workers, such as freedom from abuse and the right to regular rest periods. By May 2020, twenty-nine countries had ratified the convention, but over 100 had not (ILO 2020b).

The home is an unusual workplace not only in legal terms but also because of its intimate nature. As anthropologist Edward Hall (2011: 592) notes, the home is weighted with 'complex and embodied familial relations' and domestic workers will often need to negotiate challenging relationships with their employers inside this intimate space (Bakan and Stasiulis 1997; Green and Lawson 2011; Gregson and Lowe 1994). Employers are often conflicted about the work domestic workers do, particularly if it involves childcare and the development of loving relationships between children and carers (see, for example, Macdonald 2010). For domestic workers this means that their job may be organized and negotiated in an emotionally charged environment making it difficult to insist on what rights they have. However, the emotional content of the work, particularly caring for young children, is also identified by these workers as the aspect which makes otherwise isolated and difficult work bearable.

WORKING ON THE FABRIC OF HOME

In the first two sections, I have examined the organization of work that goes on inside the home to keep household members fed, clean, and cared for, and the house itself clean and tidy; in this section, I examine the work of physically repairing, maintaining, and improving the fabric of the home. While 'do-it-yourself' (DIY) is carried out by both men and women, it is particularly associated with men's role in the heteronormative home. For some people, and in some places, doing the physical work of maintaining and improving the home is part of the expectations of what it means to be a man, and a good man at that. The amount of work that the fabric of home demands varies across time and space. In some instances, this work may be extensive and can encompass the repair and renovation of whole buildings or the building of a home in the first place.

Carrying out DIY can be an important part of relationships with others; it can display care for family, be part of spending time with groups of friends, and can be part of culturally celebrated fathering. Like housework, home maintenance can seem unremarkable but is in fact entwined in the most significant social relationships. This section looks at the examples of DIY in New Zealand up to the present day and in the United States in the first half of the twentieth century to examine the ways that DIY builds not only homes but also community and nation. When working on your home is what makes you a good citizen or a good person, then people who cannot afford to buy a home, or who are excluded from homeownership through practices such as colour bars, are also excluded from inclusion in the nation.

Working on home and nation in New Zealand

New Zealand has a housing history which links working on the home to a sense of national, gendered identity and belonging for white New Zealanders (white people of European descent are known as Pākehā in New Zealand). This is part of a history of settlement that was based in part on an ideal of Pākehā settlers building their own homes and providing for their families through self-provisioning (Cooper 2008). Today, New Zealanders are thought to do more DIY than any other nation, and DIY is an important part of being a good homeowner, a good family member, and a good New Zealander. Although figures are hard to come by, it is suggested that New Zealanders are more likely to be involved in DIY projects than any other population in the Western world (Mackay, Perkins, and Gidlow 2007; Morrison 2012). As Perkins and Thorns comment, 'The significance of particular forms of home-based domestic work, do-it-yourself maintenance and building, has meant that many New Zealanders have developed a special type of relationship with their houses which has seen them continually renovating and changing the physical shape of house and garden' (2001: 43).

From the mid-1930s, the New Zealand government supported the notion that the ideal 'family' home was a detached house in the suburbs. After the Second World War, large suburbs were built made up of mostly timber-framed, single-storey, detached dwellings on quarter acre plots of land. Between 1954 and 1964, 207,700 such houses were built with government support (Mackay 2011) and the three-bedroom, single-storey suburban home on a large plot became the 'typical' New Zealand home (Perkins and Thorns 1999, 2001; Morrison 2012). Homeownership (with or without a mortgage) is considered both the norm and most desirable form of tenure; homeownership has consistently been associated with positive virtues (Perkins and Thorns 2001). Ownership has given people

FIGURE 5.5: A typical single-storey New Zealand house built on a timber frame, covered in weatherboard with a tin roof. Photograph by Michal Klajban via Wikimedia (Creative Commons).

relatively high levels of control over their dwellings and enables activities such as DIY (Perkins and Thorns 2003). In turn, research has found that there is a strong relationship between housing tenure, collective identity, and the way New Zealanders create a sense of home (Perkins and Thorns 1999).

The social circumstances of European settlement in New Zealand, the opportunities for homeownership, the design of houses, and the materials used for housebuilding encouraged (and indeed often demanded) high levels of input from homeowners who could build and repair their homes in a way that was uncommon in Europe (Perkins and Thorns 2003). Thus the history of European settlement in New Zealand is not separable from a particular housing history that defined white New Zealanders, particularly white New Zealand men, as responsible for the physical provision and upkeep of their homes. It is within this context that New Zealanders live in and work on their homes today. DIY in New Zealand is therefore a particularly rich area for investigation, bound up as it is with colonial history and discourses of family, gender, and nationhood.

Within this context of a commitment to homeownership and self-provisioning and the cultural celebration of ingenuity and craft skills, working on the home has particular resonances. Michael Mackay (2011) describes New Zealanders as actively producing a 'DIY'ed' home as an outward expression of their identity; as a practice to adapt the home to the changing requirements of household members and as way of actively enjoying the home as a site of productive work. The home and the act of working on the home become part of an iterative process whereby self and desired home are made together (Mackay 2011).

This process of identity-making through DIY is also part of relationships with others. People may choose to carry out home improvement projects, or to carry them out in particular ways, so as to reinforce relationships and communicate them to others. Carey-Ann Morrison (2012) found that DIY projects are important to heterosexual couples in New Zealand as a way to establish their relationships. Couples could spend time together planning and carrying out DIY, and also saw the changes they made to their homes as a manifestation of their relationship. Taking part in DIY projects can be a way for friends to bond. Working with friends on home improvement projects is common amongst young New Zealanders, particularly men (Cox 2013; Mackay et al. 2007; Mackay 2011).

Building the American dream

Like New Zealand, the United States has a history of DIY activity bound up with suburban living and state-supported homeownership, organized and represented in a way which reproduces an image of the nation as white. This history has roots in the long, but relatively little-known tradition of families, particularly poor Americans, building their own homes. Architectural historian Dianne Harris (2013) argues that this trend has been under-estimated by historians and that many hundreds of thousands of houses were built by their owners in American cities from the 1920s to 1950s using various combinations of contract labor and 'sweat equity'. In the early twentieth century, middle-class Americans chose to rent rather than buy houses; it was working-class people, including new migrants, who were most motivated to own their own homes, even if this meant building shacks just beyond city limits, where homes did not have to conform to the same building standards and fire regulations as those within incorporated areas. The owner-occupied, single-family dwelling became part of the American dream through the active promotion of homeownership by the federal government, church groups, and business interests, all of whom offered credit to families to enable them to build their own homes. Homeownership was heralded as a route to 'freedom' in terms of both freedom from landlords and freedom of self-expression, a route to becoming one's own lord and master and, after 1918, a 'bulwark against the Bolshevik tide' (Harris 2012: 40).

In the immediate post-war, era federal housing policy supported the building of suburban housing in a way that encouraged DIY. More than five million houses were built in the United States between 1946 and 1949 (Goldstein 1998) and owner-occupation grew apace. The GI Bill of Rights made suburban homeownership affordable and accessible for more people than ever before as returning GIs were able to obtain mortgages with little or no down payment – by 1961, 5.6 million loans had been made for housing for veterans of the Second World War and the Korean War. Unlike in the earlier period, the majority of houses were built by speculative builders but they were built at low cost and many were deliberately designed to allow the new owners to expand and improve. For example, in the famous Levittown developments in Pennsylvania and New York, houses were built with staircases to unfinished attics, windows designed to be turned into doors to new rooms, and carports which could be converted to garages or living space. Levitt's promotional materials encouraged remodelling by purchasers to suit their families' needs (Goldstein 1998). By 1955, one California builder even included a 'do-it-yourself workshop' within the garage of their new houses so owners could easily continue the work of refining their new homes (Harris 2013).

The new suburban living created the ideal situation for DIY to boom and it became a mass cultural phenomenon in the United States in the 1950s. On one level, this was a result of labor market and economic conditions. Skilled labor was in short supply and the new homeowners were happy to save money to spend on other household expenses. At the same time, the new generation of homeowners, which included veterans and manual workers, had the technical skills need to work on their homes with their own hands. At another level, the appeal of DIY tapped into the desire to participate in the American dream. DIY enabled families to obtain the house and lifestyle to which they aspired and 'resonated as a quintessential expression of that dream, especially as it was defined by the dominant values of the 1950s: domesticity, leisure, and independence' (Goldstein 1998: 37). The ability to work on one's own home was also seen as morally uplifting and as offering 'ways by which men and boys especially can make themselves useful when they would otherwise be idle' (Kyrk 1933, quoted in Harris 2012: 39). Working on one's own home was also portrayed by early manuals as the way to be a member of a neighbourhood or community and the way to be the right sort of man – one who took pride in his house and in working hard to provide a home for his family (Harris 2012).

As the strong ties to government policy suggest, homeownership, suburban living, and the work on homes, in the form of DIY and home improvements, that went with this were represented as an ideal form of Americanism, which in its whiteness implicitly excluded African Americans (Harris 2013). The exclusion of African Americans from this 'ideal' form of Americanism was not only implicit: from the 1870s, racially restrictive covenants existed that barred anyone not identified as white from purchasing homes in specific neighbourhoods. These were backed up by the requirements put on builders in order to qualify for federally insured financing, meaning that, for example, only 3.3 percent of the federally subsidized suburban housing built in Southern California's 1950s housing boom was made available to people not identified as white (Harris 2013: 29–30). Homeownership, citizenship, and whiteness became synonymous. In her analysis of popular culture representations of mid-twentieth-century housing in the United States, Harris found that: 'a pervasive iconography of white, middle-class domesticity that circulated widely in various media and that became instantiated in thousands of houses nationwide served to reinforce and to continuously and reflexively create and re-create midcentury notions about racial and class identity, and specifically about the rightness of associating white identities with homeownership and citizenship' (2013: 12). Working on the home and creating a 'perfect' home became activities which allowed men and women to perform gendered, classed, and racialized identities.

DIY, home and identity

Research on DIY and home maintenance from around the world suggests that working on the home is an important arena for the negotiation of identities, particularly masculinities, and relationships, as well as being a way to gain a home that better conforms to the household's needs and desires. DIY is not necessarily undertaken to save money, and not always or only to produce a particular end result, but also because the act of carrying out DIY produces and confirms valued identities and relationships (see Cox 2013, 2014, 2016). Historian Steven Gelber has argued that in the early decades of the twentieth century in the United States, the rise of DIY was a key component in men's renegotiation of their place in their homes and 'part of the definition of suburban husbanding' (1997: 67). Household repairs and maintenance were free from any hint of gender-role compromise and allowed men to reassert their masculinity at a time when women's entry to the workplace made that space a less definite source of masculine identity. DIY was not undertaken to save money but as a way to be a proper man and a good father. Andrew Jackson, writing with reference to the rise of DIY in Britain in the twentieth century, found that 'household repairs and maintenance allowed men to stay at home without feeling emasculated. They replicated and reinforced work values and gave a sense of psychological fulfilment. Because jobs around the house had an economic value attached to them, they also carried the legitimacy of masculine skilled labor' (2006: 61). Similarly, geographer Andrew Gorman-Murray (2011) found that an increased focus on home repairs can be a way for men to negotiate anxiety produced in the world of work following the Global Financial Crisis (see also Wolf and McQuitty 2011 on the United States). In his classic study of self-provisioning on the Isle of Sheppey, sociologist Ray Pahl (1984) showed home maintenance activities to be an expression of a particular, valued, identity. Self-provisioning was a result of relative affluence rather than poverty as only those with their own homes and resources to buy equipment could do DIY (on the need for resources to carry out self-provisioning, see also Nelson 2004; Shove et

FIGURE 5.6: DIY can be a way for men to 'do' fatherhood and express care for their families. Photograph by Cade Martin and Dawn Arlotta via Pixnio (Creative Commons).

al. 2007; Williams and Windebank 2002) and his work locates DIY within class and gender divisions, a very specific history, and material circumstances.

DIY work at home can also be a way that identities can be communicated across generations and fatherhood can be performed. Jackson (2006) comments on the importance of father/son relationships in DIY activities; taking part in DIY was seen as a healthy way for respect to be built amongst male members of the household. Performing DIY in New Zealand offered some men a way to 'do' fatherhood as it both expressed their care for their families and allowed them to spend time with children passing on skills (Cox 2014). In contrast, a recent study in the UK found that expectations on men to be 'hands-on' fathers can underpin a move away from DIY and towards the employment of paid handymen (Kilkey, Perrons, and Plomien 2013). The study found that ideals of 'hands-on' fatherhood could create a time squeeze for men similar to that faced by working women. In order to be the 'right' sort of father, men would outsource activities such as home repairs and gardening in order to spend more time with their children (see also Ramirez and Hondagneu-Sotelo 2009 on the outsourcing of gardening in the United States).

These cultural and emotional aspects of DIY suggest that people may welcome opportunities to work on their homes as well as using DIY to achieve a particular outcome. Working on the home is not necessarily a cheap alternative to employing tradespeople, nor always an unwelcome chore; DIY activities can be embraced as a means by which to realize valued identities and relationships and to make a home. For men as well as women, home is a place to labor, a place to carry out tasks that, like those women carry out in the home, are expected of men by virtue of their gender and which are bound up in definitions and imaginings of appropriate masculinity.

CONCLUSION

Throughout this chapter, I have argued that in many different ways, home is not separable from work. The home is not only a place where very large amounts of work take place, but it is also a site that shapes opportunities for and experiences of work outside the home. Work at home organizes and reflects social hierarchies, most obviously of gender but also of race/ethnicity and class. The unequal division of work at home provided the foundation for the feminist movement, which dramatically changed experiences of work and political life outside the home. Yet the imagining that work is something which happens outside the home still shapes our lives, which makes the work of home invisible and lowers the status of people who do that work.

In the period since 1920, there has been both dramatic change and surprising continuity in the relationship between work and home in the West. Women are still overwhelmingly responsible for reproductive labor – spending more than twice as much time on these tasks as men – but men's contribution to housework has grown in most countries. While women are involved in paid work outside the home in higher numbers than ever before and in much more varied roles, there is still stark segregation in many jobs with women concentrated in occupations that are related to caring. The association of caring work with women's 'natural' role means these occupations are generally considered to be less skilled and are less well paid than the occupations which are dominated by men.

In 1920, if women were employed they were more likely to be domestic servants than anything else, a trend which continued through the depression of the 1930s. Despite the huge changes brought about in the wake of the Second World War, in the twenty-first century, at a global scale, more women than ever are employed as domestic workers. In the West, numbers of domestic workers have grown in recent decades, although they are below their pre-war high. Paid domestic work is now organized at a global scale; the work of home is networked into international flows of people and money (through the sending of remittances) and part of broader political and economic relationships. Domestic workers are the group that suffers most from imagining that work is something separate from home. Their labor is not seen as 'real' work in legal terms and despite intervention from the ILO, the majority of countries in the world do not assure domestic workers the same rights as other groups.

The strong association of home with women's traditional role as carers has meant that men's work at home and the importance of this work to broader social trends and inequalities is less well-known than that of women. Yet, throughout the period since 1920, this work has been important in shaping masculinities, building communities, and, in the United States and New Zealand at least, in distinguishing 'good' men who are recognized as part of the nation.

Work and home are not distinct realms or activities and the work of home is linked to life outside home in myriad ways. This domestic work shapes and reflects the most profound social and economic inequalities in society but it also offers a route to organize against them, to express care for family and friends, and to express oneself in a valued and valuable way.

CHAPTER SIX

Gender and Home: (Re)scripting Domestic Life and Design

BARBARA PENNER

To open this discussion of gender and home, I begin with a film: the much-loved children's classic, Walt Disney's *Mary Poppins* (1964). Having first seen the film when I was a child, my encounter with it again as an adult (feminist, mother, academic) was a revelation. Of course I remembered Mary Poppins, with her umbrella and sticking-out boots, and Bert, the vaudevillian chimneysweep. The chocolate-box prettiness of 17 Cherry Tree Lane stayed with me, too. But other details were a surprise. While I vaguely recalled that the children do not have a happy relationship to their parents – the mother is flighty; the father, stern – the specific reasons for the parents' neglect never made an impression.

On re-viewing the film, I became very aware that Mary Poppins, a magical domestic *deus ex machina*, has floated down from the sky to correct some well-defined social 'ills'. The mother's inattentiveness to her children and home is caused by her commitment to 'the cause': Women's Rights. The father's distance stems from his rigid adherence to a patriarchal and capitalist system: 'A British bank is run with precision', he declares, 'A British home requires nothing less!' In fact, the eponymous Banks is a banker and, in songs like 'Feed the Birds', the film suggests that capitalism has destroyed his sense of compassion. Banks's humanity is only revived when he says a nonsense word (Supercalifragilisticexpialidocious), tells a joke, loses his job, undoes his tie, and makes a kite to fly with his children.

Similarly, Mrs Banks's full embrace of her maternal responsibilities only occurs when she offers up her beloved 'Votes for Women' sash to serve as a kite-tail. Thus, the final number, 'Let's Go Fly a Kite', depicts the triumph of child-oriented familism and togetherness (Penner 2009).

While we will leave our analysis of *Mary Poppins* there, it is hopefully clear why it serves as a useful starting point for considering the relationship of gender and home in this essay. For the film represents the home as a key site for the modern definition and enactment of gender roles. Indeed, the home as portrayed in *Mary Poppins* might be described as an incubator of gender relations, generating normative ideas about the roles of men, women, and children; but, as the film also makes very clear, the gender relations established within the home are also operative outside of it, undergirding capitalist, colonialist, and imperialist ideologies. The link between the patriarchal family unit and empire is memorably affirmed in 'The Life I Lead', when Banks sings, 'A British nanny must be a gen'ral!; The future empire lies within her hands . . .'

Even if the resolution of *Mary Poppins* is deeply conformist, some subversive messages are nested within it. Ironically, the film underscores in a cautionary way the fragile nature of the nuclear family unit and emphasizes how gender roles and relations are in a constant state of negotiation and contestation. In particular, Banks's claim to have 'lordly' rights as a patriarch and breadwinner comes to seem borderline delusional, as his wife, children, and servants rebel against his authority, and Mary Poppins openly rejects it; while in the end, Banks is able to resume his place as head of the family, he does so only by exercising love and care, rather than by virtue of any inherited or abstract set of rights. In a similar way, rather than fixed or timeless, gender roles and relations are represented in the film as highly contingent: powerful and pervasive, but also in need of constant reinvention, adaptation, and assertion (within limits). This essay focuses on dissecting and understanding how exactly these gendering operations have historically operated within the 'sacred precincts' of home.

SEPARATE SPHERES

It is important first to put this discussion of gender and home into context. An initial and perhaps obvious point involves nomenclature: when speaking of 'gender', I am following a line of feminist scholars since the 1980s who use the term not to refer to the biological sexes and any associated and essentialized traits but rather to the way in which the relationship between the sexes is organized socially. As historian Joan Wallach Scott, one of its most acute expositors, has noted, the use of gender:

> explicitly rejects biological explanations, such as those that find a common denominator for diverse forms of female subordination in the facts that

women have the capacity to give birth and men have greater muscular strength. Instead, gender becomes a way of denoting 'cultural constructions' – the entirely social creation of ideas about appropriate roles for women and men.

—[1988] 2000: 77

This rejection of 'natural' roles determined by sex is crucial, as it insists we understand that gender roles are not defined by some eternal or biological logic. Instead, the way the relationship between the sexes is configured at particular moments in time and in particular places is treated as a strategic construction, supporting certain forms of social and sexual organization and/or certain economic and political systems.

Whether our historical focus is on patriarchy, heteronormativity, capitalism, or imperialism (or the way in which these operate in concert), the home quickly emerges as a crucial nexus for the formation and regulation of gender relations. But as with the term 'gender', we should also be clear that we are using 'home' in this essay in a very specific sense. Home at its most basic may be a physical site – a house – but it may also be a symbol of individual and collective ideals, aspirations, and memories that can act upon and attach people just as surely as a physical dwelling may do: consider, for instance, how the notion of a *home*land fosters patriotic attachment. Looking at home in this way – as both space and symbol – complicates our account because it highlights a potential gap between the idea of home and its lived reality.

While we will soon discuss these issues in relation to the twentieth century, it should be noted that in Anglo-American society some of the most powerful ideas about home and gender roles were established earlier and continue to exert a strong influence now. To identify their origins, we need to go back to the mid-eighteenth century, when the rise of industrial capitalism resulted in the separation of places of production (work) from spaces of reproduction (home). As it was removed from the public spaces of production, home became more clearly defined as a private sphere, a place of retreat from the outside world and, crucially, its economic relations – a place that sheltered individual self-expression and family life. The essential fact from the perspective of this essay, however, is that this private sphere was one that incontrovertibly belonged to the male head of the family.

The husband's position as the head of the household – and his right to direct his spouse and children – were enshrined in law. As the legal historian Hendrik Hartog reminds us: 'The law created marriage as the husband's private sphere. Law gave him vested rights and limited duties within a domestic space that he owned' (2000: 136). The moment a woman in Britain or America was united with her husband in marriage in the eighteenth or nineteenth century, she lost her independent legal status under the principle of coverture; as a 'feme covert', her legal rights were incorporated into those of her husband and her identity was literally 'covered over' by his. Once married, a wife could no longer bring legal action against parties in her own name, own personal property or real estate, or have custody over children in the event of a separation. Her husband was responsible for paying her debts, supporting her and any dependents, and overseeing her behaviour (Hartog 2000: 93–135).

Yet the wife's subordination to her husband in law was partially mediated in practice by the emergence of a particular model of marriage in the nineteenth century: the companionate model. This model of marriage established that husbands and wives were to function as equal partners in the operation of the household, each with a distinct arena of responsibility. Already in the 1830s, the political and social commentator Alexis de Tocqueville compared the specialization of labor he witnessed within American homes to the specialization of labor within American industries, noting that wives and husbands were trained through education and public opinion to take charge of different facets of household management ([1840] 1968, vol. 2: 778). While husbands managed the external relations of the family, wives managed the domestic realm: housekeeping, food preparation, laundry, nursing, and children's education in practical and spiritual matters, labor that was at once physical and emotional and that feminist scholars today refer to as 'affective' (Weeks 2007).

The aptitude of women for these caring domestic roles was justified by biology: as women were weaker, and supposedly more emotional than men, they were seen as being more in tune with spirituality, religion, and beauty. As ministering 'angels of the household', women came to exert considerable moral influence and a degree of autonomy within the family sphere (though, of course, they still had few legal rights and little economic independence.) Women – as wives and mothers – were praised for selflessly performing these labors of love; and their voluntary submission to husbands was lauded as a model for how society itself should be organized. As Catharine Beecher, the most influential early domestic advisor, maintained: 'There must be the relations of husband and wife, parent and child, teacher and pupil, employers and employed, each involving the relative duties of subordination' (quoted in Sklar 1979: 158). The consensual model of social relations established in the household struck American commentators especially as a larger principle around which a unified national identity could be built.

Due to the national and nationalistic importance given to household units, it was vital that they be free from outside interference or meddling. The private sphere of the family was thus often visualized as a kind of sacred or inviolable circle into which outsiders were not admitted. While this private sphere did not correspond exclusively to any one space, the single-family home emerged as a kind of ideal, especially from about the 1830s, and it still retains a certain aspirational valence today. Only the single-family home could provide the spatial privacy needed to guarantee individual and familial autonomy and freedom from outside interference.

Seen in light of the aspiration for spatial privacy, we can understand why a specific vision of home came to be favoured in contemporary architectural writers from Andrew Jackson Downing ([1850] 1969) to Calvert Vaux (1864), who were remarkably consistent in their prescriptions. The house, built for a single family and detached from its neighbours, required a property of fifty to one hundred yards in order to guarantee familial privacy. The house's property line – and, hence, the extent of the family's sovereignty – was to be visually demarcated by an entrance-gate. Further protection from neighbours and the casual eye of passers-by was to be provided by yards and lawns (aptly dubbed 'verdant moats' by historian Kenneth T. Jackson), as well as by trees and shrubbery that created a natural screen around the house (1985: 58).

No less important than securing physical boundaries externally was establishing clear internal ones. However much the nuclear family was held up as an ideal social arrangement, most rural and working-class families still shared their homes with paying boarders, relatives, and hired help, and lived, ate, and slept in rooms with multiple functions. For this reason, from the 1830s, reform-minded architects began to subdivide internal spaces more rigorously to differentiate between particular activities (say, bodily cleansing and sleeping) and between groups of occupants. The sexes were now explicitly segregated: for instance, in working-class housing, girls and boys were given their own bedrooms, separate from their parents. This gendered geography was further elaborated in the bourgeois suburban villas sprouting up at the borderlands of most Western metropolitan centres that provided distinctly feminine spaces such as dressing rooms and masculine spaces such as studies (Wigley 1992).

Part of the moral project of domestic reform, however, was always to bring family members and friends together again in appropriately respectable ways. As budgets allowed, architects began to include a series of specialized rooms dedicated to leisure, entertaining, and hospitality (parlours, dining rooms, and spare bedrooms). Proper appropriation of these spaces consisted of reading aloud, writing, sewing, singing, and having edifying conversations – never of washing, dressing, or working for pecuniary gain. Creating suitable settings for these activities required a high level of staging; supported by a new market in mass-produced goods and furnishings, the interior became an index of familial character and values, status, and aspirations (Ames 1992; Grier 1988).

The living room and parlour thus encouraged a self-referential familial performance that reinforced the illusion of the household's autonomy from the public realm – an illusion that Jürgen Habermas argued was essential to providing 'the bourgeois family with its consciousness of itself' ([1962] 1991: 46). Far from being separate from the world, however, this carefully cultivated and introverted model of domesticity became a colonizing force. As literary

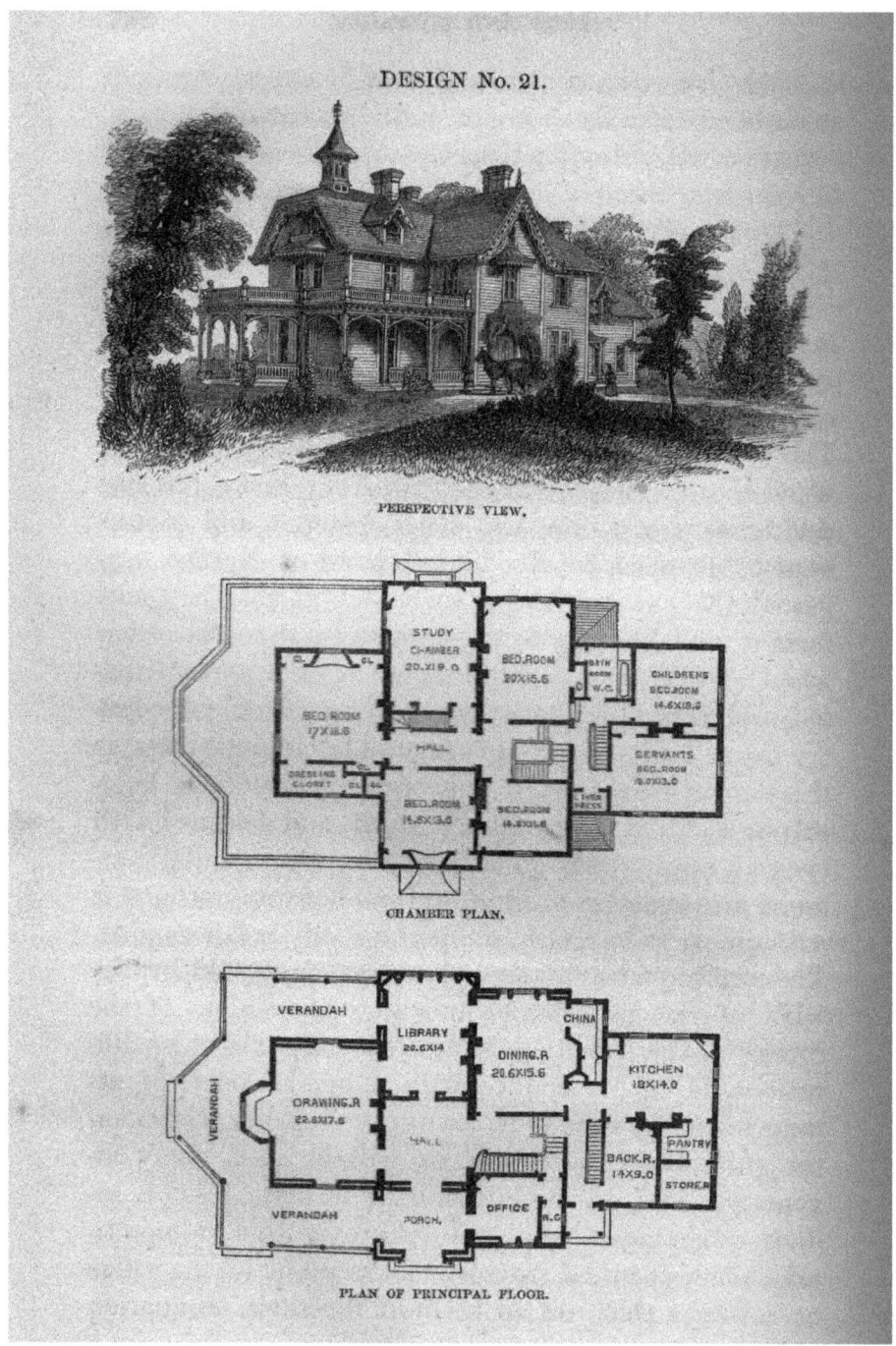

FIGURE 6.1: Calvert Vaux, 'Design No. 21: Irregular Wooden Country House', 1864. Calvert Vaux, *Villas and Cottages* (New York: Harper & Brothers, 1864).

FIGURE 6.2: Picturing ideal middle-class family relations: Asher B. Durand's engraving, 'The Wife', 1830. From *The Atlantic Souvenir* (Philadelphia, PA: Lea & Carey, 1830).

critic Lori Merish notes, the consequence of making this attachment to home seem both morally and socially 'progressive' meant that those with other models of living – indigenous peoples or those of different ethnicities – could be disenfranchised and brutally subjugated as 'uncivilized' or 'savage' (2000: 15). The single-family, decorously divided, detached house proved to be a powerful mechanism that shaped the larger gendered moral, economic, and political order – one of the most effective tools of patriarchy, capitalism, and imperialism.

SUBURBAN DREAMS

The model of the single-family detached home would prove to be remarkably enduring. Speculative suburban developments made up almost entirely of single-family homes were by no means the invention of the twentieth century, but as mass production techniques in construction began to make a suburban home more economical, it became a more realistic aspiration for a much wider swathe of the population. This form of development was also favoured and supported by government policies to encourage homeownership in many countries in the wake of the First World War. In America particularly, initiatives like President Herbert Hoover's 'Own Your Home' programme saw homes built with federal monies sold to war veterans (Wright 1981: 196). Considering these national campaigns, in which governments and employers promoted individual homeownership and patriarchal families as the best guarantor of social and economic stability, it is hard to sustain the fiction that the home and its organization is ever a purely private matter. As Hoover stressed, 'We must remember that the home is the backbone of the nation . . .' (quoted in Wheeler 1932: 25).

Campaigns to encourage homeownership were very successful and certainly, in America, they proliferated, thanks to a combination of innovative financing and the efforts of a growing number of developers who, as architectural historian Gwendolyn Wright notes, now had a vastly enlarged scale of operations (1981: 200–1). Developers undertook to provide all the elements of a community, planning for amenities like streets, water reservoirs, and transportation systems, as well as creating certain standards to determine the area's overall look. These standards and regulations, which might specify anything from the size of each house's lot to the height of its fence, was the reason why suburban developments often had such uniform, bland, appearances. They aimed to encourage conformity among residents, a social homogeneity further enforced through mortgage lending practices that discriminated against those of other races or ethnicities, or those who did not fit the norm of the nuclear family (Cohen 2003: 200–55; Harris 2013).

From the perspective of our main focus, gender and the home, we also see that this configuration of domestic space had a significant impact in perpetuating patriarchal social organization. Due to the separation of suburban developments from most workplaces, a culture of commuting sprang up: husbands, as the main (ideally sole) breadwinners, travelled often considerable distances each day to and from work. For them, home was the place to which they returned at the end of a workday, a place of relaxation and repose; for wives, however, the home was a workplace. The fact that servants or domestics were becoming a luxury by the end of the First World War meant that comparatively little paid help was available and ensured that women did most housekeeping themselves.

This workload was heavy, constant, and physically demanding (Strasser 1982; Cowan 1983). As it had evolved, the twentieth-century suburban house had become a highly individuated space – each house had its own kitchen, laundry area, bathroom, etc. – which meant that in each house, every day, wives were separately carrying out similar cleaning, caring, and maintenance routines to support their own family. The growing discourse around hygiene within the home since the late nineteenth century, along with the highly emotive marketing of cleaning products to women, not only made cleaning routines more onerous than previously, but more emotionally charged, as a failure to meet acceptable standards of cleanliness supposedly meant that a wife was exposing her family to germ- and potentially tubercular-harbouring nooks and crannies (Adams 1996: 36–102; Forty 1986: 156–81).

The particular way in which architectural form, in this case, the single-family home, exacerbated the female burden did not go unremarked. Proto-feminist or feminist critiques of the single-family house typology and the broader separation of private and public spheres have been around since the birth of feminism itself, as has a keen awareness about the injustice of women's lack of remuneration for their domestic work. Friedrich Engels in *The Origin of the Family, Private Property and the State* (1884) had in mind women's unpaid yet necessary labor in the home when he declared, 'Within the family, he [i.e. the husband] is the bourgeois and the wife represents the proletariat' (quoted in Buchli 2013: 117). This was an incredibly charged comparison, as it underlined that, like proletarians, women were economically exploited in order to benefit a ruling class – men.

As the architectural historian Dolores Hayden has chronicled in her classic study, *The Grand Domestic Revolution* (1981), in response to these issues, a committed group of 'material feminists' emerged between the 1860s and 1920s who specifically focused their energies on tackling economic and spatial issues connected to the organization of family life. These feminists worked from the premise that single-family homeownership effectively condemned women to a life of uncompensated drudgery rather than acknowledging the value of their work and freeing their potential as human beings. Hayden describes the way in which material feminists designed and sometimes built a wide range of architectural alternatives to the single-family dwelling in their pursuit of social and economic justice:

> In order to overcome patterns of urban space and domestic space that isolated women and made their domestic work invisible, they developed new forms of neighborhood organizations, including housewives' cooperatives, as well as new building types, including the kitchenless house, the day care center, the public kitchen, and the community dining club . . . For six decades the material feminists expounded one powerful idea: that women must create feminist homes with socialized housework and childcare before they could become truly equal members of society.
>
> —1981: 3

As Hayden focuses mostly on communal and un-iconic architectural typologies, her discussion of feminist interventions into the built environment has been usefully extended by the architectural historian Alice T. Friedman. In *Women and the Making of the Modern House* (2006), Friedman argues that in order to understand key innovations of modernist domestic design, we must acknowledge the influence of reform-minded feminists. In recounting the story of how five modernist icons came into being, from Frank Lloyd Wright's Hollyhock House (1921) in Los Angeles to Robert Venturi's Vanna Venturi House in Philadelphia (1964), Friedman notes that these were mostly commissioned by women who did not suit or openly rejected the conventional domestic typology. These 'atypical' female clients were mostly single or widowed women, often with children. All had strong feminist convictions and recognized, in Friedman's words, 'that conventional building types and patterns of domestic planning were inadequate responses to . . . needs, both programmatical and ideological' (2006: 130).

Through long and sometimes tense discussions with their famed architect-collaborators – who responded with varying degrees of sympathy, ambivalence, or indifference – these clients demanded domestic spaces tailored to their own needs and beliefs. A good example is the second-floor living space of the Schröder House in Utrecht, Holland (1924), which reflected Truus Schröder's progressive ideas about childrearing (see Figure 0.2): in place of fixed internal walls, the space had flexible partitions separating bedrooms from the living room to allow for the freer flow of conversation and greater sharing between children and adults (Friedman 2006: 74–85).

Yet even if the modernist homes that Friedman describes went on to become highly celebrated, they never constituted a serious threat to the dominant model of social organization. And while some of the material feminists' socialized designs gained a certain amount of traction – for instance, urban apartment blocks with collective kitchens – they did not revolutionize domestic arrangements at large. Instead, as Hayden notes, material feminism declined in the 1920s during the 'Red Scare' when the fear of Communism was rife and a new generation of conservative and commercially minded home economists emerged, such as Christine Frederick, who were not ideologically opposed to capitalism (1981: 281–86).

This did not mean that concerns about female drudgery in the home went away, but rather that the idea of how to tackle the problem shifted at this time, with a preference for reforming existing space rather than challenging the underlying single-family model. Instead of arguing for change at a structural level, or considering socialized approaches to childcare, laundry, and food preparation, the exhaustion of women was now more commonly blamed on their failure to approach housekeeping rationally or to adopt modern technologies and equipment. If women were to be 'saved', to use the highly charged language of reformers, then housework had to be rationalized and homes modernized – convictions that sustained a zeal for microscopic efficiency studies, labor-saving devices, and functional domestic planning well into the 1960s. Nowhere was this consensus felt more than in the space that was seen as women's primary workspace: the kitchen.

KITCHEN STORIES

It is worth considering twentieth-century efforts to reform the kitchen in greater depth as they demonstrate precisely how the relationship between gender and home has been consistently – if not always successfully – mediated by various external agents from government agencies to home economists, manufacturers to industrial designers and architects. In these attempts to reshape the kitchen, we also see how it became a privileged entry point for new technologies and for new regulatory regimes for female behaviour in the home.

In most nineteenth-century middle-class homes, the kitchen was regarded mostly as a 'back-stage' space, a functional behind-the-scenes necessity for domestics; by contrast, the parlour was a 'front-stage' space par excellence, the primary marker of respectability in which one's taste and status was displayed. In the twentieth century, however, the kitchen displaced the parlour to become the most important room in the house. The reasons for the kitchen's elevation in status were multi-fold, but one factor was the new concern with hygiene, which became a major preoccupation for both working- and middle-class housewives in this period.

While reformers had tried to instil ideas of cleanliness and order since early Victorian times, Adrian Forty argues: 'Only when advertisers, designers, and manufacturers began to make use of the imagery of hygiene did the general public fully assimilate the lessons which the hygienists had been teaching' (1986: 161). From the 1920s to present, manufacturers and designers imbued their products with the 'look' of hygiene through the streamlined surfaces of domestic appliances such as refrigerators and the use of white, easily wiped surfaces (Lupton and Miller 1992: 41–64); and, significantly, consumers came to value hygienic imagery in products because they increasingly equated cleanliness with beauty. Hence, according to Forty's still seminal account, products imbued with the 'aesthetic of cleanliness' became 'objects of desire' (1986: 180).

While the aesthetic of cleanliness affected other rooms of the house, most notably the bathroom, it made a particular impact in the kitchen, which had by this period become the main workspace for women of all but the elite classes and had the greatest concentration of appliances. Crucially, it was also the place where new forms of 'clean' fuels like gas and electricity were introduced into the home and it contained the expensive mechanical systems necessary to pump water and circulate heat. All of these factors ensured that the kitchen emerged as a primary focal point for home economists and manufacturers alike: the former saw the kitchen as a testing ground for practices that maintained the health of the family (that is, where sound principles of nutrition, hygiene and sanitation were applied and efficient routines were enacted to 'save' the housewife); and the latter saw kitchens as vital to stimulating domestic consumption of all kinds.

In fact, home economists and manufacturers frequently joined forces to promote new technologies in the home. For instance, home economists played important roles in campaigns to encourage rural electrification in America: to increase domestic electrical usage, they worked to persuade farmers to buy more labor-saving devices to rescue their wives from sanity-endangering housework. (There was a long-standing, if apocryphal, myth that insane asylums held a disproportionate number of farmers' wives [Kline 2000: 87–112, 131–214].) Even more commonly, home economists acted as consultants to corporations or were employed by them to help with the development, testing, and marketing of domestic appliances to make them more effective and appealing (Blaszczyk 1997). As it happened, however, the proliferation of these mechanical servants did not reduce the number of hours that women spent on domestic chores overall: most time studies show that they had the effect of simply raising standards of cleanliness (Kline 2000: 266–70).

But home economists did not invest all their faith in labor-saving devices alone. From the time of Catharine Beecher and Harriet Beecher Stowe's *The American Women's Home* (1869), it was argued that kitchen spaces and women's housekeeping routines themselves could become more efficient. By the 1910s, Taylorist principles of scientific management and time-and-motion studies were being deployed to rationalize kitchen plans and housework. Two

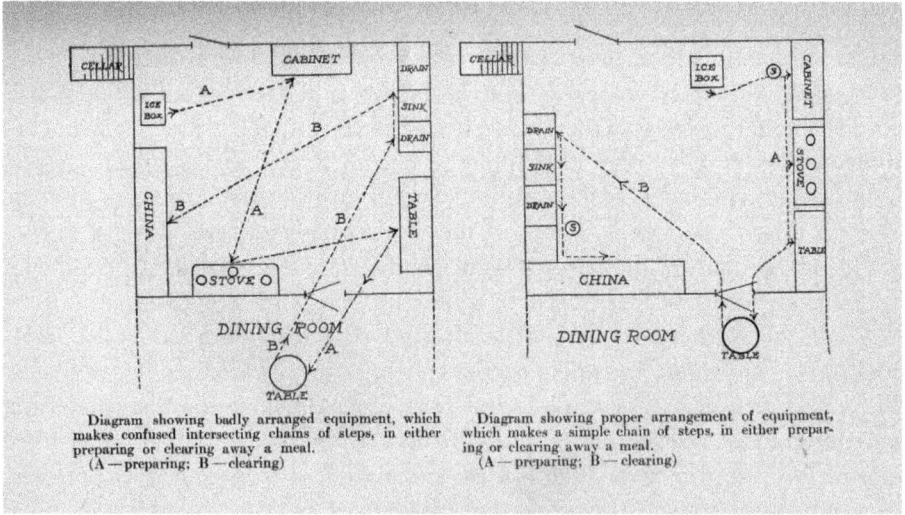

FIGURE 6.3: Diagram in Christine Frederick's *The New Housekeeping* (1913) showing badly arranged equipment (left) and proper equipment (right). Christine Frederick, *The New Housekeeping: Efficiency Studies in Home Management* (Garden City, NY: Doubleday, Page, 1913).

of the most influential figures in this endeavour, Christine Frederick and human engineer Lillian Gilbreth, closely studied kitchen activities and workflows – Frederick even had her own testing laboratory – with the aim of eliminating fatigue caused by wasted movements (Frederick 1913; Gilbreth 1938). Their findings were then used to plan kitchen spaces more economically, designing 'work centres' devoted to particular activities, and devising rules about arranging and working in the space.

While European home economists and women's organizations watched developments in America closely, they pushed the rationalization of the kitchen further still. The most influential example is Austrian socialist architect Margarete Schütte-Lihotzky's Frankfurt Kitchen from 1926. Schütte-Lihotzky had developed this prefabricated kitchen for use in the modern public housing estates designed by Ernst May in Frankfurt, the largest building programme of its kind in Germany. In this context, home economists' preference for compact kitchens (to save steps) coincided with local government's push to improve housing standards at reasonable cost, making Schütte-Lihotzky's prefabricated

FIGURE 6.4: Margarete Schütte-Lihotzky's Frankfurt Kitchen, from the Ginnheim-Höhenblick Housing Estate, Frankfurt am Main, Germany, 1926. © The Museum of Modern Art, New York / Scala, Florence.

galley-type kitchens a logical solution. Over 10,000 kitchens were installed between 1926 and 1930 in Frankfurt and they had a long legacy, as they were adapted for use in other European countries, and remained in use in the Federal Republic of Germany until the 1970s (Heßler 2009: 163).

At 1.9 by 3.44 metres, the standard-type Frankfurt Kitchen was the first scientifically calculated fitted kitchen. Schütte-Lihotzky studied the flow of activities in the kitchen with a stopwatch and tried to ensure that a housewife-worker's tools were in easy reach: all surfaces were continuous and seventeen essential features were built-in, from dish-drying rack to fold-out ironing board to overhead light to gas stove (Bullock 1988; Henderson 1996; Hochhaeusl 2013). A lower work surface and a height-adjustable swivel chair were provided for tasks like chopping vegetables that could be done while seated. The kitchen made abundant use of aluminium, tiles, linoleum, and glossy enamel paint – materials that were easy to clean and gave the kitchen that all-important hygienic look. Finally, as architectural historian Susan Henderson astutely remarks, the kitchen's separation from the eating and living areas by a sliding door also ensured that smells, noise, and equipment did not intrude into the flat's spaces of (husbandly) leisure and relaxation (1996: 236).

This separation from the home's living spaces ultimately resulted in the most vociferous criticism of compact kitchens and of home economists' efficiency methods: that in order to enforce rational workplace conditions in kitchens, they banished most of the activities that actually took place in them, from laundering to childcare to family socializing. Critics complained that this resulted in alienated homemakers and historical studies support their objections, highlighting that rational kitchens were often intensely disliked as users resisted the types of technology, work, and sociality inscribed within them. Writing about the Frankfurt Kitchen's reception, for instance, historian Martina Heßler noted how the tenants attempted to circumvent its separation from the living areas (2009: 163–84).

By the time Sigfried Giedion wrote *Mechanization Takes Command* in 1948, the isolated kitchen was regarded as problematic even by many committed modernists: Giedion instead championed 'living-kitchens', which were more integrated into the home's living spaces, balancing efficiency with sociality (1948: 620–25). And in the post-war period, the living-kitchen model gained traction, as kitchens expanded, became more open-plan, and made room again for family gatherings. One design is worth mentioning in this context: the Cornell Kitchen, designed between 1950 and 1954. The product of a pioneering interdisciplinary university-based research project, the Cornell Kitchen set out to reconcile elements of the rational kitchen with the living-kitchen paradigm.

The Cornell Kitchen had many by-now expected rational features to optimize workflow. It had five prefabricated work centres – Oven-Refrigerator, Mix, Sink, Range, and Serve – each with necessary features built-in, including electrical appliances, ventilation, lighting, and wiring. The oven and fridge were installed at waist height to reduce bending; the range had four electric burners in a line to reduce reaching. The Cornell Kitchen provided a place for seated work and a task chair; and work surfaces at other centres could be raised by up to six inches to fit different user heights and tasks (the kitchen's most unique feature). The design was customizable in other ways, too: cupboards were a single size, 24 inches, so all parts were interchangeable and interiors could be reorganized as desired; and the modular work centres could be compactly arranged to fit existing spaces, such as farm kitchens, while leaving ample room for other activities.

In sum, the Cornell Kitchen shared the user-centred ethos of the Frankfurt Kitchen and, in its height-adjustability and flexibility, went well beyond the latter in accommodating user needs. Like the Frankfurt Kitchen, the Cornell Kitchen also made use of the latest technology and, as an industrial product, was itself a consumer item (although it never was commercially produced). Yet unlike the Frankfurt Kitchen, which Schütte-Lihotzky explicitly hoped would free women to take on paid work outside the home, the producers of the Cornell Kitchen claimed that their more integrated design would act as a buffer

FIGURE 6.5: 'New Kitchen Built to Fit Your Wife'. Article on the Cornell Kitchen in *Popular Science* (1953). Gardner Soule, 'New Kitchen Built to Fit Your Wife', *Popular Science* (September 1953): 172–73. © 1953 Bonnier Corporation. Used with permission via Copyright Clearance Center.

against 'outside agencies' that might otherwise 'destroy' traditional rural life (Kinchin 2011: 94–95; Beyer 1953: 10).

This social conservatism comes through in a *Popular Science* article, 'A New Kitchen to Suit Your Wife' (Soule 1953: 172). Explicitly addressing a male readership ('Your Wife'), the article clearly saw the Cornell's Kitchen purpose as being to ease the burden of tired wives *and* to keep them happily immersed in family life, not to emancipate them. (On the contrary, with its rather menacing graphic of an apron-clad woman held by callipers, the article seemed to promise that the kitchen would more precisely pin wives in place.) The comparison between the Frankfurt Kitchen and Cornell Kitchen is instructive because, for all their genetic resemblance, they were deployed to very different ideological ends, nullifying any straightforward association we might be tempted to make between advanced technology, scientific design, and social progress. And the rejection of the Frankfurt Kitchen by at least some of those it was intended to liberate reminds us that architectural innovations cannot alone revolutionize existing gendered relations unless supported by corresponding changes in the structures of everyday life.

A NEW FEMINIST WAVE

It is worth dwelling for a moment on the dark if vague invocation of 'outside agencies' that might 'destroy' traditional social patterns above, as it reveals something fundamental about the operations of patriarchy and capitalism and the organization of home. That is, for all of their resilience, authorities always presented patriarchy and capitalism as being under siege or assault. The autonomy of the patriarchal family in particular was supposedly weakened by almost every major social change – the increasing ease of divorce, free-lovers, lesbians, feminists, working women, socialists – and with some reason. As Hendrik Hartog notes, over time, 'A structure of understandings [about the husband's rights] that had once been hegemonic – tacit and presumptively true – was on its way to becoming ideological – contested, challenged, and recognizably partial' (2000: 211). These challenges to marriage were extremely threatening to the existing social order, given that the nuclear family and the home supposedly lay at its very foundation. This perpetual sense of threat also explains why the single-family home was so often described in protective or defensive terms: it was a fortress, a castle, a retreat.

In the specific case of the Cornell Kitchen, the phrase 'outside agencies' was likely meant to invoke the forces of modernization as embodied by suburban or urban lifestyles, which were seen to be less healthy, authentic, and moral than rural ones. Yet the Cornell Kitchen made itself attractive to rural families precisely by adopting elements of a commercial suburban kitchen – for instance, by incorporating electrical appliances and the more open plan. At one stroke, and in one prefabricated package, the kitchen thus attempted to remake thrifty rural families as post-war consumers.

Such a move was logical because, in the late 1940s, a consensus had emerged that corporate capitalism and mass consumption was the best means of ensuring American peace and prosperity (Cohen 2003: 112–65). Mass consumerism was fuelled by domestic consumption, which is why the largest corporations in the period, apart from automakers, were electrical appliance companies like General Electric. It is also why, in the brewing standoff with the Soviet Union and the ideological confrontation between capitalist and socialist ways of life, the American home – specifically its kitchen – became so symbolically central. As Greg Castillo, Ruth Oldenziel, and Susan E. Reid have demonstrated, the American 'technokitchen' was a major weapon in Cold War propaganda and hosted one of the most memorable encounters of that period: Richard Nixon and Nikita Khrushchev's Kitchen Debate in 1959 (Castillo 2010: 139–70; Oldenziel 2009: 325–29; Reid 2009: 83–112). Standing before a General Electric-supplied kitchen at the American National Exhibition in Moscow, Nixon asked Khrushchev, 'Would it not be better to compete in the relative merit of washing machines than in the strength of rockets?' (quoted in Henthorn 2006: 1).

Nixon was here suggesting that a privatized and, let us not forget, *feminized* form of consumption could underlie national strength and even a new world political order. He was certainly claiming that domestic consumer goods underpinned the superiority of the American way of life. Although Khrushchev did not deny the value of labor-saving devices, and the Soviet Union was then in the midst of a new housing programme that aimed to improve the efficiency of homes for Soviet women, he explicitly rejected the notion that consumption could bring them fulfilment. As Reid notes, for the Soviets, 'The freedom gained through "labor saving" in the home was not freedom to be a leisured ornament but to become a fully rounded person, and this entailed participation in social life and production outside the home' (2009: 90). Khrushchev's long-term goal was precisely to eliminate 'petit-bourgeois consciousness' defined by commodity fetishism, the nuclear family, and an attachment to the traditional domestic hearth (Buchli 1999: 137–47; for the contradictions of Khrushchev's stance in practice, see Reid 2005).

There is little doubt that, as the ambivalent Soviet response highlighted, the American post-war regime of mass consumption put women in an ambiguous position. Although sociologist Thorstein Veblen had long before highlighted the link between bourgeois women and 'conspicuous consumption', women's everyday role as tastemakers and as consumers was now increasingly celebrated and normalized across the social spectrum (Veblen [1899] 1970: 60–87). As design historian Penny Sparke notes, the post-war period saw the 're-energised domestification of women', as the age of marriage dropped and the birth rate boomed. Women were urged on all sides to be 'nurturants, beautifiers and consumers', and to interest themselves in home decoration (Sparke 1995: 166, 194); but as the operators of many of the domestic technologies driving mass consumption, they also had a growing say in the purchase of appliances (Lupton 1993). With the help of market researchers, manufacturers and industrial designers now designed products to appeal specifically to them, which in this period translated into streamlined contours, coordinated colours, and soft décor. We can see this softening, for instance, in the bathroom. Clinical white was banished by matching coloured fixtures, colours that were then carried through in 'ensembles' of towels, bath mats, and toilet seat covers. (To complete the look, coloured toilet paper was introduced in 1957 [Penner 2013: 173–78]).

But the increased prominence of women as the home's ceremonial consumers of goods still did not equate to equality in the home in terms of equal pay or equal rights, and many women found themselves both privileged and oppressed by the 1950s cult of domesticity. In the wake of Simone de Beauvoir's devastating account in *The Second Sex* (1949) of how female housework denied subjectivity to women, a new, polemical wave of feminists emerged, putting the home and its gendered social relations in the spotlight. In *The Feminine Mystique* (1963), Betty Friedan famously attempted to diagnose the growing sense of malaise or, as she called it, 'the problem that had no name': the feeling that women, as wives and mothers, were missing something fundamental, despite always being told they'd never had it so good. 'I do not accept . . .', declared Friedan, 'that there is no problem because American women have luxuries that women in other times and lands never dreamed of . . .' (Friedan 1963: 26)

The Feminine Mystique also puts *Mary Poppins* in a new light. Appearing in 1964, just a year after Friedan's book, it does not require a giant leap of the imagination to relate the Bankses' Edwardian villa to the contemporary American suburbs critiqued by Friedan. With its respectable façade shielding deep familial discontents, 17 Cherry Tree Lane reflects the turmoil then being revealed within the typical suburban home. The film even lampoons the suffrage movement, the mother to the American Women's Liberation Movement, a link made explicit when Winifred Banks invokes the legacy of 'the cause' ('our daughters' daughters will adore us . . .') (Mayhall 1999: 1–24). In the film's conclusion, of course, Mrs Banks gives up suffrage for the sake of her family – that act of voluntary submission so crucial to patriarchy – and Mary Poppins' departure re-establishes familial autonomy. As she exits, she reasserts traditional boundaries by shutting the front door behind her and noting, firmly, 'That's as it should be'.

While this new wave of feminists represented a wide range of positions, they would have been united in rejecting Mary Poppins' insistence on the autonomy of the home and 'as-it-should-be' relations, identifying the public/private binary as one of the most destructive weapons of patriarchy. They attacked this binary in different ways. Liberal feminists like Friedan refused to accept the gendered division of labor – which relegated women to the domestic realm and childcare – and began to agitate for women's right to participate on equal terms in paid work outside the home. Meanwhile, radical feminists such as Catherine MacKinnon and Andrea Dworkin attacked the sexual objectification of women and male control over the female body, one of the most extreme manifestations of which was domestic violence and marital rape. (In this period, let us not forget, the police and other social authorities remained reluctant to intervene in domestic abuse cases because of the 'privacy' of marital relations and the lingering notion that husbands legally 'owned' the bodies of their wives.)

Above all, the rejection of the separate spheres ideology led to the feminist rallying cry, 'the personal is political', meaning that what happened behind closed doors could no longer be regarded as being outside of politics; rather, the relations, work, routines, and values of the home were transformed into sites for political intervention and action. No longer could marital privilege, husbandly rights, or domestic privacy be used to justify unequal power relations or abuse. Even if the division of private and public spheres could not be completely dismantled, the fundamental interconnection of these spheres needed to be acknowledged and related associations systematically challenged – that is, the automatic association of women with reproduction, caregiving, and the home; and the association of men with production, breadwinning, and the public realm.

For a playful and still inspiring example of feminist strategies to overturn gender roles in this period, we turn to artist Martha Rosler's brilliant video, *Semiotics of the Kitchen* (1975). Sited in the kitchen, which, as we have seen, was at the frontline of efforts to improve and control women, Rosler performs a series of routine actions with a lexicon of kitchen implements running from A to Z. By the time she demonstrates 'Fork' and 'Ice pick', her actions have become irrational, exaggerated, and violent – as far from the efficient, seamless motions of the Taylorized housewife as one could imagine. But this is Rosler's point: the Taylorized housewife is herself a kind of fictional construction, a compliant patriarchal dream, whose highly programmed and controlled domestic actions needed to be made visible and strange in order to be re-choreographed (for another inspiring instance of labor-saving techniques being rebelliously performed, see Diller 1996: 74–94). Housework needs a new language; domestic roles, a new script.

HOME AS SITE OF RESISTANCE

Women's Liberation, alongside the other civil rights movements, made important strides in the 1970s and 1980s. Nonetheless, we cannot claim that these immediately changed the dominant patterns of domestic life or housing preferences; domestic roles were not rewritten straight away. Single-family homeownership remained, for many, an aspiration. Moreover, women who did take on waged labor outside the home quickly discovered the sting in its tail: as men continued to do – and mostly continue to do – proportionately less in terms of housework and childcare, many wives found themselves carrying 'the double burden' of paid work *and* unpaid domestic work. As one bitterly noted, 'They have told us, "Liberate yourselves through work outside the home" and we have found ourselves working 16–18 hours a day' (Fortunati 1975: 14). In response, an international coalition of Marxist feminists revived the Wages for Housework campaign, which, despite clear-sightedly linking the increased pressure on women to the growing precariousness of wage labor in a post-industrial world, failed to generate widespread support from male comrades (Cox and Federici 1975: 1–16: Edmond and Fleming 1975: 9–12).

Yet, even if changes in housing and living patterns did not happen overnight, as more women entered the professions, including architecture, planning, and engineering, they sought to exert greater control over the 'man-made' built environment. A new generation of feminist architects and designers explored types of non-sexist dwelling, community planning, and city design (including, notably, Dolores Hayden in the United States and Matrix in the UK), and revived a commitment to communal amenities and inclusive spaces. And although they were not necessarily undertaken with feminist aims in mind, many countercultural experiments in collective living or informal practices such as squatting also took place across Anglo-America and Western Europe at this time, which directly opposed mass consumerism, planned obsolescence, and their environmental consequences. Other developments in this period, from the popularity of mobile homes to the interest in self-build and traditional vernacular dwellings, equally questioned the permanent, fixed, and speculative model of private housing and searched for other means of accommodating and empowering users.

The point of the brief summary above is that the construction, organization, and materiality of the home became a key space for intervention and protest in a wide but interlinked series of political movements. Most worked from the premise that the dominant model of home was a major source of oppression, waste, and false consciousness. Yet, as these debates entered the 1980s and 1990s, and these various movements themselves evolved, an important counter-position also emerged, which was more open to the pleasures or possibilities of home and its importance historically as a space of political resistance or of everyday creative expression for women. Feminists such as American author Alice Walker began to celebrate the artistry of earlier generations of homemakers, finding value in 'domestic arts' such as gardening, sewing, and quilting (Walker 1983). Scholars associated with this counter-position tended to occupy a broader range of subject positions than second-wave feminists; often informed

FIGURE 6.6: Cover of Matrix, *Making Space: Women and the Man-Made Environment* (London: Pluto Press, 1984). Used with permission of Matrix and Pluto Press.

by post-colonial critiques, they were far more sensitive to difference in shaping identity – factors such as sexuality, age, religion, ethnicity, race, and class.

The counter-position was most forcefully and eloquently set out by feminist philosopher bell hooks in the 1990s. As hooks argued, there are cases where other allegiances and circumstances – race or class, for instance – become just as, if not more, important than gender, a claim that is vital to opening up discussions around difference and to producing more nuanced and relational accounts of space and power relations generally. Drawing on her memories and experiences of her grandmother's homeplace, hooks demonstrated how race intersects with gender to change the meaning of home for Black American communities. As opposed to the straightforward site of subjugation that white, mostly middle-class feminists described, hooks described home in almost primordial terms – as a shelter from threat and a place of maternal nurturing, care, and warmth. But this sheltering quality was not an innate, stable property of home as classic phenomenological accounts like those of Gaston Bachelard or Martin Heidegger would hold (Bachelard 1958; Heidegger [1954] 1971). Rather, Black women had to dig deep within themselves every day to carve out a sustaining home in an innately hostile environment. As hooks wrote:

> Black women resisted [patriarchal white supremacist society] by making homes where all black people could strive to be subjects, not objects, where we could be affirmed in our minds and hearts despite poverty, hardship and deprivation, where we could restore to ourselves the dignity denied us on the outside in the public world.
>
> —[1990] 2015: 42

hooks reversed normal feminist formulations in that she valued the private realm and praised the nurturing role of women. Even if caretaking was not necessarily the choice of Black women, she stated, it remained central to liberation struggles because, in the maternal home, a strong and *resistant* subjectivity was cultivated and renewed.

Like hooks, political philosopher Iris Marion Young has more recently attempted to argue for the way in which 'homemaking' generally gives meaning to individual lives through the 'materialization of identity', that is, through the arrangement of objects which hold personal narratives mostly told by women (2005: 139–40). Young revisits philosopher Martin Heidegger via Luce Irigaray, to argue that homemaking should be understood as 'preservation', an act of constant (female) making and remaking, and a necessary counterpart to (male) dwelling. While Young agrees with many feminist critiques of home, she wants to hold on to what she sees as the critical potential of preservationist homemaking. She asks, 'Is it possible to retain an idea of home as supporting the individual subjectivity of the person, where the subject is understood as fluid, partial, shifting, and in relations of reciprocal support with others?' (2005: 124–25, 130). She believes that it *is* possible – in fact, it is necessary (without home, she says, 'we are, literally, lost'); however, in her account, home should be understood to anchor, rather than fix, identity through female acts of remembrance (2005: 140).

Young tries to negotiate a fine line. She wishes to hang on to certain elements of phenomenological readings of home and to acknowledge the importance of embodiment, time, and memory to identity formation. As homemakers, traditionally and today, women, she believes, stand to lose the most from an impoverished understanding of home. But Young's reading of homemaking requires a bracketing-off of certain kinds of activity that she does not acknowledge to be authentic or valuable – for instance, any act of furnishing or decoration that stems from a desire to accumulate goods, exhibit status, or increase property prices. She notes that it is possible to live in other ways – that our mode of 'civic privatism' is the result of capitalism – and cites other cultures and traditions where alternative paradigms of dwelling and communal living exist (2005: 131–32).

Without denying the allure of the vision of homemaking Young conjures, it seems hard to believe that our varied motives for cleaning, decorating, and furnishing homes can ever be separated out so neatly in our daily lives, not least because, as Young herself notes, many objects exist at multiple registers: many are at once items of display *and* bearers of memory (think of weddings gifts). Material culture scholars, who have produced some of the most nuanced ethnographic studies of homemaking practices to date, would likely be wary of attempting to bracket off meaning in this way. In a well-known study of working-class English female homemakers, for instance, Alison J. Clarke describes their acts of home decoration as a process of constant negotiation between personal narratives and communally held ideals. As Clarke concludes, her female subjects' relationships to their home environments cannot be characterized simply as normative or coercive, emulative or expressive, but rather involve 'a more complex process of projection and interiorization that continues to evolve' (2001: 43; see also Pink 2004).

We might equally say that the way in which the relationship between gender and home is understood has also evolved considerably over the period covered in this essay – and no doubt, will continue to do so. To sum up crudely, the more uncompromising critiques of early material feminists and second-wave feminists of the patriarchal-capitalist home have not been forgotten, but have now been supplemented by scholarship that also acknowledges the meaningfulness, rewards, and gains of home for women and others. This may be, quite simply, a response to the fact that, for all the criticisms, the idea of home so obviously remains as desirable as ever for many social groups, but especially for disenfranchised ones. In a globalized age of migration and vast inequalities of wealth, the very act of critiquing the idea of home – when so many are going to great risks to secure one – feels like an uncomfortable privilege. The same can be said of the determined campaigns for same-sex marriage in many Western European countries: despite the critique that marriage (and by extension, its locus, the home) perpetuates heteronormativity, it remains a desired goal of many LGBTQ people (Pilkey et al. 2017).

In short, it is evident that home remains operative culturally, as a symbol, a space, and a set of values and practices. The explanations for why it endures, however, are as varied as the accounts of its nature: if we see it as an essential part of spatial and cultural patterning under capitalism, imperialism, patriarchy, or heteronormativity (or all of these), then home will dominate so long as our current social order remains; or if we see it as a central structure in our psyches, as phenomenologists would hold, then it will remain so long as we are human. However, some common ground emerges between these more recent accounts of home and its gendered relations. Specifically, regardless of their theoretical perspectives, scholars all tend now to insist upon a relationship to home that is defined by movement and open-endedness: most now reject the idea that identity formation and gender relations are determined and essential and instead allow for a kind of negotiation or play between idea and reality.

One of the most powerful theoretical supports that underpin this fluidity relates to the idea of performance, as articulated by philosopher Judith Butler. In the repetition and accumulative performance of daily life, Butler at once affirms the embodied and sedimented nature of identity formation (that, say, Young insists upon) *and* locates possibilities for subversion, no doubt why it has been so rich a concept for feminists and many other scholars as well (Butler 1990, 1997). The idea of performance acknowledges the significance of gestures and routines and finds in homemaking the potential for reorienting ourselves towards new objects, spaces, feelings, relations, and identities (Ahmed 2006). Home and its gendered relations may still have a commonly understood 'as-it-should-be' script, but it is now one that homemakers of all kinds have some say in performing.

CHAPTER SEVEN

Hospitality and Home: British and American Cultures of Entertaining

GRACE LEES-MAFFEI

INTRODUCTION

Domestic privacy and the history of the home

The eighty years from 1920 to 2000 saw tremendous changes in the ways that hospitality was practised in people's homes, informed by simultaneous shifts in class, increased homeownership, informalization, the development of the hospitality industry, greater media attention paid to the home, and changing perceptions of domestic privacy. Today, we think of the home as private, a place in which to retreat from the public sphere, at least in the West. Sure, we invite friends and extended family into our homes. We practise our hobbies at home, with or without others, and work at home too, domestically and more formally. But these diverse uses of the home do not obscure the fact that the contemporary home is ostensibly our space to control. This was not always the case: the perceived, and actual, privacy of the home has waxed and waned over time.

Medieval and early modern households were small communities working together and living together. They accommodated immediate and extended family, staff and retainers of various kinds such as apprentices. Rather than the entire home being perceived as a private space, therefore, medieval householders attributed varying levels of privacy to particular rooms or spaces. The view of the home as a private place more generally intensified in the West in the nineteenth and twentieth centuries as the notion of a household became more firmly associated with the immediate family only. In the Victorian period, room usage became more specialized so that separate morning rooms, dining rooms, parlours, sitting rooms, billiard rooms, and smoking rooms were variously found in homes of different scales. These differentiated rooms managed sociability in the home so that the remaining rooms – and the home overall – were increasingly perceived as a private realm. This model of domesticity continued throughout the twentieth century. In the current century, however, the physical privacy of the home is compromised by online social interactions. It is no longer accurate to consider the home a private place; Western children, for example, are as vulnerable to bullying and abuse from school peers within their homes via social media as they are in the school playground. Even though such online interactions increasingly challenge domestic privacy today, the home is still represented as a private place and a refuge.

In fact, the very privacy of the late modern home has made it hard for historians to access. What we know about homes of the past is limited by the lack of historical sources, which in turn results from varying ideas about what is, and has been, important. For these reasons, the home has long been ignored by historians. However, that situation has now altered and the economic, political, social, and cultural significance of the homes of the past is increasingly recognized. If information about past homes is hard to find, there is a wealth of information available in books of domestic advice. These books offer us insights into the 'real ideals' (Lees-Maffei 2014a: 51) that readers bought in to when they purchased, and read, them. And they tell us, if not what actually went on in people's homes, then what notions of acceptable and aspirational hospitality at home were shared by advisors with their readers. When we read domestic advice books accordingly, as fictions to which home dwellers have aspired – or not – we can understand what was possible and desirable in domestic hospitality, and what was not.

The literature of hospitality: Domestic advice books

Domestic advice literature has a long history. Historical sociologist Norbert Elias ([1939] 1994) traces the roots of twentieth-century advice books back to Greco-Roman antiquity, and even earlier. Some of the earliest advice books addressed children and behaviour at royal courts, with a notable example being Erasmus of Rotterdam's *De civilitate morum puerilium* (on civility in children), of 1530 (Elias [1939] 1994: 42–43). The form and content of advice literature, as a discourse that mediates between society and the individual, have been shaped in response to social and cultural changes throughout the modern period (Lees-Maffei 2014a: 31). Elias's focus is on guides to manners, specifically, and these have much to tell us about how people behaved in their homes, as well as outside the home. But we can add to that corpus of writing the other literatures of domesticity. Early cook books, for example, are important forerunners to the domestic manuals of the twentieth century. Domestic advice literature first developed from its roots in guides to courtly life, books on husbandry and housewifery, and recipe books, to holistic texts on domestic economy, akin to the catch-all nature of the almanac. The genre of domestic advice literature has undergone increasing specialization as those general household guides divided into guides for ladies and for gentlemen, manuals on housewifery and husbandry, books on home decoration, which guide readers in constructing their domestic spaces, and books about home entertaining, which cover cookery, and the creation of a hospitable environment. To understand hospitality in the past, it is useful to read three specialized and differentiated sub-genres: etiquette books aimed at harmonizing social interaction, homemaking books concerning the establishment and maintenance of homes, and home decorating books which have guided readers in the design of their homes.

As well as becoming more specialized so that its constituent categories multiplied, in the twentieth century domestic advice literature was published in greater numbers of titles and in an increasingly wide range of formats. During the post-war period, domestic advice literature expanded across the cultural and literary landscape, aided by increased literacy and affluence, cheaper formats such as paperbacks, increased choice in consumer goods as a result of developments in manufacture, distribution, marketing, advertising, and retailing, social developments that created an extended market for advice, and cultural developments including lifestyles and the aestheticization of everyday life. Perceptions of increased social transition, and increasingly rapid shifts in behaviour, produced a significant market for domestic advice.

Gender roles in the home

The market for domestic advice has been largely female, because the association of woman and home is fundamental in Western patriarchal society. In the post-Second World War period, girls were given conduct manuals and brides received household manuals and etiquette books. Although men are stereotypically associated with homebuilding, DIY, and home maintenance, home decorating guides have also been aimed at women. The stereotypical roles for men and women in our society have been reflected in the advice books written for them, with very few changes over the period from 1920 to 2000. Sexism pervades the literature of hospitality and the roles assigned to women and men in the practice of home entertaining (Lees-Maffei 2007). Women and men performed distinct roles on a day-to-day basis in the home, and when guests came to visit. In families with domestic staff, the lady of the house would oversee the food and accommodation; every aspect of the experience would be her responsibility even if she did not actually do the physical domestic labor. In families without staff, typically a woman undertook the cooking, cleaning, and presentation of the home for hospitality.

Children are not mentioned as playing a role in domestic hospitality unless it is their friends, rather than their parents' friends, who are visiting. In that case, children and teenagers are encouraged to assist with the preparations for home entertaining, or even to take full responsibility for it, in consultation with their parents. Many post-Second World War domestic advice guides, which address issues arising from the demographic increase in teenagers and their increased prosperity, relative to their parents, complain about the lack of assistance offered by children around the home, especially when friends visit (Lees-Maffei 2014a: 151–60).

Men's role in home entertaining has traditionally been to provide drinks and carve the meat. However, the host remains a key figure particularly if we understand him, as sociologist Thorstein Veblen suggested, as the provider (Veblen [1899] 1970). Veblen observed the status accruing to the male head of the household as he, and the people around him, engaged in conspicuous consumption of his wealth. So a wife providing a luxurious meal is making use of his resources. A guest enjoying an aperitif given to her or him by the host is also conspicuously consuming the host's wealth. Home entertaining, in these terms, becomes an expression of the host's wealth and status.

DEMOCRATIZING HOSPITALITY: INTER-WAR HOSPITALITY AT HOME, 1920–39

In post-industrial Western society, aristocratic authority has diminished, and so has the role of aristocrats as tastemakers. In the United States, models of hospitality ceased to follow French and British courtly models from the 1820s onwards (Schlesinger [1946] 1968; Lynes [1949] 1980: 5). In Britain, a feudal hierarchy in which power resided with a landowning aristocracy persisted until the 1870s. Between the 1880s and the 1930s, however, the dispersal of the great estates, comprising a great house, gardens, parks, and extensive land, unlocked a triangle of power, prestige, and property (Cannadine 1990: 18, 343), while the sale of titles and honours allowed new money into high society. Plutocrats, such as the press barons Lord Beaverbrook and Lord Rothermere, 'lived far more loudly, lavishly, and luxuriously than the patricians, and ... increasingly set the social tone' (1990: 345). At the same time, an influx into British high society of foreign-born brides – especially the tenfold rise in American peeresses between 1880 and 1914 (1990: 347) – further functioned to relax conventions.

In the United States and the UK alike, the twentieth-century middle class was swelled by a newly affluent portion of the working class.[1] Describing this expansion, British sociologist Anthony Giddens (1981: 111–97) popularized the term 'new middle class'. For Giddens, lifestyle choices have become increasingly central to the construction of social identities (1991: 50). This newly expanded middle class presented new problems of hospitality at home on both sides of the Atlantic based on the relative unavailability of resources including time, staff, and finance, when compared with their upper-middle and upper-class models of hospitality. Domestic advisors recommended scaled-down, cheaper, modes of home entertaining suited to middle-class, rather than upper-class, elite, or aristocratic lifestyles. Indeed, domestic advice itself can be seen as a middle-class cultural form: 'the very profusion of etiquette books, their large sales, and the insistent flow of collateral advice in periodicals suggests a demand for and preoccupation with gentility among middle class people' (Ohmann 1996: 152–53), while new broadcast media such as television disseminated education and entertainment across the population, whatever the social class.

In the UK and the United States, during the period between the two world wars, Victorian domestic hospitality practices persisted. The domestic hostess was still presented as a conspicuous consumer of her husband's wealth and status, and of the great number of goods and services that formed her home, including the labor of her staff (Veblen [1899] 1970: 68). Before the Second World War, the ideal hostess depicted in domestic advice was seemingly disengaged in her demeanour (Lees-Maffei 2007) as shown in *The A.B.C. of Etiquette by a Society Lady* of 1923, published a year before economist Thorstein Veblen's *Theory of the Leisure Class* first appeared in Britain:

> When receiving callers, it is necessary that the lady should rise or lay aside the employment in which she may be engaged ... The duties of hostess at dinner are not onerous; but they demand tact and self-possession in no small degree. She does not often carve. She has few active duties to perform; but she must neglect nothing, put all her guests at their ease, and pay every possible attention to the requirements of each and all around her. No accident should ruffle her temper. No disappointment ought embarrass her. She ought to see her old china broken without a sigh, and her best glass shattered with a smile.
>
> —A Society Lady 1923: 38

Here the hostess's success in hospitality is dependent upon her skill in 'emotional labor' (Hochschild 1983; James 1989), meaning her attentiveness to others and suppression of her own reactions. Her only apparently active role is symbolic, as exemplified by the practice of the formal procession to the dining room, which was as much about status hierarchies as it was about moving guests from one room to another. Dinner parties would have begun with drinks in the drawing room, followed by a formal procession to the dining room for a meal

FIGURE 7.1: 'The perfect example of a formal dinner table in a great house'. From Emily Post's *Etiquette in Society, in Business, in Politics and at Home* (New York: Funk & Wagnalls, [1922] 1940), plate between 236 and 237.

of five or more courses, after which the ladies withdrew (to the withdrawing, or drawing, room) leaving the men to their own amusements for a while. The men's activities might involve cigar smoking, games such as billiards, and conversations not thought suitable for the ladies. The ladies would subsequently re-join the gentleman. Doyenne of American manners, Emily Post, illustrates 'The perfect example of a formal dinner table of wealth, luxury and taste' in her 'Blue Book' of Etiquette, first published in 1922, noting that it 'involves no effort on the part of the hostess of a great house beyond deciding upon the date and the principal guests who are to form the nucleus of the party' (Post 1922: caption to plate between pages 236 and 237). Post here overstates the hostess's lack of involvement, perhaps to underline the staffed grandeur with which some members of society entertained. Although the hostess was relatively uninvolved in the overt labor of hospitality, her guests would have held her responsible for every aspect of their experience.

The A.B.C. of Etiquette offers remarkably similar advice to guests as it does to hostesses and hosts: 'Should you break or upset anything, do not apologise for it. Show your regret by your facial expression. It is not considered well-bred to put it into words' (A Society Lady 1923: 36). Veblen observed that the guest 'consumes vicariously for his host at the same time that he is a witness to the consumption of that excess of good things which his host is unable to dispose of singlehanded' ([1899] 1970: 65). Guests and hostess each consumed the host's wealth. At the highest levels of what Veblen termed the 'leisure class', the host, as the male head of the household, also engaged in conspicuous consumption of his staff's labor and he, like his female counterpart, had very little to do, except perhaps carve meat. In this situation, the lack of active labor on the host's part, and his leisure, communicates status.

If the hospitality shown in inter-war advice literature emphasized disinterested leisure for the host, hostess, and guests, it was extremely labor-intensive for staff. From 1920 to 1939, domestic advice writers continued to assume that their readers would have domestic staff, whether permanent or employed for specific occasions. During wartime, and in the post-war period, such an assumption became untenable, and domestic writers addressed both staffed and unstaffed households or, increasingly, solely the latter. However, a pre-Second World War ideal of leisurely hospitality based on social ease persisted. Even as late as 1959, sociologist Erving Goffman emphasized the social importance of the hostess's 'secret consumption' and hidden, 'backstage' labor (Goffman [1959] 1990: 39). Labor is secret and hidden in order to maintain the illusion of ease associated with an aristocratic model of status.

Early efforts at rationalizing the burden of the homemaker without staff began with increasing specialization of kitchen design. Historian Ian Bullock has noted that the development of gas-powered lighting and cooking allowed the separation of food preparation from living quarters, and the subsequent replacement of the 'living kitchen', celebrated by architect and author Hermann Muthesius among others, with the 'cooking kitchen' (Bullock 1988). The cooking kitchen bore the influence of 'New Housekeeping' advocate Christine Frederick, whose *Household Engineering* (1919) appeared in Britain in 1923. Influenced by Frederick, Grete Schütte-Lihotzky designed what has commonly been regarded as the first fitted kitchen for the Frankfurt am Main housing settlements created by city architect Ernst May in 1926, in which cooking equipment and supplies were readily at hand and no extraneous activities were accommodated (Henderson 1996). In the rationalized domestic spaces designed by Frederick and Schütte-Lihotzky, the wife – and despite the fact that women were increasingly working outside the home, gender roles within the home remained traditional – acted both as hostess in the 'front-region', or public space, of the home, and as domestic worker in the 'back', or off-stage region, where the unseen labor of cooking took place. Thus, while Frederick, Schütte-Lihotzky, and their followers attempted to rationalize and make easier household work, they failed to address the fact that in performing the conflicting roles of both entertaining guests and cooking, the unassisted hostess was simultaneously expected to perform in the front and backstage regions of the home (Goffman [1959] 1990: 110, 114). Distinct from the solutions produced by followers of Frederick's New Housekeeping, were a range of solutions dependent not upon rationalization, but rather upon the informalization of domestic practices. What has been accepted today as common sense may for hostesses of the inter-war and post-war periods have seemed to fall short of proper hospitality.

SECOND WORLD WAR HOSPITALITY, 1939–45

In the UK, aristocratic influences on the ways in which hospitality was practised and expressed waned between the wars and during the Second World War. Grand houses were requisitioned for use as hospitals and other institutions. Food and cooking ingredients were severely rationed, as were fabrics, clothes, and furniture. What was available often differed considerably from inter-war market offerings, so that shop-bought eggs were replaced with powdered eggs, and fashionable clothing was replaced with 'Utility' scheme options that echoed the simple geometric aesthetic of military uniforms. The British government's Utility scheme aimed to provide economical clothing and furniture which used the minimum of materials while also being well made and hardwearing. Utility furniture introduced a reluctant British buying public to the clean lines of continental modernist design. Wartime rationing did more than reduce the options available to those wishing to entertain others at home: it also had a

FIGURE 7.2: Two women sitting down for a meal in a display room of the Utility Furniture Exhibition, held at the Building Centre in London in 1942. Ministry of Information, Imperial War Museums, D11053.

levelling effect. Ministry of Information propaganda campaigns in the UK warned against waste of food and other resources through the figure of the Squander Bug, while the notion that 'careless talk costs lives' was promoted in order to regulate sociability and keep gossip in check. The Ministry of Food, under Lord Woolton, worked to improve health during the Second World War through the provision of canteens, civic 'British restaurants', and meals in schools as well as through rationing and price controls to guide eating and nutrition education. In fact, eating out, rather than at home, increased from 79 million meals per week in 1941 to 170 million by the end of 1944, and the transformation 'shifted a quarter of the average individual's leisure time away from the home' (Hardyment 1995: 10).

The question of how to express hospitality at home when faced with the challenges of war and associated rationing taxed domestic advice writers and householders alike. However, more positively, rationing, patriotism, and a desire to succeed during wartime deprivations produced a strong commitment to thrift, ingenuity, and keeping up appearances. Truly skilled hosts and hostesses could make their guests feel indulged notwithstanding wartime deprivations, advisors reassured their readers. 'Victory pudding' made a virtue of necessity, comprising 'eggless sponge plumped out with grated carrot, potato and breadcrumbs' (Hardyment 1995: 11). Constance Spry's 1942 book *Come into the Garden, Cook* was part of a trend for kitchen gardening in order to supplement rationed food, while Marguerite Patten guided 18 million radio listeners to 'The Kitchen Front', a daily dose of food and cooking advice. In addition, the war brought people together in ways that would not have occurred during peacetime. From the crowded bomb shelters and London Underground stations of the air raids, to communities pulling together to host social events in spite of wartime conditions, camaraderie was given a boost by the very unusual circumstances.

Margaret Merivale's inter-war home decorating book, *Furnishing the Small Home* of 1938, begins with a letter to the reader, addressed 'Dear Virginia . . .'. Virginia is shown to have expressed an interest in homemaking advice for people on reduced incomes (Merivale [1938] 1944: 5). Merivale's solution is fashionable, modernist design. 'In just the same way that you would not think for one moment of wearing a hat bought fifty years ago, you must not collect Victorian atrocities if you are furnishing a modern home'. She goes on: 'I want you to see what is of our own times in furniture and accessories, and to consider their merits in the light of to-day's requirements' ([1938] 1944: 5). However, the 1944 edition has the following postscript:

> My letter to you was written in the spacious days of peace, and now we are at war your choice is temporarily much more limited . . . and if you cannot furnish as you wish immediately, I hope my book will help you to weave the

picture of the ideal home which you are going to have when the war is won. You will not only be very patriotic but very wise if you confine your purchases to absolute essentials. In war-time, the choice is restricted, labor is scarce, and prices are bound to be high. Many of the items shown here will not be obtainable to-day, but they will help you formulate your own ideas.

—Merivale [1938] 1944: 15

Merivale presents the war as beneficial for introducing new design 'developments in plastics, glass and metals' and concludes, 'Weave your dreams with the aid of this book: work out your plans; then when the time comes, you will be ready to complete your scheme . . .' ([1938] 1944: 15). Dining room solutions include a dining cabinet, from which a table pulls out and, using an idea from Sweden, 'a dining alcove, enclosed by draperies of striking design' ([1938] 1944: 50).

The setting for domestic hospitality during the Second World War was complicated by the fact that for many people in Western Europe at that time, their furniture was destroyed as homes were routinely bombed. The need for furniture was increased by relocation as well as bombing. In Britain, the government's Utility furniture scheme (explained above) catered for the wartime mass market as far as possible within the constraints of manufacturing and materials shortages. Utility furniture, like Utility garments and rationed food, was purchased with rationing coupons. The furniture was economical with materials and labor. Utility design was informed both by the design reformers of the nineteenth century and by continental modernism, and it was offered to consumers who had little alternative. While Norman Hartnell's Utility clothing enabled the whole country to be dressed in patriotic quasi-militaristic styles by the Queen's dressmaker, Utility furniture has been seen as a route through which a British public notoriously resistant to continental modernism was persuaded to accept a pared-down practical aesthetic (Lees-Maffei 2010: 131). In Britain, rationing continued until 1954, so that the privations of war continued well into the post-war period, notwithstanding its much-vaunted optimism, Americanization, and consumerism.

POST-WAR HOSPITALITY, 1945–59

The impact of conflict continued to be felt in the home following the Second World War as the Cold War replaced the frontline carnage of trench warfare and the air raids of the First and Second World Wars with newly developed nuclear weapons. These were largely kept on standby rather than being detonated, their symbolic threat fuelling a war of competing ideologies in which socialism and capitalism, as represented by their respective leaders, the Soviet Union and the United States, sought to gain global dominance. The quality of life experienced by ordinary people became highly politicized, with each superpower seeking to show that it offered superior living standards. Cultural historian Susan Reid has shown that the Cold War was fought through public debate about the domestic interior as well as through the space race. Scientific communism was embedded in household advice, domestic science education, rational planning of the kitchen or 'scientific management', and the domestication of the scientific-technological revolution through the mechanization of housework (Reid 2005). The home was a crucial tool in the armoury of ideology and iconography, whether directly – for example, in the flexible and space-saving furnishings developed to meet the needs of citizens of the new apartment blocks showcased by Soviet city planners – or indirectly, from the space-inspired fashion of Frenchman Pierre Cardin to the application of new materials in furniture and interior design. The latter is exemplified by the fiberglass chairs of leading American designers Charles and Ray Eames, and the anonymous pattern designers at Formica (Lees-Maffei 2010: 132).

Key determinants of hospitality at home during the period following the Second World War included economic changes that allowed greater employment opportunities to women. While working-class women had always worked, a new job market offered them alternatives to domestic service, thereby transforming both their lives and the lives of those they had served. In post-war Britain, even women in a position to afford full-time live-in domestic assistance sometimes experienced difficulty finding staff (Lees-Maffei 2007). Writing of the United States, Susan Strasser notes that domestic service was never as prevalent as 'the literary evidence' suggested and that 'people of limited means – that is, most people – employed household help [only] in emergencies' (1982: 164). A shift 'from service to self-service' impacted upon both those members of the middle classes who needed to revise their domestic practices as a result of losing their staff *and* a new group of socially mobile readers keen to entertain in a manner different to the one they had known at home (Lees-Maffei 2001). The latter group might be, for example, those brought up within working-class cultures who sought to participate in the newly enlarged middle class.

So in this period, when women managed work inside and outside the home in ever-greater numbers, advisors suggested that the work of hospitality should be distributed among the guests. A clear example from the period is American industrial designers Russel and Mary Wright's *Guide to Easier Living* (1950, revised 1954). The Wrights' book shows that far from dispensing with a need for published advice, informalization necessitated what they termed the 'New Hospitality'. They recognized that 'we live in a transition period in which there are few established rules' (Wright and Wright 1954: 187). Their introduction rails against the 'Old Dream' of gracious living inherited from 'the stilted ritual of the English manor house': 'Subtly preached by that able evangelist Emily Post, the Dear Old Dream dominates writing and merchandising concerned with the home, haunts domestic architecture across the country, and tyrannically rules American family life' (1954: 2). The *Guide to Easier Living* was as important as Russel Wright's tableware designs in prompting curators Donald Albrecht, Robert Schonfeld, and Lindsay Stamm Shapiro to assert in 2001 that 'more than their fellow modernists Charles and Ray Eames or George Nelson, the Wrights influenced the post-war home in an all-encompassing way' (2001: 19). Russel Wright began his career designing for the theatre, like Norman Bel Geddes, for whom he worked as an apprentice, and this training may have influenced the way he sought to design domestic behaviour as well as household goods. A retrospective at the Cooper-Hewitt National Design Museum in New York in 2001 sought to communicate 'both the formal and social dimensions of Russel and Mary's work, from individual objects to scripts for entertaining', and presented their interior design, landscaping, and architectural output as 'Stage Sets for American Living' (Albrecht et al. 2001: 21). But while they were explicitly engaged in scripting 'the new hospitality', Mary and Russel Wright tried to sidestep the paradox of replacing one set of rules with another: 'Once you've shaken free of traditionalism, don't, for heaven's sake, go looking for a new type of Dream House, or for a new Emily Post to put yourself in bondage to. Don't swallow anyone's ideas whole, not even the ones in this volume' (Wright and Wright 1954: 9).

Aspirations to informality are particularly highlighted in the act of home entertaining, which not only requires a considerable effort on the part of the hostess and/or host, but also demands that such effort be concealed or denied, for the avoidance of embarrassment (guests feeling discomfited by their friends serving them). Thus, informal patterns of home entertaining have not diminished the work of the hostess and/or host, but rather forced it into hiding, under the pretence of nonchalant ease. As Mary and Russel Wright state, apparently without intended irony: 'We can plan for that informal, relaxed kind of entertaining' (Wright and Wright 1954: 166). Although the authors would probably deny it, their book shows that, because it is undertaken without hired help, entertaining informally is no less demanding of the hostess and/or host than earlier formal models. Their emphasis is on planning and simplification ('perhaps the most important consideration of all in the new etiquette') of both menu and service: 'We believe that your degree of nonconformance to useless convention determines the extent of your meal's smooth service, plus meaning less work for you. Any of these simplifications, if executed thoughtfully, can be in good taste, can even have "style"' (1954: 167, 169).

The Wrights' recommendations for informal hospitality included 'the Kitchen Buffet' ('quite the most unconventional and informal variation, if your kitchen is large enough to permit it') and a T-shaped setting termed 'the Cafeteria Table'. The latter is described as 'a worksaver for family meals; it is easily adapted to company meals', in which guests move along the short side of a table collecting flatware, plates, bread, butter, and a drink and then sit down

FIGURE 7.3: An illustration by James Kingsland of guests helping themselves at a kitchen buffet, published in Mary and Russel Wright's *Guide to Easier Living* (New York: Simon & Schuster, [1950] 1954).

at the long sides of the table to help themselves to food set in the middle (Wright and Wright 1954: 173, 174). This recommendation is followed by a chart in which the eighty-two items carried to and from the table for a conventional setting are compared with the thirty-six pieces needed for the 'Cafeteria' setting. So the designers of 'by far the best known [tableware] in the country' (as claimed on the flyleaf for *Guide to Easier Living*) were influential in the art of doing without unnecessary table items.

By the 1950s, service hatches were a feature of new homes and a commonplace improvement in old ones. Like the 'dumb waiter' lift between floors of a home, the hatch physically connected the backstage kitchen and the social parts of the home. It saved steps, obscured labor or its material evidence in the kitchen from guests, and 'catered to the growing feeling that it was somehow not quite right for mum to be shut away in the kitchen' (Hardyment 1995: 57). In subsequent decades, hatches did not disappear through disuse; rather, they were incorporated into more ambitious architectural solutions such as the kitchen-diner and open-plan living solutions. Howard Robertson's *Reconstruction and the Home* of 1947 shows an inter-war example of a hatch built in to a storage unit dividing kitchen and dining room, called a 'buffet-dresser fitting' (Robertson 1947: 31–32). Mary and Russel Wright's *Guide to Easier Living* presented similar open-hatch solutions, allowing greater interplay between food preparation and dining areas. One image from the Walker Art Center's *Idea House II* – built in Minneapolis, Minnesota in 1947 – shows a peninsular breakfast bar, which

FIGURE 7.4: A contemporary kitchen design with hatch by the German firm MTB Schreinerei. MTB Schreinerei GmbH, Edingen.

allows serving directly from the kitchen and easy return of crockery, although it was probably not intended for anything other than family dining, as the seating is in a linear rather than conversational arrangement.

On a larger scale, the fashion for open-plan interiors and zoned living preoccupied post-war architects, interior designers, and domestic advice writers. There is little scope for the cover and refuge provided by a backstage environment in a kitchen-diner, a bedsitter, or a home with few internal walls. For the Wrights, these open environments necessitated new forms of entertaining: 'Who would think about wearing an evening gown on the golf course? Isn't it just about as ridiculous to set a traditional table, complete with starched white damask and all the trimmings in the dinette, or in a combination living-dining room?' (Wright and Wright 1954: 189). They recommend enlisting help from guests, so that whether in conventional homes with clearly demarcated front and backstage spaces, or in homes where front and backstage are collapsed, guests will find their way into the kitchen, thereby necessitating new etiquette. As an example of 'present-day good manners', the Wrights cite the importance of hostesses/hosts cleaning up after meal preparation and before guests arrive, so if a guest offers to help with the post-meal cleaning, you 'don't inflict your unwashed before dinner pots and pans on them' (Wright and Wright 1954: 171). Whatever the material makeup of the home in which hospitality was to take place, hostesses or hosts were encouraged to set the scene with care, considering everything in the home as evidence of their personalities, and therefore as being of potential value in supporting their hospitality (Lees-Maffei 2007).

HOSPITALITY AT HOME IN THE SWINGING SIXTIES, 1960–70

Solutions to the problem of hospitality without staff at home ranged from changes in the food served, the methods of serving, the transportation of food between regions of the home, and the locations for the service of food, as well as in the practice of allowing guests to assist, as discussed above. The period from 1960 to 1970 saw some of the most innovative approaches to lessening the labor of hospitality through the design and architecture of the home.

Public health scholar John Coveney has noted: 'During the 1950s and 1960s "convenience" foods were increasingly promoted as cooking in the "modern" way' (2000: 133). These relied on a number of developments which occurred during the first half of the twentieth century: increased production capacity, the availability of dietary supplements and vitamins, the consolidation of supply into multiple retailers, and the importance of refrigeration technology for the types of foods sold, their distribution, and domestic storage. Additional advances in branding, marketing, and packaging foods were aided by emergent materials and techniques such as cellophane and canning and by the development of television advertising from 1955 onwards (Oddy 2003). Supermarkets proliferated during this decade. The demographic shift towards smaller households and, in Britain, the development of commercial food provision in motorway service stations from 1959, fuelled the spread of the ready meal in advance of the acceptance of microwave technology in the 1980s. Along with eating outside of the home, convenience foods were a major trend in food preparation during the twentieth century, in the United States and the UK alike, and both of these trends have been associated with women's increasing participation in paid work outside the home (Lees-Maffei 2014a: 125–26).

One response to the increasingly widespread availability of convenience foods was a contrary taste for home-cooked dishes. The desirability of culinary authenticity underpinned Elizabeth David's influential *A Book of Mediterranean Food* of 1950 and the traditionalism of the French Cordon Bleu cookery school alike. Floral designer Constance Spry, and cook Rosemary Hume, ran a Cordon Bleu cookery school in Britain and published accompanying books on cookery and home entertaining (Spry and Hume, 1956, 1961), just as Julia Child popularized methods she had learned at Le Cordon Bleu in Paris, for an American audience in *Mastering the Art of French Cooking*, co-authored with Simone Beck and Louisette Bertholle (Beck, Bertholle, and Child 1961). The year after David's *Mediterranean Food* appeared, the Festival of Britain introduced UK visitors to the milk bar, a café serving milkshakes among other things, which served as a location for teenage sociability, and the *Good Food Guide* was launched (Lees-Maffei 2014a: 126).

Aside from the simplification of menus and the use of convenience foods and buffets, the designers of domestic goods joined architects and home economists in promoting solutions to the expanded burden of the unassisted hostess centred upon innovative uses of domestic space, particularly the provision of flexible spaces. New tools facilitated domestic practices that bridged the backstage region of the working kitchen, and the social front of the reception rooms in the home of the 1960s (Lees-Maffei 2007). A basic example is the recommendation of simple, sturdy designs for ceramic or Pyrex oven-to-tableware, which saved time that would otherwise have been spent plating food for presentation on serving dishes. Another practical solution was Tupperware's 'Party Susan'; akin to the 'lazy Susan', which can be rotated to allow food to be passed between diners, the Party Susan featured six compartments for separating foods, a lid to keep food fresh, and a handle which allowed it to be carried between kitchen and buffet. More complex solutions took the form of gadgets and appliances such as electric plate-warmers and hot plates. These enabled advanced preparation of food that could be kept hot and freed women performing the dual role of cook-hostess from having to coordinate the simultaneous readiness of meal components as well as allowing food to remain warm when left out for guests to help themselves, as noted in the UK Design Council publication, *Tableware* of 1969:

> With smaller houses, better planning of kitchens in relation to eating-serving, and the growing tendency to eat at least some meals in the kitchen, keeping food hot is no longer the problem it was when protocol and several flights of stairs separated kitchen from dining room. Nevertheless there are occasions when equipment for keeping dishes hot can be useful . . . for parties to save constant trips to and from the table.
>
> —Good 1969: 53

Plate-warmers and hot plates, however, merely preserve what has been achieved in the kitchen. A next step is the use at the table of portable cooking equipment such as 'electric skillet, rotisserie or a thermostatically controlled cook-and-serve unit' (*Woman's Own* 1967: 85). These turn the dining area into a temporary kitchen. Similarly, while the standard hostess trolley functions as a bridging device, easing the transition from kitchen to dining room, a more complex model with a hot plate can function almost as a portable kitchen, especially when combined with a small cooking device of the type mentioned.

In advising the unassisted hostess, domestic advisors prescribed modifications to the design and layout of the ideal home, which first bridged front and backstage regions, and then collapsed the distinction between them. Discrete kitchens, sitting rooms, and dining rooms, popularized prior to the twentieth century, were bridged with designed goods ranging from oven-to-tableware, hot plates, portable cooking appliances, and hostess trolleys, and the distinctions between the separate spaces were collapsed through architectural solutions such as transitional service hatches and a variety of hybrid kitchen and eating spaces like living-dining rooms, kitchen-diners, and an open plan. Domestic advisors of the 1960s went further in presenting even more flexible solutions. Joyce Lowrie is not alone in recommending that that the hall be used as 'a tiny, formal dining room for grown-ups' (1965: 18). Ilana Henderson's ingenious revolving kitchen is just one of a number of examples (most notable among them Joe Columbo's 'Mini-kitchen' of 1963) which negate the existence of the kitchen as a discrete space and redefine it as an object for use in any room (Good 1969: 57). It was developed with Bird's Eye Foods, a collaboration which associates the company with a future of convenience food and the decline of a more traditional ideal kitchen. These novel domestic solutions engage the modernist design virtues of space-saving, flexibility, multifunctionality, informality, and practicality. The prevalence of the kitchen-diner by the end of the 1970s constituted a rejection of the upper- and middle-class Victorian ideal home, in which separate rooms for discrete functions had been enshrined as standard, and resembled much more the experience of working-class Victorians. Thus the period witnessed a return to multi-purpose flexible rooms that preceded the Victorian ideal.

In an era in which broader influences of food preparation and interest in new cuisines encouraged a redefinition of home cooking as creative, the collapse of front and backstage produced a situation of greater visibility and continuous performance for the cook-hostess, thereby increasing her social labor. The design solutions offered promoted the juggling of multiple, competing roles and domestic advice writers thereby avoided the more radical and effective proposition that labor might be distributed more equally between the members of the household than the stereotypical and sexist distribution of labor, as discussed in the introduction, allowed (Lees-Maffei 2007).

ASPIRATIONS: MEDIA ATTENTION TO HOMES AND HOSPITALITY, 1970–90

Private domestic practices have not been recorded to the extent that public events have, nor have they been as visible. The ways in which hospitality has been practised and expressed in the relatively private realm of the home is, therefore, difficult for historians and others to access. However, a key distinguishing feature of domesticity in the period from 1920 to the present is the abundance of printed and broadcast sources about the home. The further expansion of print culture in the twentieth century and the introduction of new media technologies such as television, and more recently the internet, have meant that hospitality and home are the subject of significant media attention in books, magazines, radio and television broadcasts, websites, blogs and social media posts. Some figures associated in various ways with the practice of domestic hospitality have attained the status of intertextual reference points – advisors who are referred to in the books of other advice writers – from Constance Spry in the post-war UK, to Martha Stewart and Donna Hay in the millennial United States and Australia respectively.

One such reference figure, albeit imagined, who has been instrumental in representing domestic hospitality in 1970s Britain, is the hostess Beverly, from Mike Leigh's play *Abigail's Party*. The play was first performed at the Hampstead Theatre, London in April and July 1977, and broadcast on television as part of BBC 1 series 'Play for Today' in November of that year. Leigh's satire was developed through improvisation with the cast, including his then-wife Alison Steadman who played Beverly. The stage directions give an insight into the specificity with which the details of Beverly and Laurence's party are captured by Leigh:

> Laurence and Beverly's house, the ground floor. Room-divider shelf unit, including telephone, stereo, ornamental fibre-light, fold-down desk and prominently placed bar. Leather three-piece suite, onyx coffee-table, sheepskin rug. Open-plan kitchen, dining area with table and chairs. Hall and front door unseen.
> Lights up.
> Enter Beverly. She puts on a record (Donna Summer: Love to Love You Baby). Lights a cigarette. Places a copy of *Cosmopolitan* in magazine rack. Pours a gin-and-tonic. Gets a tray of crisps and salted peanuts from the kitchen and puts it on the coffee table. Sits.
> Pause.
> Enter Laurence, with executive case (Leigh 1983)

Beverly's party, characterized by 'the stifling charade of social etiquette: cocktail napkins, pineapple chunks, and party sausages on sticks, "nibbles" and "little fillups,"' which ultimately proves fatal for her husband Laurence (Brottman 2007: 323), is compared with the imagined lasciviousness of the off-stage party of neighbouring teenager Abigail. The play remains a salient study of the pretensions of domestic hospitality and the ways in which the extension of hospitality engages social power dynamics. Reviewing the play for the *Sunday Times*, writer Dennis Potter railed against Leigh's snobbery, describing the play as 'a prolonged jeer, twitching with genuine hatred, about the dreadful suburban tastes of the dreadful lower middle classes'. He concluded: 'As so often in the minefields of English class consciousness, more was revealed of the snobbery of the observers than of the observed' (Potter 1977: 35).

The UK and the United States both took a turn to the right politically during the 1980s with Margaret Thatcher, British Prime Minister from 1979 until 1990, in a 'special relationship' with Ronald Reagan, US President from 1981 to 1989. For those who could afford it, Thatcherism in politics translated into domestic life in terms of an emphasis on homeownership and new conspicuous consumption patterns for the mass middle class. Thatcherism fostered acquisitiveness among a wider proportion of the British market. Working-class people were actively encouraged to become homeowners through the right-to-buy scheme that depleted Britain's social housing infrastructure, and a (doomed) property boom rewarded existing owner-occupiers. Even the ensuing slump in the property market meant that people focused on improving their current homes and leisure became more home-centred (Lees-Maffei 2014b: 291–92).

Aspirations to continental European culinary excellence found expression in the influence of French nouvelle cuisine, an exercise in culinary skill, product freshness, and dietary restraint. Nouvelle cuisine attracted satirical responses highlighting the inadequate portion sizes, and influenced mass market convenience foods such as American manufacturer Stouffer's 'Lean Cuisine' brand, introduced in 1981. Research into the obesity epidemic in the West in the later twentieth and early twenty-first centuries has shown that portion sizes at home vary greatly when compared with catering industry portioning. In any case, the expression of hospitality through largesse in provisioning was at odds with the reductive approach of nouvelle cuisine and remains so when set against calorie- or otherwise controlled diets which have refusal at their core, rather than acceptance.

Although media coverage of homes and hospitality increased throughout the twentieth century, it accelerated sharply in the period from 1980 to 1995. In the British magazine market, several new titles were introduced, while circulation figures for existing titles grew. Both *What's New in Interiors* and *House Beautiful* reached circulation highs in 1993. Simultaneously, the trade publications *Interior Design* and *Kitchens and Bathrooms* increased their circulations by around 50 percent. While *Homes and Gardens* and *Home Improvements Journal* fell victim to the increased competition, there was nevertheless a boom period in magazine circulation between 1986 and 1992, indicative of real and increased interest in the home (Lees-Maffei 2014b: 292–95).

In 1982, Martha Stewart, today seen as a leading authority on matters of hospitality, published *Entertaining*, the first of what now amounts to around 100 books on home entertaining and decoration. With a degree in history and architectural history, Stewart worked as a model and then as a Wall Street stock trader before restoring a house in New England. She subsequently set up a catering business, which led to the publication of *Entertaining*. The style of home entertaining promoted in the 1982 book differs from Stewart's more recent book on the subject, *Martha Stewart's Dinner at Home: 52 Quick Meals to Cook for Family and Friends* (2009), with the later book forming yet another exemplar of informalization. Stewart's considerable influence on the homes and hospitality practices of American householders relies on her astonishing reach, in terms both of the breadth of content (entertaining, cooking, gardening, interior design) and the multiplicity of platforms. Martha Stewart Living Omnimedia (MSLO) worked across and interwove publishing (books and magazines), media (TV, radio, web), and merchandising (product lines, promotions, and licensing deals). Stewart's own extensive use of social media means that Martha Stewart the woman is almost indistinguishable from Martha Stewart the brand.[2]

MILLENNIAL HOSPITALITY, 1990–2010: TECHNOLOGY AND REACTIONS

Hospitality at home in the final decade of the twentieth century can be characterized as having been dominated by two competing trends: the domestic impact of new technologies, and reactions to that impact. In this sense, the turn of the twentieth century into the twenty-first resembles the *fin de siècle* one hundred years previously, in which a long process of industrialization in the West had provoked a far-reaching movement of social and design reform that looked to a pre-industrial past for the succour needed to face the new century. Then, proto-modernism and high modernism in design influenced the design and decoration of people's homes, if not the behaviours practised within them. However, in the period leading up to our own century, the domestic impact of new technologies and reactions to them has been largely behavioural, rather than impacting the material make-up of the home.

In terms of home design and hospitality, this period therefore represents a continuation of innovations in open-plan interiors introduced in the post-war period and given a boost by post-industrial 'loft' living in the 1980s and later. While open-plan living is ostensibly less formal than domestic practices based on the segmentation of space, and through that, the separation of distinct practices and even family members, it is also demanding on hosts and hostesses. Open-plan and multi-functional domestic spaces form part of a wider aestheticization of everyday life (Bourdieu 1984) in which all of one's home is available to guests for inspection and judgement. Open-plan kitchens, flexible kitchen-dining, and living-dining spaces provide no refuge for flurried hosts and hostesses and their domestic messes. Happily, however, while the trend in home design – as evidenced by consumer and trade magazines alike – is strongly in favour of open-plan homes, in practice millennial householders continue to meld an informal, open-plan approach to domestic life with the discrete rooms that many houses provide. In socializing, they move from room

FIGURE 7.5: Friends in Montreal gather with their computers in a suburban basement for a LAN (local area network) party and play an online game together. © Karl Erfle, 2016.

to room, using them in a variety of different ways rather than as separate spaces with discrete functions. They follow this pattern both in the secondary market of the existing built environment with existing room arrangements, and in new build developments.

Twenty-first century hospitality at home extends beyond the physical borders of the house. The introduction of relatively affordable hardware for personal computing in the 1990s and the technical developments that allowed for extremely widespread market penetration of mobile phones and, later, smartphones has had a huge impact on the ways in which people conduct their social lives. From video chat services such as Skype, Facetime, and a raft of apps, to social media sites such as MySpace and Facebook, these new technologies have enabled people to interact socially with others who are not present, or even known to them. They build, therefore, on the remote social interactions enabled by forerunners of various kinds such as the telegram, telephone, and citizens' band radio (local radio communication in which a number of users share a channel). However, the effect of social media in the home has been more impactful in recent years, as more people, globally, have participated. Today, it is not accurate to regard the home as private, although apparently many people continue to do so. In addition to other members of the household, individual home dwellers engage with friends, colleagues, acquaintances, and strangers via social media based in text, image, and video, to conduct a range of interactions and relationships from maintaining family ties and sharing common interests to pursuing romantic and sexual liaisons. The extent to which this activity stands in for, or replaces, hospitality at home, is variable and currently uncharted.

However, in so far as social media allow the initiation and maintenance of relationships in the home as well as outside of it, they do fulfil something of the function of hospitality and home at this time.

As well as facilitating sociability, information technologies have facilitated the exchange of information about homes and hospitality as noted above. Internet users can access a plethora of advice about homes and hospitality via subject-specific blogs, advice from friends, family, colleagues, and a wider contact group via social media posts and amateur films, for example on YouTube. Providers of online advice, such as Martha Stewart's team, encourage readers and viewers to post evaluations of the advice they offer. With the introduction of web 2.0, the Read-Write web, internet users have begun to publish a vast array of online content, from Facebook profiles, and family snaps on Flickr, to home movies on YouTube, opinions on blogs, and product reviews on Amazon.

FIGURE 7.6: As social media posts attest, baking experienced a surge in popularity among people confined to their homes during the Covid-19 pandemic. In this Instagram post, design historian D.J. Huppatz parodies the competitive aesthetics of domestic sourdough baking by humorously photographing a shop-bought loaf, complete with tell-tale paper bag, in his home oven. @dj_huppatz (April 2020) [Instagram post].

An immense resource has been created, at once intimate and widely seen, which allows unparalleled access into the homes and lives of billions of web users. In the online environment, in which anyone with access to a smartphone or a computer (whether at home, at a library, or in an internet café) has the potential to become a producer, as well as a consumer, of domestic advice the problem is not finding advice, but rather judging its value based on the advisor's expertise.

A range of technological developments changed the way food was presented and sold during this period. Innovations in convenience foods continued, including that of freshly washed bagged salads removing the need for the domestic cleaning and preparation of leaves and servicing a trend for healthier, lighter foods. Food manufacturers and restaurateurs alike responded to, and shaped, new culinary tastes in the West, such as Pacific Rim and Asian-American fusion foods. In the twenty-first century, food purchasing has shifted online to a significant extent, from bulk buying with the major supermarkets to weekly deliveries from local farmers in 'vegetable box' schemes that foreground seasonal produce and cooking from scratch. These online subscription box schemes service a need for time-starved customers who are unable or unwilling to grow their own food, in spite of the exhortations of a number of prominent gardening and food writers to do just that (Don and Don 1999; Oliver 2007). At the same time, this return to seasonal food, increased awareness of nutrition and health issues, and pressing ecological concerns, have combined to make convenience foods and supermarket shopping unattractive for some consumers.

The Slow Food movement, which promotes seasonal local foods, authenticity, and heritage, was founded in 1986 in response to a proposed McDonald's fast food restaurant in Rome (Slow Food 2015). It also opposes convenience foods at home. Slow Food's first international congress was held in Venice the following year, and the Slow Food publishing house, Slow Food Editore, was launched at the same time. International branches of the movement followed (Slow Food 2015). Campaigning has centred upon eco-gastronomy and the availability of food such as raw milk cheeses, which have suffered from large retailing methods, practices such as pasteurization, and associated food safety legislation (Lees-Maffei 2016). Today, cities and towns committed to slow food, improving conviviality, and preserving gastronomical diversity are found around the world, including in Korea, South Africa, and the United States (Cittaslow 2019). Improved transport and urban infrastructures facilitate increased sociability, including hospitality at home. Home entertaining has always privileged homemade food, even at the height of the trend of convenience foods (the latter would only have been served covertly or apologetically by some hosts and hostesses). Slow food entertaining, however, increases the burden of the host and hostess by demanding daily, local, seasonal shopping in place of bulk buying at supermarkets, and by celebrating home cooked food, however simple or elaborate.

The practice of cooking from scratch further increases the domestic workload for householders, and in particular women. The battery of devices designed to assist food production in the home increases year on year, as manufacturers and retailers continue to promote bread makers, ice cream machines, waffle makers, yogurt- and cheese-making equipment for the mass, rather than specialist, markets. Each of these appliances implies a further process to be undertaken in the domestic kitchen, thereby increasing the domestic workload, rather than reducing it, in a manner Ruth Schwartz Cowan has noted (1983). Concern about the amount of time involved in cooking, when people perceive themselves to be too busy to cook, is expressed in a number of cook books. For example, Martha Stewart has attempted to show how entertaining, which has traditionally relied on home cooking of labor-intensive meals as expressions of regard for the guests, can be approached in a more relaxed, and less time-consuming way (Stewart 2009).

CONCLUSION

Just as homes have changed, so have expressions of hospitality in the home. Notwithstanding a range of technological innovations and shifts in standards of relative formality and informalization examined in this chapter, entertaining at home is still an act of labor, however considerable or inconsiderable, and therein lies its value. To invite someone into your home to experience your hospitality remains an act of esteem embedded in effort, even if the occasion is casual, the food bought-in, and the entertainment streamed without forethought. Indeed, in the era of digital social media, in which hospitality need not mean actual physical presence in someone's home, and need not mean, therefore, physical co-presence, the instances in which people do physically go to one another's homes to enjoy their hospitality become even more meaningful, regardless of the nature of that hospitality. This chapter has shown that hospitality at home is a complex practice in which the physical and material composition of the home supports or denies the behavioural practices of sociability. Hospitality, in these terms, is nothing less than care manifested socially and materially. In these terms, hospitality at home, in the intimate familial spaces of everyday life, is surely more meaningful than hospitality as it is practised industrially in hotels, restaurants, and other settings, however competent and professional the commoditized affect might be in those settings.

CHAPTER EIGHT

Religion and Home: Sites of Sanctuary and Suspicion

PAMELA E. KLASSEN

INTRODUCTION

Home, as concept and as material space, evokes a profound mix of desire and dread.[1] Longings for a space of shelter, comfort, constancy, and care may contend with fears of inhabiting a place of constraint, secrecy, privation, overabundance, or even violence. In times of pandemic, some people 'shelter in place' in great comfort, while others quarantine in a crowded room and worry about paying the rent (Keller and Dobby 2020; Muñoz 2020). Home provokes existential questions about security, justice, and relationships – who has a home and who does not, who has enough in their home and who has too much, who experiences love and care in their home and who lives in fear or is a cause of fear in their home? As Sigmund Freud noted in his essay on the 'uncanny', the German word *heimlich*, or 'belonging to the home', has two interrelated but distinct meanings: 'the one relating to what is familiar and comfortable, the other to what is concealed and kept hidden' ([1919] 2003: 132). So too does the English word 'home' contain this ambiguous mix of consolation and concealment.

For as long as people have lived together in dwellings, they have made homes: spaces to which they can return, where they keep their worldly goods, and where they sleep, cook, eat, make love, play, fight, care for animals, and create families. Home is a material space in which people gather and an ideal to which people aspire. Not surprisingly, then, home has often been the focus of religious prescription and the ground of religious formation. In this chapter, I tack between home as an aspirational goal and as a lived reality to examine the ways in which 'religion', as both practice and ideology, has formed what counts as home in twentieth-century North America. This requires not only thinking about local practices of homemaking, but also examining the material and ideological basis of what counts as a home and who can afford one.

Asking what counts as home requires questioning all the way down to the ground, both conceptually and literally, by asking how 'property' is conceived and accessed, and by whom. In the context of North America, a settler society in which Europeans came to what they saw as a 'new world' and claimed it as their home, this question can be asked in (at least) two ways.

First, how do Indigenous and settler understandings of 'home ownership' reflect very different cosmologies of land and how to inhabit it? In both Canada and the United States, Indigenous peoples have long traditions of collective land ownership, which often included homes that were movable, depending on the season and the demands of hunting or fishing. When colonial settlers arrived, they called this a 'nomadic' life, and considered it to be a lesser form of home, even though it was a highly adaptive pattern of life for Indigenous peoples (Darnell 2008). In this view, not being a 'settler' – quite literally someone who has settled in a fixed dwelling place – made one a 'savage'. Oriented by a tradition of political theory that understood property to be a fixed spot of ground which had to be 'improved' in order to be owned, settlers saw buildings – especially houses – as necessary to property ownership (Turner 2011). Over time, repeated stories of placement and replacement helped to turn the settler story into the dominant story of 'homeland' in North America (O'Brien 2010).

From Indigenous perspectives, however, home was not tied to a building situated on a patch of land. Instead, home lay in a much broader relationship to land: rocks, rivers, trees, mountains, and the spirits who lived around and within them (Marsden 2002). Ironically, over time many settlers have become more migratory than Indigenous peoples, moving frequently across the continent and the globe in search of work, religious utopias, or an idea of freedom, selling one home to buy another. As Aileen Moreton-Robinson has written in *The White Possessive* (2015), a book about Indigenous cosmologies of land in relation to settler colonies, this kind of settler nomadism has ignored how specific lands, or homeplaces, matter to Indigenous peoples.

A second way to ask about the relationship of home and property is to ask how religion has shaped the basic ability or inability of people to own or to inhabit a home. Being housed or homeless is a profound distinction in

North American society, at the level of lived experience and ideological value. Within the scope of being housed, gradations of status accrue: being a renter, living in subsidized housing, living alone, in a co-op, with family, or even extended family, living in an apartment, a house, a mansion, multiple homes across the continent or the world. Many people in North America live in accommodations characterized by surveillance or constraint, such as a hospital, a prison, a 'halfway house', or migrant worker residences. These people live under conditions of coercion that challenge the very notion of home as a place of sanctuary or refuge. Thinking at these limit points helps to clarify the naturalized, or sometimes romanticized, qualities of what counts as a home.

Oriented by an awareness of property and power, and with the help of concepts such as ritual, domesticity, and gender, I consider the relationship of religion and home at multiple scales, from the domestic to the national to the heavenly. I focus in particular on two broad categories of homes: (1) family homes as sites for creating domestic ritual subjects, and (2) 'not-family' homes, or religiously sponsored institutional homes, such as maternity homes and residential schools. While some of these homes have met the profound needs of their inhabitants for shelter, love, and care, others have deeply traumatized those who live within them. I frame my discussion with an on-going pressure that cannot escape home life: the tension between home as a profoundly intimate, if idealized, sanctuary and home as a site of suspicion, trauma, and concealment.

Sanctuary and suspicion

Sanctuary is a word used conventionally within Christianity and Judaism to describe ritually consecrated spaces in churches and synagogues, sometimes known colloquially as the 'house' of God (Stiefel 2014). In a church, a sanctuary is the place where the most powerful rituals happen: bread and wine are turned into the body and blood of Jesus Christ by the Eucharistic service, babies, children, and adults are baptized, two people are wed, and dead people are mourned and commemorated. For Jews, a sanctuary also houses the 'Holy of Holies'; it is the place where the Torah scrolls reside and are read, and where important life-cycle rituals of weddings and bar and bat mitzvahs take place. In both churches and synagogues, the house of God is also where one prays and sings.

In both medieval and modern contexts, a Christian sanctuary – meaning the inner sanctum of a church – has also meant a place where someone might find refuge safe from the legal power of the state. From the 1980s onwards, Latin American, Roma, and other refugees have revived this practice in both Canada and the United States, as churches and synagogues have offered them refuge from deportation (Cunningham 1995; Lippert 2011; Nepstad 2004). In both Christianity and Judaism, then, the sanctuary is at once a place set apart – a place made sacred – and a place idealized as refuge from external forces.

The idea of a sanctuary can also be applied to the family home, as a place where children are nurtured, meals are cooked and shared, and families gather. A fertile site for nostalgia, hope, and the sacralization of family, the sanctuary of home also has a flip side: suspicion of what might be going on behind closed doors. Though some may claim that a 'good' home is the genesis of piety and good character, the same people may also consider a 'bad' home to be a site of suspicious activity, malformed character, a threat to both neighbour and nation. The dividing line between a good home and a bad one has often fallen along other lines by which people construct difference, including religion, ethnicity, sexuality, class, and racialization. White flight, crack house, ghetto, barrio, parish hall, halfway house, homeless shelter, reserve: the language of home and neighbourhood often carries within it histories of religious and racialized patterns of organizing where people live, and with whom.

Even gentrification, if one looks back far enough, comes from a word that once had a spiritual cast. In Ireland, 'gentry' once meant fairies, whose homes, the 'gentry bushes', were supposed to be protected: they were 'sacred to the "good people", and are therefore let alone' ('Gentry' 2020). As people stopped giving credence to the idea that fairies needed a place to dwell, the word slowly changed meaning. The fairies eventually lost out to those gentry 'of gentle birth and breeding', when in post-war Europe and North America gentrification came to mean the displacement of poor and vulnerable residents in the wake of so-called urban renewal that transformed a neighbourhood according to 'middle-class taste' ('Gentrify' 2020). This etymology, though fascinating, is an ironic reminder that older traditions of sanctuary – whether leaving green space for the fairies or commons for the common folk – have disappeared in the face of 'development'.

The patterns of social organization that group nearby homes into neighbourhoods often have the effect, whether intentional or not, of organizing people according to race, religion, and class. Neighbourhood groupings have fostered community at the same time as feeding suspicion and division, often at great cost to those with the least amount of power (Orsi 1999, 2010; McGreevy 1996; Radforth 2014). A collection of so-called 'bad' homes becomes a 'bad' neighbourhood, and a host of inequalities and surveillance follow.

Like the word 'home', religion is a concept that carries a great deal of ideological and historical freight. In the way that I use it here, religion means a kind of authoritative knowledge and practice that appeals to a transcendent or ancestral source for its legitimacy (see also Klassen 2016). Held collectively by groups of people, but also challenged from within and without, religion is never a fixed essence. The ways that religion is deployed and remade through the home is a question not only of the relationship of 'private' practices and 'public' traditions, but also of the choices and constraints on the ways that people live their daily lives as economic, sexualized, and racialized beings shaped by the laws and rituals of nations.

Considering home and religion via the intersection of sanctuary and suspicion and through the frames of ritual subjects and institutionalized homes requires thinking across scales of the individual, the family, the religious community, and the laws and zoning that shape how people live together. I do this by considering the prescribed, forbidden, and creative ritual practices that people make in the space of home, as well as the ways that religions have established institutions for people to live in – for example, orphanages – in what some might see as quasi-homes, or 'not-family' homes. I close with a brief reflection on the materiality of homes as built forms that have their own 'force of design' that shapes both what can happen in homes and how they are remembered.

DOMESTIC RITUAL SUBJECTS

Home is an important site for rituals – daily, weekly, or seasonal embodied practices by which people orient themselves in relation to each other, in space, story, and time, within emotional valences, and often in relation to spirits, deities, ancestors, or otherworldly places (Klassen 2008a). For example, Christmas dinners, Passover Seders, breaking the fast during Ramadan are all examples of ritualized kinds of eating in the home shaped by the calendars and stories of religious traditions. Homes are also places where people design and implement rites of passage, that is, particular kinds of rituals whereby people mark transitions in their bodies, in their families and wider social relations, and in their educational or work lives. Births and birthdays, showers and weddings, wakes and funerals, and initiations and graduations are all rites of passage that cut across various religious and popular traditions. Drawing from scriptures and fairy tales, rites of passage are not 'only' religious. The aesthetics, location, and cost of rites of passage are influenced as much by the popular culture of fashion magazines and movies and the therapeutic cultures of biomedical and other kinds of care as they are by religious manuals of practice.

When thinking about religion and home in the twenty-first century, it is hard to judge the comparative weight of religiously inspired ritual calendars *vis-à-vis* commercial purveyors of ritual advice, such as Martha Stewart's home-focused media empire or Marie Kondo's counsel to 'spark joy' through decluttering. One constant remains across both religious and commercial visions of the ritualized home: women do most of the work to make domestic ritual happen. Many scholars have pointed to the role of women work's in preparing the food, decorations, and ritual implements required to mark religion during both the everyday and holidays (McDannell 1994; Joselit 2002; Kurien 1999; di Leonardo 1987; Iacovetta, Korinek, and Epp 2012; Gardner 2002). Women also take a primary role in turning their children into ritual subjects who participate actively – if sometimes reluctantly or belligerently – in a wider religious tradition and the seasonal ritual life of the home: fasting, joining household devotions and prayers, giving gifts, cooking and baking, lighting candles, and cleaning the house (see Ridgely 2006). This is not to say that men do not perform these important roles in rituals of the home, but simply to acknowledge that in many homes, especially those of heterosexual couples, women have often done more of the domestic and childrearing labor.

Sometimes, the burden on women to perform a much greater role in domestic labor and childcare even has religious sanction, as in more conservative religious traditions that deem men the 'head of the household'. Feminist scholars of women and religion have long noted the profound significance of domesticity – in both practical and idealized forms – as a powerful and ambivalent metaphorical tool that shapes the labor of women both inside and outside of the home (McDannell 1994; Joselit 2002; Sered 1986). Susan Sered, in a book analysing the ritual practices of Middle Eastern Jewish women in Jerusalem, focused on what she called 'domestic religion' in order to bring more prominence to the religious labor of women. If only public ritual work is acknowledged, Sered argued, scholars of religious ritual would largely pay attention to men (which, until relatively recently, was the case). For Sered, domestic religion is 'the arena in which the ultimate concerns of life, suffering, and death are *personalized* – domestic religion has to do with the lives, sufferings, and deaths of *particular*, usually well-loved, individuals' (1996: 32). Insisting that domestic religion is not necessarily opposed to non-domestic, or 'official' religion as practised outside the home in religious institutions, Sered focused on the everyday labors of women in the home as directed to others, especially with regard to cooking, childcare, and ritual observance.

Women's historians, anthropologists of gender and reproduction, and religious studies scholars focused on women have all clarified different aspects of the political and gendered significance of religion and domesticity. As historians such as Nancy Cott (1997) have shown, in the late nineteenth century and into the twentieth, white middle-class Christian women often asserted their ties to the domestic sphere, even if they were not wives and mothers, in order to engage in public political action. Similarly, Jewish middle-class women who had immigrated to the United States from Germany in the nineteenth century were called 'priestesses of the home', in a nod to their importance for bourgeois households and childrearing. These so-called priestesses also became active in movements for women's suffrage and women's access to higher education (Baader 1998).

Conversely, for many Black, immigrant, or rural women, the homes of middle-class women were their workplaces, whether as nannies, housekeepers, or 'hired girls' (Weisenfeld and Newman 1995; Stansell 2012; Epp 2011; Klippenstein 2011). Women activists from many backgrounds rooted calls for reform, including temperance legislation, women's suffrage, and the fight to abolish child labor, in a special authority derived from their experiences of childcare and practical householding. This authority was often further justified by claims from biblical or theological texts and traditions.

While earlier scholars focused on the concept of 'separate spheres', which understood the private life of the home and the public life of the world as two domains of women's lives, later scholars have argued that separate spheres were rarely that distinct (Klassen 2009). In the case of Black women who worked in white women's homes, for example, the domestic was a sphere of labor, not a family sanctuary (Carby 2007). As Nancy Cott (2009) has shown in her research on marriage in the United States, the very legality of only certain people having the right to form a family and to live in a home together, whether in the case of outlawing 'interracial' unions or 'same-sex' unions, meant that public law profoundly shaped private lives.

When thinking about ritual, religion, and the home, then, it is always revealing to ask some basic questions: Who is doing the work to make rituals happen (including cleaning the house)? Are these people also invited to the party? Who is supposed to participate and who is not allowed to participate, whether by means of social or legal exclusion? How do gender, race, class, age, sexuality, and religious orientation shape the answers to these questions?

Religion and domestic labor

Whether or not a woman worked or works outside the home, religious observance has long required her domestic labor, especially where food was concerned. Jewish Shabbat dinners, Christian grace before meals, puja with food offerings at a home altar dedicated to Hindu gods or goddesses, or the nightly breaking of the fast during the Muslim observance of Ramadan are all revealing examples of the ways that religiously inflected rhythms of eating and food preparation may set the pace of domestic ritual life.

Images of domestic piety richly exemplify the home as sanctuary ideal – and usually place a woman at the centre of the scene. Picturing religion in the home, while not widespread in popular culture, can take many forms. As anthropologist Michaela di Leonardo (2006) noted, however, the homes of non-white, non-upper-class women long remained largely unrepresented in the visual cultures of television, movies, and magazines. Religious difference, I would add, also remains unseen in most popular culture depictions of the ideal home.

In twentieth-century North American popular culture, the dominant image of a religious home was that of a Christian home inhabited by a heterosexual couple and their children. Images of families at prayer and at table, however, go

FIGURE 8.1: An illustration by Leonard Weisgard of a mother and daughter at home reciting the blessing over Sabbath candles, in Hyman Chanover and Evelyn Zusman, *My Book of Prayer* (New York: United Synagogue Commission on Jewish Education, 1959), 44–45. Special Collections, Michigan State University Libraries.

FIGURE 8.2: An extended family pictured at the Sunday dinner table, from *The Mennonite Treasury of Recipes* (Steinbach, Manitoba: Derksen Printers, [1961] 1980). Photograph by Pamela Klassen.

FIGURE 8.3: Family at the dinner table in Los Angeles, perhaps on a Sunday, *c.* 1916. Shades of L.A., Los Angeles Public Library.

beyond the dominant representation of 'white Anglo-Saxon Protestants'. For example, a Mennonite cookbook from the mid-twentieth century illustrated the saying of grace before meals with a scene of mother, children, and grandmother, with the father at the head of the table. A Jewish handbook for children depicted a mother teaching her daughter how to light the candles at the beginning of Shabbat. An early-twentieth-century photograph of a Black family enjoying a meal in their Sunday best shows smiling faces around the table.

Ethnographic studies of religion have drawn particularly rich portraits of religious practice in the home, noting that women are often the primary curators of domestic shrines to saints, goddesses, or ancestors, whether in Italian-American Catholicism, Haitian Vodou, or North American Hinduism (Orsi 2010; Brown 2001; Kurien 2007). Responsibilities as caretakers not only of children but also of deities may bring a certain authority and even power to women, but may also conflict with their responsibilities outside of the home. As sociologist Prema Kurien found when researching diasporic Hindu communities in North America, 'women's greatly enlarged responsibilities as cultural custodians in the immigrant context can be empowering but can also be limiting because this model only views women as wives and mothers' (1999: 665). There are only so many hours in the day, and cooking and caring for gods, men, and children while carrying a full-time job can take its toll.

Homes as in-between religious mediums

As spaces that mediate consumption (the buying and consuming of goods), labor, and ritual practice, homes are fascinating liminal spaces in between religion writ large, material culture, and people's everyday lives. The ever-increasing presence of communication media within homes makes this liminality even more porous and profound. A hundred years ago, a city newspaper and a church newspaper might have arrived daily to bring news of the world to a household's breakfast table; today, a person could listen to the radio, watch a television, check a smartphone, and open her laptop all before a morning coffee. These domesticated media practices also have ritual implications, blurring the line between home and religious institution (Klassen 2008b).

Anthropologist Marla Frederick explains this well in her ethnography of Black Pentecostal women, *Between Sundays* (2003). Frederick shows that for these women the distinction between one's 'home' and one's 'church home' was never a sharply drawn line. The rise of televangelists, making their way into a woman's living room to appeal for donations on the television screen blurred this line further. But contrary to many popular depictions of gullible donors, the women Frederick spoke with were critical supporters of televangelists, insisting that they would pull their support if televangelists improperly used their donations. Making moral decisions about what causes they wished to support from the space of their own living room, these women engaged in ethical deliberation about where and to whom their offerings should go (Frederick 2003: 177).

Religion and ritual practice in the home cannot be understood without considering practices of consumption. For example, in the past two decades, the Chinese cosmology of *feng shui*, in which the design of a house and the placement of furniture and objects within it are considered to either block or enhance harmonious 'energetic flows', has grown increasingly popular in North America, well beyond Chinese communities. As interior designers and home builders take up the practice of *feng shui* – and market themselves as having done so – the 'spiritualizing' of the home through these principles becomes a lucrative business proposition (Bonaiuto, Bilotta, and Stolfa 2010; Langdon 1991). In the wake of the commodification of *feng shui*, some critics have labelled it a 'new age fad' that re-fetishizes commodities through a logic that claims to simplify life (Binkley 2008). As controversies over Marie Kondo's lightly Shinto-inspired 'life-changing magic of tidying up' demonstrate, mixing domesticity, consumption, and religion can provoke hostile critics and staunch defenders, both of whom deploy racist and gendered tropes to make their point (Thomas 2019).

Feng shui may well be a fad or even a scam in celebrity versions in which it promises to transform one's life and livelihood. Its commodified version may also rightly be criticized for appropriating Chinese traditions without sufficient understanding or respect for wider historical or cosmological context. But it should not be set apart as less legitimate when compared to other more 'established religions' simply for the fact that adhering to its domestic ritual requirements causes someone to spend money. The home is a central way station for the goods we buy – whether food, clothing, media, or other objects. Religious rituals almost always increase the level of consumption of a household, especially when it comes to food.

No matter what cosmology of home one endorses, within a capitalist system the desire to 'consume simply' is very difficult to achieve. Even people living within highly circumscribed communities, such as the Old Order Amish, Ultra-Orthodox Jews, or Kibbutzim, must grapple with the question of whether a practice of consumption – especially regarding media technology – is appropriately simple or religiously appropriate (Tharp 2007; Livio and Weinblatt 2007; Ribak and Rosenthal 2006).

The history of Hanukkah and Christmas in North America offers a fascinating window onto the question of the role of consumption in the home as a site of religion. Christmas is, arguably, the Christian holiday most firmly ensconced in the North American home. This is partly because, for many people, it has become more about gift exchanges, family gatherings, house parties, and festive dinners than attending midnight mass or Advent services. A holiday that roots itself in a biblical story about a pregnant woman who could find no shelter in which to give birth, Christmas moved with aplomb from stable to home in the late nineteenth and early twentieth centuries in both Europe and North America (Klassen and Scheer 2019; Miller 1995b).

The rise of department stores in urban centres and Christmas cards circulating through the mail helped to turn Christmas into a ritual of consumption, gift

FIGURE 8.4: A Christmas event held at the home of Superior Court Judge Earl C. Broady (standing, left) in Beverly Hills, *c.* 1950. Shades of L.A., Los Angeles Public Library.

exchange, and 'season's greetings' (Schmidt 1997). For many Christians, Christmas is still an important celebration of the Christian story of the incarnation of God into the body of a baby boy via the womb of a virgin mother. But for others who may be nominal Christians, or not Christian at all, Christmas has become a 'secularized' holiday celebrating home, family, and social harmony.

A secular Christmas is, of course, a lot more convincing to people who come from Christian backgrounds than to those who grew up or participate in other religions. As historian Jenna Weissman Joselit has shown, the popularity of Hanukkah rose dramatically in twentieth-century North America as Jews interacted more regularly with Christian neighbours, co-workers, and an implicitly Christian popular culture (Joselit 2002; see also Plaut 2012). Jewish parents faced an overwhelmingly child-focused Christmas home invasion – from Santa Claus sliding down a family's chimney laden with gifts to the Grinch entering via the television (Weiner 2019). Faced with the ubiquity of the story of Christmas told not only in churches and Bibles, but also in department stores and television shows, some Jews turned to Hanukkah as a Jewish winter celebration that could stave off the Christmas onslaught.

Hanukkah, a ritual rooted in a story about re-sanctifying the Jewish Temple, became a powerful tool for rededicating the Jewish home. Based on an account in 1 Maccabees about a band of brothers in the second century BCE who fought against Hellenistic rulers who were desecrating the Temple with idol worship, Hanukkah marks eight nights of their vigil to restore the Temple. As religious studies scholar Dianne Ashton writes, the creation of Hanukkah as a festival to remember the Maccabean revolt 'marked a successful effort to restore Jewish practices, an innovation that signaled devotion to Jewish community' (2013: 23). Repurposed in the twentieth century to counter the hegemony of Christianity in popular culture – and in the minds and hearts of many Jewish children – Hanukkah restored Jewish practices through reinventing them with menorahs, latkes, and dreidels in the North American and European home.

And then there is the question of 'Chrismukkah'. Some of the most interesting points of conflict and creativity in terms of domestic rituals occur in the context of 'interfaith families'. How does a family comprised of people adhering to multiple traditions decide on which holidays and what domestic rituals will be celebrated? Samira Mehta, a scholar of American religions, has written about the emergence of Chrismukkah as a response to Jewish-Christian families dealing with the dilemma of celebrating Christmas and Hanukkah, winter holidays that can sometimes overlap (Mehta 2015, 2018). The dilemma is not only about scheduling dinners or gift-giving, but also about how to understand what it means to celebrate multiple rituals within one family (see also Nathenson 2013; Shandler and Weintraub 2007). According to Mehta, Chrismukkah (a neologism coined on a television show) was a solution to the problem of dual religious loyalties by way of a discourse of multiculturalism. This discourse turns Christmas and Hanukkah into cultural, and not religious, traditions: 'Chrismukkah itself, then, serves as a (sometimes minimally) reconfigured holiday that points to "cultural" heritages rather than "religious" truths, allowing interfaith families to shape a family-based, multicultural practice' (Mehta 2015: 83).

Combining ritual creativity with practices of consumption is a reality of everyday life in families, friendship networks, and workplaces throughout North America (Lofton 2017). When families can be comprised of people related to each other through biological kinship, through what anthropologists call 'fictive kinship', as well as via a wide variety of other social relations, it is no surprise that religious diversity may become a source of conflict and creativity in the home. The 'nuclear' family of parents and children may include people of multiple religious affiliations; larger extended families across multiple generations likely also include people of varying religious commitments. Perhaps the most fraught yet affecting occasions for this kind of ritual creativity in the home come as people and families negotiate the transitions of life, from birth to death.

Rites of passage

At the beginning of the twentieth century, most people were born and died at home. Birthing women were assisted by midwives or doctors, and dying people were cared for by family members or a visiting physician. In a Christian home, both the newborn and the corpse were washed and clothed by the women of the home, readied for their rituals of transition to a new phase of existence, whether baptism or a funeral. By the end of the century, most people were born and died in hospitals. The institutionalization of caring came with the rise of biomedicine, and moved the most significant life-cycle rituals of birth and death out of the home and into hospitals and funeral 'homes' (Klassen 2001a; Laderman 2003).

In twenty-first century North America, however, many of the rites of passage that were slowly institutionalized over the past century are making a comeback in the home. Home birth, home dying, and even home schooling (which I will not address here) are movements with complicated religious and/or spiritual roots and motivations (Stevens 2009). Why is it that a significant and vocal minority of people across a range of religious commitments have come to the position that these critical moments in the life of a human being in community – birth, death, and education – need to be 're-housed'? The answer to this question is not simple, but one theme that ties together the home birth and home death movements is the desire to return birth and death to domestic spaces in ways that are not necessarily de-professionalized, but are instead re-personalized. In this, the movements to return birth and death to the home fit well within Susan Sered's definition of domestic religion as 'the arena in which the ultimate concerns of life, suffering, and death are *personalized*' (1996: 32).

In North America, the home birth movement has its roots in a mix of feminist-oriented women's health activism, counter-cultural experiments with communal living, and the growing critique of the medicalization of childbirth (Klassen 2001a). Arguing that childbirth was usually not a pathological condition, the 'natural childbirth' movement struggled against the routinization of medical procedures such as anesthetizing women to sleep, surgically cutting women's vaginas during birth, and a growing rate of planned caesarean sections. For some of its proponents, this led to arguing that natural birth could be returned to the home, so that a woman could be cared for not only by professionals such as midwives and doctors, but also by her family and friends. Countries such as the Netherlands and Great Britain had always retained the option of home childbirth, along with flourishing midwifery professions, and Canadian and US midwives looked to these examples for guidance (Benoit, Bourgeault, and Davis-Floyd 2004).

In both Canada and the United States, a religiously diverse cross-section of women has turned to home birth: conservative Catholics, Pentecostals, Ultra-Orthodox Jews, liberal Protestants, goddess feminists. Convinced that the vast majority of women were equipped to give birth with little intervention save for the support of others, these women have largely understood the return of birth to the home as an acknowledgement of the spiritual significance of birth as a rite of passage even in a biomedical age (Klassen 2001b). For Indigenous women living in areas remote from major hospitals, the revitalization of midwifery has been understood as a restoration of both sovereignty and spirituality. For many years pregnant women were automatically transported from their 'fly-in' communities to urban hospitals weeks before giving birth, which was a considerable strain on their personal and family lives (Olson and Couchie 2013). The home birth movement, then, means very different things for a woman living in a city and one living in a home considered 'remote' (Rutherdale 2010).

The home dying movement, similarly to the home birth movement, is rooted in shared convictions that critical moments in the passage of a life are more than medical events. Aiming to bring palliative care from the hospital to the home, advocates of home dying insist that a person with a terminal illness who is actively waiting to die can do so with dignity when provided with the necessary supports to stay at home. The question of supports is key, as in some places home dying has grown more frequent because medical systems have turned to home care as a cost-saving mechanism (Donovan et al. 2011).

Similar in another way to the home birth movement, the home death and home funeral movements cut across a range of religious identities for both doctrinal and 'personalized' reasons. Most Muslims consider a 'good death' to be one that takes place at home, where a family has been able to care for their loved one as he or she passes on to the next life. Due to a religious obligation to bury a dead person as quickly as possible, many Muslims forgo funeral homes and wash and wrap the bodies of their dead at home (Gardner 2002). More widely, people from many backgrounds are turning to home dying as a way to care for their loved ones in death as they did in life – personally, intimately, carefully (Jones 2019). A challenge to medical and funeral industries, home dying shows again the ways that home is a shifting space for the intersection of religion and the market.

HOME AS INSTITUTION, OR THE 'NOT-FAMILY HOME'

Religious groups have long made homes that were based not on the model of the biological family but on visions of fictive, or perhaps better put, spiritual kinship. Monasteries, convents, and other places of asceticism or celibacy are examples of communal homes that take various forms and various names within Christianity, Buddhism, Hinduism, and many other religious groups. These 'institutionalized' homes have been organized both by principles of 'voluntary association', in which someone joins a group out of a sense of vocation or desire, as in some monasteries or ashrams, and by principles of need, in which the religious group provides homes for those who would otherwise have none, such as an orphanage or a homeless shelter (Weisenfeld 2018). Sometimes, institutionalized homes founded with the best of intentions were also places of surveillance and even imprisonment. Quakers, for example, were influential in developing the very first prisons in the United States, as they sought to provide spaces of rehabilitation for those convicted of crimes. For the Quakers who established these early jails, imprisonment was to be an experience of sanctuary and solitary reflection, not suspicion and solitary confinement (Graber 2011).

The institutionalization of caring work done in the home was not necessarily an act of 'secularization'. Across Europe and North America, many hospitals were funded and staffed by religious organizations, Protestant, Roman Catholic, and Jewish (Klassen 2011). Often founded quite literally in houses, the small-scale beginnings of many hospitals had the actual appearance of home. Understanding their mission as extending beyond the sanctuary and into society, religious groups proliferated the institutionalization of the home quite literally, through orphanages, maternity homes, and halfway houses. Addressing a wide range of human needs, as well as what many religious groups considered to be deviance, institutional homes constructed their social relations not on the model of the biological family, but on notions of spiritual kinship or responsibility.

Indian residential schools

In North America, the 'Indian residential school' or boarding school is perhaps the most trenchant example of the interplay of sanctuary and suspicion in the

FIGURE 8.5: Photograph by Oliver Buell of the Fort Qu'Appelle Indian Industrial School in Lebret, Saskatchewan with tents, carts, and teepees outside the fence, c. 1885. This image demonstrates how parents travelled to be close to their children in residential schools. O.B. Buell / Library and Archives Canada / PA-182246.

not-family home. One of the most devastating outcomes of the colonial assertion that nomadic lives were inferior to settled ones was the institution of residential schools, which forcibly took Indigenous children away from their families, languages, spiritual traditions, and homelands. In both Canada and the United States, the church and government leaders who established residential schools held deep suspicions of Indigenous models of homemaking as supposedly 'pagan' and problematically migratory (Child 2018; Milloy 1999; Kelm 1999). Missionaries argued that because 'the habits of the Indian are nomadic', children needed to be taken from their parents to attend school on a consistent daily schedule (Whittington 1906).

Nineteenth- and early-twentieth-century residential schools in Canada and the US were established through partnerships between the government and Christian churches. These schools, designed to be group 'homes' where Indigenous children would be transformed into Christians, were, in the words of Ojibwe historian Brenda Child, 'symbolic of American colonialism at its most genocidal' (2018: 38). Similarly, in 2015, the Truth and Reconciliation Commission of Canada declared these residential schools to be a form of 'cultural genocide'. Often forcibly taken from their families, forbidden to speak their languages, and abused both emotionally and sexually by their teachers and guardians, these children suffered from a most profound sense of homesickness, quite literally. Many children died at residential schools, from starvation, violence, or disease (Miller 1996; Milloy 1999). 'Housing' children without providing them with a home, residential schools have had devastating intergenerational consequences.

The materiality and movability of Indigenous dwellings was only one justification offered by missionaries and government officials for residential schools, but it was a powerful rationalization that was backed up by arguments from both 'hygiene' and religion (Lux 2001; Kelm 1999). Residential schools were the large-scale imposition of a colonial Christian vision of religion and home on Indigenous children and their families; this vision was oriented by convictions about sanctuary and suspicion that carry legacies of trauma and injustice that are still on-going.

Maternity homes

Notorious thanks to movies such as *The Magdalene Sisters* (2002) and *Philomena* (2013), 'maternity homes' (in the limited sense I use it here) were institutions for unmarried pregnant women. 'Unwed mothers' were often sent to these homes by their families, so that their time of 'confinement' (i.e. childbirth) would occur in secret. The babies would usually then be given up for adoption. A home in only the most perverse sense of the word, these institutions were found throughout North America and Europe. Called 'Magdalene Homes' in Ireland in homage to Mary Magdalene, often considered a prostitute in Christian tradition, these homes were places where young 'fallen women' deemed inappropriately sexually active were hidden away so that the mark of their supposed shame – their pregnant belly – would go unseen by their community, even if their absence from their own natal homes did not go unnoticed.

The vision of maternity homes for unwed mothers grew out of a particular theological premise shared by both Christians and Jews, which has understood female sexuality as requiring containment inside heterosexual marriage (Marks 1992: 121). In the context of England, historian Lara Marks has shown that when combined with poverty, immigration, and religious diversity (i.e. not only Anglican or other Protestant women, but also Jewish and Catholic women), unwed pregnant women faced serious challenges. In an era of the growing hospitalization of childbirth, even by the 1920s many hospitals did not admit unmarried pregnant women for care. In the breach, Protestant, Catholic, and Jewish charitable organizations established maternity homes out of a complex mix of motivations: to care for vulnerable women and their babies, for the purpose of 'saving souls', and to preserve the 'respectability' of their religious communities (Murray 2004: 262; Marks 1992).

Maternity homes and forced adoption practices grew out of a mix of religious motivations and social service approaches. Indigenous communities were particularly hard hit by the practice of forced adoption, in what has come to be called the 'sixties scoop'. This refers to a time, especially during the 1960s, when Indigenous children under the care of child protection services were taken from their families and communities and placed among settler families (Sinclair 2007). Even today, a large number of Indigenous children in Canada live under the care of the state, outside of Indigenous homes, in part because of on-going racism and inequitable government funding for Indigenous child welfare (Blackstock 2011; CBC News 2016).

With changing sexual mores and the rise of feminism in the 1960s, the idea that a young unmarried woman needed to hide her pregnancy and to automatically give up her child for adoption has fallen by the wayside. But a generation of young women who relinquished or lost their mid-century babies has not forgotten, as a growing number of both church-based and government inquiries demonstrates (Carlson 2013; Galloway 2016). In one downtown Toronto neighbourhood, the shifting sensibilities around women's roles as mothers, wed or unwed, can still be read on the side of a building. What is now the 'Carmelite Day Nursery', a daycare centre and preschool housed within a Carmelite convent, was once the 'Carmelite Girls' Home', an orphanage for girls and young women. There are no longer enough Carmelite sisters with vocations to work in the daycare, so it is privately staffed; orphanages and maternity homes are similarly in decline, for a complicated set of reasons, including the rise of foster care for children.

In-between homes

Another model of religiously oriented homes not based on family ties includes the homeless shelter, which provides a liminal space for people who are 'in-between' homes. The homeless shelter may provide a space for a night or two, or even longer, for a resident who has no other place to stay. Some of these residents considered 'hard to house' may prefer living on the streets to inhabiting a home, at least within the social and economic constraints they face (Gurstein and Small 2005). Others may strongly desire to find more permanent dwellings. But as religious studies scholar Amy Fisher (2015) has argued, there are ways that even a homeless shelter could be understood as a 'homeful' place, depending on the circle of people who inhabit it.

Another example of a religiously based institutional home that disrupts the idea of what counts as 'family' is the network of L'Arche homes found throughout North America and Europe. Founded in the 1960s by Catholic theologian Jean Vanier and others, L'Arche is a non-profit organization made up of homes in which people with and without intellectual disabilities live together not as professionals and patients, but as a community, or even family. With prayer, shared meals, and the work of home life shaping their days, the people living in a L'Arche home attempt relationships of 'mutuality' that bring risk and emotional commitment to all participants (Cushing and Lewis 2002; Whitney-Brown 2019). It was all the more devastating, then, for members of L'Arche to learn of the revelations, shortly after the death in 2019 of Vanier at the age of ninety, that he had sexually preyed on many non-disabled women living in L'Arche homes. A revered leader with many accolades, Vanier manipulated these women through a mix of spiritual authority and emotional violence, often within the space of their own shared home (Brown 2020; L'Arche International 2020). When I first included L'Arche homes in this chapter, I did so to exemplify home as sanctuary. By the time of copy-editing, L'Arche had also become an example of home as a place of suspicion, fear, and violence.

CONCLUSION: HOME, RELIGION, AND THE FORCE OF DESIGN

As built spaces, homes and institutions assert the 'force of design' on ritual practice (Klassen 2012). Whether a woman gives birth in a home or hospital, a couple is wed in a backyard or a sanctuary, or a father dies in his living room or in a hospital ward, the domestic or institutional qualities of the space matter for who participates in these life transitions and how they do so. As people perform rites of passage with both creativity and obedience to tradition, they do so in designed spaces that shape their ritual practice, their bodily experience, and their social relationships. Buildings, structures, and landscapes are commodified and historicized artefacts that constrain and encourage diverse choreographies of ritual.

Architectural historian Neil Harris argues that even buildings have life cycles shaped by 'architectural ritualism', in which rites of passage mark their construction, 'opening', preservation, decay, and even destruction. Both homes and institutional religious buildings can be marked by rituals of blessing, consecration, deconsecration, and willed destruction. Harris shows the importance of paying attention to the ways that built forms are not simply sites for ritual, but also 'contribute so powerfully to the mythification of social reality' (1999: 165). To think about religion and home at the levels of both family and institution requires attention to the materiality of the built forms that shape ritual practice.

In recent years, some survivors of residential schools for Indigenous children have decided that the destruction of school buildings is a necessary ritual response to the trauma of such schools. In Alert Bay, a community on a small island north of the larger Vancouver Island in British Columbia, this decision took a while to emerge. After considering whether or not to turn the Anglican St. Michael's Residential School into a community centre, the Kwakwaka'wakw community decided to destroy the building in a 'ceremony of demolition'

(Lehmann 2015). The residential school no longer looms over the bay from its perch on the hill, as a reminder of a time when the church and the state collaborated on a vision of a 'home away from home' that would 'civilize' Indigenous children. This vision of home was meant to strip away their language and their rituals, teaching them to forget their relationship to land, to family, and to their own stories of creation.

Even when St. Michael's School remained standing, the 'Namgis First Nation had built new communal structures in which to remember and ritualize their nation's past. One of these buildings is the U'mista Cultural Centre, housing a remarkable collection of bentwood boxes and ceremonial regalia which had been stolen or seized under the Canadian anti-potlatch law, and which the 'Namgis First Nation had successfully repatriated from museums (U'mista Cultural Centre 2020). The former United Church has become a hostel for tourists who have come to the island, where they can visit the new Big House. There, they will learn about Kwakwaka'wakw traditions and watch the dances of the women, men, and children of the T'sasala Dance Group.

Considering the complicated relationship of religion and home at different scales of analysis – including the individual, the family, the institution, the religious community, the law, and the state – requires telling particular stories about particular homes. Such a consideration also requires reflecting more broadly on home as a concept and ideal for which people and communities strive. At once sustained and disputed, rehearsed and improvised, material and imagined, religion and home are concepts that share much in common: both carry great power, comfort, pain, and love. As sites of relationships and rituals, homes are necessarily complicated places that can foster creativity but also coercion; much the same could be said for religion itself, as a site of memory, practice, and imagination.

NOTES

Chapter 2

1. I am grateful to doctoral candidate Ipek Mehmetoglu, School of Architecture, McGill University, social historian Peter Gossage, and recent teenager Charlie Adams-Gossage, for assistance and inspiration.

Chapter 3

1. Many thanks go to Matt Lasner for his incisive comments on multiple versions of this manuscript and for pointing me towards much of the relevant reading, as well as for our many conversations about housing over the past years. This chapter has also benefited enormously from the critical feedback of Despina Stratigakos, Max Hirsh and Alexander von Hoffmann. A final word of thanks goes to Reinhold Martin and the organizers of the Wohnungsfrage workshop at Haus der Kulturen der Welt in October 2015, which helped me to refine my ideas.
2. At the same time, Wright's houses were envisioned as part of a larger suburban plan, the Quadruple Block Plan. Made up of clusters of four single-family homes on a grid, this plan can be read as an idealistic re-imagination of America's rapid suburban development, which subdividers and speculative developers, rather than architects, were leading. See Levine 2015.
3. This account is based on Seebohm-Rowntree 1910.
4. The Federal Housing Administration was not interested in underwriting experimental house forms, and 'non-conforming plans' were ineligible for government loans (Harris 2010).
5. I am referring here to discussions about 'technology transfer' in STS Studies. For an example of how ideas about dwelling culture travelled across the networks of the Cold War, see Oldenziel and Zachmann 2009; Anderson 2009.
6. Thanks to Max Hirsh for pointing this out to me.

7. For overview histories of mass housing, see Dufaux and Fourcaut 2004; Urban 2011.
8. For France, see Horne 2002.
9. For example, Jean Renaudie's star-shape, angular design for Ivry was a collection of more than one hundred unique dwelling units and collective amenities (Cupers 2014).
10. Although the image of rental housing in the United States is apartment blocks and slabs, the largest number of rented units are single-family homes.
11. An example is the multifaceted history of the condominium, which challenges neat typologies of private and common housing. See Lasner 2012; Rao 2013.
12. Thanks to Matt Lasner for this point.
13. I use the term *shantytown* to refer to an aggregation of self-built dwellings on squatted or pirated land, to distinguish it from *slum* as a more general term that can denote any type of built environment.
14. Among other data sources, Davis (2006) uses reports such as that of the United Nations Human Settlements Programme 2003.
15. Nevertheless, particularly during the late colonial period, some administrations built housing for colonized subjects as a way to organize urbanization and development, for example in Kenya, where thousands were housed in bachelor as well as family housing. See Harris and Hay 2007.
16. Thanks to Max Hirsh for pointing this out to me.

Chapter 5

1. Anonymous rhyme quoted in Oakley ([1974] 1976: 5–6).

Chapter 7

1. From 1911 to 1981, white-collar workers rose from less than 14 percent of the British working population to 43 percent. In the United States between 1900 and 1980, they increased from 17.5 to 52 percent (Edgell 1993: 66), reaching perhaps as much as 70 percent (Goldthorpe et al. 1968–69) of American society.
2. This remains the case even after Martha Stewart's enforced hiatus from MSLO leadership following her 2004 conviction for obstruction of justice and subsequent return to MSLO as Chief Creative Officer. In October 2014, MSLO production was outsourced to Meredith Corporation in a ten-year fixed-term deal with MSLO staff continuing to deliver the content. MSLO was sold to Sequential Brands Group in 2015 (Sebastian 2015) and Sequential Brands agreed to sell the loss-making MSLO to Marquee Brands in April 2019.

Chapter 8

1. I am very grateful to Magdalene Klassen for her editorial suggestions, including the recommendation to reread 'The Uncanny'. I also thank Despina Stratigakos for her comments and patience, Judith Weisenfeld for pointing me to the Umbra image database, and Amy E. Fisher for thinking over the topic of religion and home together with me.

BIBLIOGRAPHY

Primary sources

A Society Lady (1923), *The A.B.C. of Etiquette by A Society Lady*, London: Drane's.
Beck, S., L. Bertholle and J. Child (1961), *Mastering the Art of French Cooking*, New York: Knopf.
Beecher, Catharine E. and Harriet Beecher Stowe (1869), *The American Woman's Home*, Boston, MA: A.H. Brown.
Beyer, G.H. (1953), *The Cornell Kitchen: Product Design Through Research*, Ithaca, NY: New York State College of Home Economics in association with The Cornell University Housing Research Center.
Brown, C. (1962), 'Two Houses in One: A Wing for the Children and a Wing for You', *House Beautiful*, August: 55–62, 115.
CBC Digital Archives (1967), 'There's no place for the state in the bedrooms of the nation'. Available online: http://www.cbc.ca/archives/entry/omnibus-bill-theres-no-place-for-the-state-in-the-bedrooms-of-the-nation (accessed 20 May 2020).
Christie, A. (1920), *The Mysterious Affair at Styles*, London/New York: John Lane/Bodley Head. Available online: http://www.gutenberg.org/files/863/863-h/863-h.htm#linka2HCH0013 (accessed 20 May 2020).
David, E. (1950), *A Book of Mediterranean Food*, London: Lehmann.
de Beauvoir, S. ([1949] 1997), *The Second Sex*, ed. and trans. H.M. Parshley, London: Vintage.
Doherty, P. (1965), 'Give your Child a Room for Christmas', *House Beautiful*, December: 155–59.
Don, M. and S. Don (1999), *Fork to Fork*, London: Conran Octopus.
Downing, A.J. ([1850] 1969), *The Architecture of Country Houses*, New York: Dover.
Du Bois, W.E.B. ([1903] 2014), *The Souls of Black Folk*, New York: Pocket.
Engels, F. ([1872] 1988), 'The Housing Question', in *Marx/Engels: Collected Works*, vol. 23, 317–91, Moscow: Progress Publishers.
Forrester, S. (1943), 'Ready-Sliced Bread Favored', *New York Times*, 26 January: 18. Available online: https://www.nytimes.com/1943/01/26/archives/readysliced-bread-favored.html (accessed 20 May 2020).

Frederick, C. (1913), *The New Housekeeping: Efficiency Studies in Home Management*, Garden City, NY: Doubleday, Page.
Frederick, C. (1919), *Household Engineering: Scientific Management in the Home*, Chicago: American School of Home Economics.
Freud, S. (1992), *Letters of Sigmund Freud*, ed. E.L. Freud, trans. T. Stern and J. Stern, New York: Dover.
Freud, S. ([1919] 2003), *The Uncanny*, trans. D. McLintock, London: Penguin.
Friedan, B. (1963), *The Feminine Mystique*, New York: Norton.
Giedion, S. (1948), *Mechanization Takes Command: A Contribution to Anonymous History*, New York: Oxford University Press.
Gilbreth, L.M. (1938), *The Home-maker and Her Job*, New York: D. Appleton-Century.
Good, E. (1969), *Tableware*, London: Macdonald in association with the Council of Industrial Design.
Hitchcock, H.-R. and P. Johnson ([1932] 1995), *The International Style*, New York: Norton.
Kamprad, I. (1976), 'The Testament of a Furniture Dealer', Inter IKEA Systems B.V. Available online: https://www.ikea.com/ms/sv_SE/pdf/reports-downloads/the-testament-of-a-furniture-dealer.pdf (accessed 20 May 2020).
Keats, J.C. (1957), *The Crack in the Picture Window*, Boston, MA: Houghton Mifflin.
Klepfisz, I. (1990), *A Few Words in the Mother Tongue: Poems Selected and New (1971–1990)*, Portland, OR: Eighth Mountain Press.
Kondo, M. (2015), *The Life-Changing Magic of Tidying Up: The Japanese Art of Decluttering and Organizing*, London: Vermilion.
Kyrk, H. (1933), *Economic Problems of the Family*, New York: Harpers.
Le Corbusier ([1925] 1987), *The Decorative Art of Today*, trans. J. Dunnet, Cambridge, MA: MIT Press.
Leigh, M. (1983), *Abigail's Party and Goose Pimples*, London: Penguin.
Lewis, S. (1920), *Main Street*, San Diego, CA: Harcourt, Brace & Howe.
Loos, A. ([1913] 1970), 'Ornament and Crime', in *Programs and Manifestoes on 20th Century Architecture*, ed. U. Conrads, trans. M. Bullock, 19–24, Cambridge, MA: MIT Press.
Lowrie, J. (1965), *Practical Homemaking*, London: Oldbourne.
Magdalene Sisters, The (2002), dir. P. Mullan [film], Santa Monica, CA: Miramax.
Manners, D.X. (1962), 'What Makes a Good Room for a Child?', *House Beautiful*, August: 63–65, 113.
Mary Poppins (1964), dir. R. Stevenson [film], Burbank, CA: Walt Disney.
Masters, W.H. and V.E. Johnson (1966), *Human Sexual Response*, Boston, MA: Little, Brown.
Merivale, M. ([1938] 1944), *Furnishing the Small Home*, London: The Studio.
Mytting, L. (2015), *Norwegian Wood: Chopping, Stacking, and Drying Wood the Scandinavian Way*, trans. R. Ferguson, London: MacLehose.
Oliver, J. (2007), *Jamie at Home: Cook Your Way to the Good Life*, London: Michael Joseph.
Philomena (2013), dir. S. Frears [film], New York: Weinstein Company.
Post, E. (1922), *Etiquette in Society, in Business, in Politics and at Home*, New York: Funk & Wagnalls.
Semiotics of the Kitchen (1975), dir. M. Rosler [film], New York: Electronic Arts Intermix.

Soule, G. (1953), 'New Kitchen Built to Fit Your Wife', *Popular Science*, September: 172–76.
Spock, B. (1946), *Baby and Child Care*, New York: Pocket Books.
Spry, C. (1942), *Come into the Garden, Cook*, London: J.M. Dent.
Spry, C. and R. Hume (1956), *Constance Spry Cookery Book*, London: J.M. Dent.
Spry, C. and R. Hume (1961), *Hostess*, ed. A. Marr, London: J.M. Dent.
Stewart, M. (1982), *Entertaining*, New York: Clarkson Potter.
Stewart, M. (2009), *Martha Stewart's Dinner at Home: 52 Quick Meals to Cook for Family and Friends*, New York: Clarkson Potter.
Tocqueville, A. de ([1840] 1968), *Democracy in America*, 2 vols., ed. J.P. Mayer and M. Lerner, trans. G. Lawrence, New York: Fontana Library.
Trivizas, E. and H. Oxenbury (1993), *The Three Little Wolves and the Big Bad Pig*, London: Heinemann.
Vaux, C. (1864), *Villas and Cottages: A Series of Designs Prepared for Execution in the United States*, New York: Harper.
Veblen, T. ([1899] 1970), *The Theory of the Leisure Class: An Economic Study of Institutions*, intro. C. Wright Mills, London: Unwin Books.
Walker, A. (1983), 'In Search of Our Mothers' Gardens', in A. Walker, *In Search of Our Mothers' Gardens: Womanist Prose*, 231–44, New York: Harcourt Brace Jovanovich.
Webb, S. (1921), *The Story of the Durham Miners*, London, Fabian Society.
Wheeler, Joan (1932), *The New Home Encyclopaedia*, London: Odhams Press.
Whittington, R. (1906), *The British Columbia Indian and His Future*, Toronto: Department of Missionary Literature of the Methodist Church, Canada. Available online: http://archive.org/details/britishcolumbiin00whitrich (accessed 20 May 2020).
Woman's Own (1967), Woman's Own *Book of Modern Homemaking*, London: George Newnes.
Woolf, V. ([1932] 1975), 'Great Men's Houses', in V. Woolf, *The London Scene: Five Essays*, 23–29, New York: Hallman.
Wright, M. and R. Wright ([1950] 1954), *Guide to Easier Living: 1,000 Ways to Make Housework Faster, Easier and More Rewarding*, revised edition, New York: Simon & Schuster.

Secondary sources

Aalbers, M.B. (2008), 'The Financialization of Home and the Mortgage Market Crisis', *Competition and Change*, 12 (2): 148–66.
Aalbers, M.B. and B. Christophers (2014), 'Centring Housing in Political Economy', *Housing, Theory, and Society*, 31 (4): 373–94.
Abrams, B.L. (2008), *Hollywood Bohemians: Transgressive Sexuality and the Selling of the Movieland Dream*, Jefferson, NC: McFarland.
Adams, A. (1995), 'The Eichler Home: Intention and Experience in Postwar Suburbia', in E. Collins Cromley and C.L. Hudgins (eds.), *Perspectives in Vernacular Architecture*, vol. 5: *Gender, Class, and Shelter*, 164–78, Knoxville, TN: University of Tennessee Press.
Adams, A. (1996), *Architecture in the Family Way: Doctors, Houses, and Women, 1870–1900*, Montreal/Kingston: McGill-Queen's University Press.
Adams, A. (2008), *Medicine by Design: The Architect and the Modern Hospital, 1893–1943*, Minneapolis, MN: University of Minnesota Press.

Adams, A. (2010a), 'The Power of Pink: Children's Bedrooms and Gender Identity', *FKW: Zeitschrift für geschlechterforschung und visuelle kultur*, 50: 58–69.

Adams, A. (2010b), 'Sex and the Single Building: The Weston Havens House, 1941–2001', *Buildings & Landscapes: Journal of the Vernacular Architecture Forum*, 17 (1): 82–97.

Adams, A. and C. Macdonell (2016), 'Making Himself at Home: Cormier, Trudeau, and the Architecture of Domestic Masculinity', *Winterthur Portfolio*, 50 (2/3): 151–89.

Adams, M.L. (1997), *The Trouble with Normal: Postwar Youth and the Making of Heterosexuality*, Toronto: University of Toronto Press.

Ahmed, S. (2006), 'Orientations: Toward a Queer Phenomenology', *GLQ: A Journal of Lesbian and Gay Studies*, 12 (4): 543–74.

Akcan, E. (2012), *Architecture in Translation: Germany, Turkey, and the Modern House*, Durham, NC: Duke University Press.

Albrecht, D., R. Schonfeld and L.S. Shapiro, eds. (2001), *Russel Wright: Creating American Lifestyle*, New York: Cooper-Hewitt, Smithsonian Design Museum and Abrams.

Alonso, P.I. and H. Palmarola (2009), 'A Panel's Tale: The Soviet KPD System and the Politics of Assemblage', *AA Files*, 59: 25–35.

Amato, P.R. and S. Irving (2006), 'Historical Trends in Divorce and Dissolution in the United States', in M.A. Fine and J.H. Harvey (eds.), *The Handbook of Divorce and Relationship Dissolution*, 41–57, Mahwah, NJ: Lawrence Erlbaum.

Ames, K.L. (1992), *Death in the Dining Room and Other Tales of Victorian Culture*, Philadelphia, PA: Temple University Press.

Anderson, B. (1993), *Britain's Secret Slaves: An Investigation into the Plight of Overseas Domestic Workers*, London: Anti-Slavery International and Kalayaan.

Anderson, B. (2000), *Doing the Dirty Work: The Global Politics of Domestic Labor*, London: Zed Books.

Anderson, M.J. (2015), *The American Census: A Social History*, 2nd edition, New Haven, CT: Yale University Press.

Anderson, R. (2009), 'USA/USSR: Architecture and War', *Grey Room*, 34: 80–103.

André, R. (1981), *Homemakers: The Forgotten Workers*, Chicago, IL: University of Chicago Press.

Annin, P. (1996), 'Slumbering Around', *Newsweek*, 128 (19): 57.

Archer, J. (2008), *Architecture and Suburbia: From English Villa to American Dream House, 1690–2000*, Minneapolis, MN: University of Minnesota Press.

Ashton, D. (2013), *Hanukkah in America: A History*, New York: New York University Press.

Attfield, J., ed. (1992), *Utility Reassessed: The Role of Ethics in the Practice of Design*, Manchester: Manchester University Press.

Attfield, J. (2000), *Wild Things: The Material Culture of Everyday Life*, Oxford: Berg.

Attfield, J. (2007), *Bringing Modernity Home: Writings on Popular Design and Material Culture*, Manchester: Manchester University Press.

Attfield, J. and P. Kirkham, eds. (1995), *A View from the Interior: Feminism, Women and Design*, London: Prentice-Hall.

Baader, M.T. (1998), 'From "the Priestess of the Home" to "the Rabbi's Brilliant Daughter": Concepts of Jewish Womanhood and Progressive Germanness in *Die Deborah* and the *American Israelite*, 1854–1900', *Leo Baeck Institute Yearbook*, 43 (1): 47–72.

Bachelard, G. (1958), *The Poetics of Space*, trans. M. Jolas, Boston, MA: Beacon.

Bakan, A. and D. Stasiulis, eds. (1997), *Not One of the Family: Foreign Domestic Workers in Canada*, Toronto: University of Toronto Press.

Balaban, U. (2011), 'The Enclosure of Urban Space and Consolidation of the Capitalist Land Regime in Turkish Cities', *Urban Studies*, 48 (10): 2162–79.

Bastia, T. (2015), '"Looking After Granny": A Transnational Ethic of Care and Responsibility', *Geoforum*, 64: 121–29.

Beecher, M.A. (2003), 'A Place for Everything: The Influence of Storage Innovations on Modern American Domesticity, 1900–1955', PhD dissertation, University of Iowa, Iowa City, IA.

Belisle, D. (2011), *Retail Nation: Department Stores and the Making of Modern Canada*, Vancouver, BC: UBC Press.

Bellafante, G. (2016), 'Airbnb and the Battle of Suitcase Alley', *New York Times*, 24 June. Available online: http://www.nytimes.com/2016/06/26/nyregion/airbnb-and-the-battle-of-suitcase-alley.html?_r=0 (accessed 20 May 2020).

Benevolo, L. (1977), *History of Modern Architecture*, vol. 2, *The Modern Movement*, Cambridge, MA: MIT Press.

Benjamin, D.N., D. Stea and D. Saile, eds. (1995), *The Home: Words, Interpretations, Meanings and Environments*, Aldershot: Avebury.

Benoit, C., I.L. Bourgeault and R. Davis-Floyd (2004), *Reconceiving Midwifery*, Montreal/Kingston: McGill-Queen's University Press.

Benton, C. (1990), 'Le Corbusier: Furniture and the Interior', *Journal of Design History*, 3 (2/3): 103–24.

Benton, T. (1987), *The Villas of Le Corbusier*, New Haven, CT: Yale University Press.

Bergdoll, B. and P. Christensen (2008), *Home Delivery: Fabricating the Modern Dwelling*, Basel: Birkhäuser/New York: Museum of Modern Art.

Berlinische Galerie, ed. (2015), *Radikal Modern: Planen und Bauen im Berlin der 1960er Jahre*, Berlin: Wasmuth.

Berner, E. (1998), *Defending a Place in the City: Localities and the Struggle for Urban Land in Metro Manila*, Manila: Ateneo De Manila University Press.

Bervoets, L. (2010), 'Defeating Public Enemy Number One: Mediating Housing in the Netherlands', *Home Cultures*, 7 (2): 178–96.

Bessel, R. (2003), 'Catastrophe and Democracy: The Legacy of the World Wars in Germany', in A. McElligott and T. Kirk (eds.), *Working Towards the Führer: Essays in Honour of Sir Ian Kershaw*, 15–40, Manchester: Manchester University Press.

Betts, J.L. (n.d.), 'Historical Divorce Rate Statistics', Lovetoknow.com. Available online: http://divorce.lovetoknow.com/Historical_Divorce_Rate_Statistics (accessed 20 May 2020).

Betts, P. (2004), *The Authority of Everyday Objects: A Cultural History of West German Industrial Design*, Berkeley, CA: University of California Press.

Bikova, M. (2010), 'The Snake in the Grass of Gender Equality: Au Pairing in Women-friendly Norway', in L.W. Isaksen (ed.), *Global Care Work: Gender and Migration in Nordic Societies*, 49–68, Lund: Nordic Academic Press.

Binford, H. (1985), *The First Suburbs: Residential Communities on the Boston Periphery, 1815–1860*, Chicago, IL: University of Chicago Press.

Binkley, S. (2008), 'Liquid Consumption: Anti-Consumerism and the Fetishized De-fetishization of Commodities', *Cultural Studies*, 22 (5): 599–623.

Blackstock, C. (2011), 'The Canadian Human Rights Tribunal on First Nations Child Welfare: Why if Canada Wins, Equality and Justice Lose', *Children and Youth Services Review*, 33 (1): 187–94.

Blaszczyk, R.L. (1997), '"Where Mrs. Homemaker is Never Forgotten": Lucy Maltby and Home Economics at Corning Glass Works, 1929–1965', in S. Stage and V.B. Vincenti (eds.), *Rethinking Home Economics: Woman and the History of a Profession*, 163–80, Ithaca, NY: Cornell University Press.

Blaszczyk, R.L. (2012), *The Color Revolution*, Cambridge, MA: MIT Press.

Blau, E. (1999), *The Architecture of Red Vienna, 1919–1934*, Cambridge, MA: MIT Press.

Blume, T. (2015), 'The Bauhaus Celebrates: Parties as Communal Art', in special issue 'Kollektiv' of *Bauhaus: Die Zeitschrift der Stiftung Bauhaus Dessau*, 7: 32–39.

Blunt, A. and R. Dowling (2006), *Home*, Abingdon: Routledge.

Bobrow-Strain, A. (2012), *White Bread: A Social History of the Store-Bought Loaf*, London: Beacon.

Bocarejo, D., M. José and A. Rivadulla (2014), 'Beautifying the Slum: Cable Car Fetishism in Cazucá, Colombia', *International Journal of Urban and Regional Research*, 38 (6): 2025–41.

Bonaiuto, M., E. Bilotta and A. Stolfa (2010), 'Feng Shui and Environmental Psychology: A Critical Comparison', *Journal of Architectural and Planning Research*, 27 (1): 23–34.

Boonyabancha, S. (2011), 'Trusting That People Can Do It', in C.E. Smith (ed.), *Design with the Other 90%: Cities*, 61–70, New York: Cooper-Hewitt, Smithsonian Design Museum.

Bourdieu, P. (1984), *Distinction: A Social Critique of the Judgement of Taste*, trans. R. Nice, Cambridge, MA: Harvard University Press.

Bourdieu, P. (1990), *The Logic of Practice*, trans. R. Nice, Stanford, CA: Stanford University Press.

Bourdieu, P. (1991), *Language and Symbolic Power*, ed. J.B. Thompson, trans. G. Raymond and M. Adamson, Cambridge: Polity Press.

Bowlby, R. (1987), '"The Problem with No Name": Rereading Friedan's *The Feminine Mystique*', *Feminist Review*, 27: 61–75.

Boym, S. (2008), *The Future of Nostalgia*, New York: Basic Books.

Bristol, K. (1991), 'The Pruitt-Igoe Myth', *Journal of Architectural Education*, 44 (3): 163–71.

Bromley, R. (2003), 'Peru 1957–1977: How Time and Place Influences John Turner's Ideas on Housing Policy', *Habitat International*, 27 (2): 271–92.

Bromley, R. (2004), 'Power, Property, and Poverty: Why De Soto's "Mystery of Capital" Cannot Be Solved', in A. Roy and N. AlSayyad (eds.), *Urban Informality: Transnational Perspectives from the Middle East, Latin America, and South Asia*, 271–88, Lanham, MD: Lexington Books.

Brottman, M. (2007), 'Debauchery Next Door: The Boundaries of Shame in Abigail's Party', *Quarterly Review of Film and Video*, 24 (4): 317–23.

Brown, I. (2020), 'The Jean Vanier I Knew, and the One I Didn't'. *The Globe and Mail*, 29 February. Available online: https://www.theglobeandmail.com/canada/article-the-jean-vanier-i-knew-and-the-one-i-didnt/ (accessed 25 April 2020).

Brown, K.M. (2001), *Mama Lola: A Vodou Priestess in Brooklyn*, Berkeley, CA: University of California Press.

Bryceson, D. (2000), 'Disappearing Peasantries? Rural Labor Redundancy in the Neo-Liberal Era and Beyond', in D. Bryceson, C. Kay, and J. Mooij (eds.), *Disappearing Peasantries: Rural Labor in Africa, Asia and Latin America*, 299–326, London: ITDG.

Buchli, V.A. (1999), *An Archaeology of Socialism*, Oxford: Berg.
Buchli, V.A. (2013), *An Anthropology of Architecture*, London: Bloomsbury.
Bud, R. (2009), *Penicillin: Triumph and Tragedy*, Oxford: Oxford University Press.
Bullock, N. (1988), 'First the Kitchen: Then the Façade', *Journal of Design History*, 1 (3/4): 177–92.
Bullock, N. (2002), *Building the Postwar World: Modern Architecture and Reconstruction in Britain*, London: Routledge.
Burns, E. (2016), *1920: The Year that Made the Decade Roar*, New York: Pegasus.
Butler, J. (1990), *Gender Trouble and the Subversion of Identity*, New York: Routledge.
Butler, J. (1997), 'Performative Acts and Gender Constitution: An Essay in Phenomenology and Feminist Theory', in K. Conboy, N. Medina and S. Stanbury (eds.), *Writing on the Body: Female Embodiment and Feminist Theory*, 401–18, New York: Columbia University Press.
Caldeira, T.P.R. (1996), 'Fortified Enclaves: The New Urban Segregation', *Public Culture*, 8 (2): 303–28.
Calleman, C. (2010), 'Cultural Exchange or Cheap Domestic Labor? Constructions of "Au Pair" in Four Nordic Countries', in L.W. Isaksen (ed.), *Global Care Work: Gender and Migration in Nordic Societies*, 69–96, Lund: Nordic Academic Press.
Campanella, T.J. (2008), *The Concrete Dragon: China's Urban Revolution and What It Means for the World*, New York: Princeton Architectural Press.
Cannadine, D. (1990), *The Decline and Fall of the British Aristocracy*, New Haven, CT: Yale University Press.
Carbone, C. (2009), 'Staging the Kitchen Debate: How Splitnik Got Normalized in the United States', in R. Oldenziel and K. Zachmann (eds.), *Cold War Kitchen: Americanization, Technology, and European Users*, 59–81, Cambridge, MA: MIT Press.
Carby, H. (2007), 'White Woman Listen! Black Feminism and the Boundaries of Sisterhood', in Ann Gray, Jan Campbell, Mark Erickson, Stuart Hanson, and Helen Wood (eds.), *CCCS Selected Working Papers*, vol. 2, 737–57, London: Routledge.
Carlson, K.B. (2013), 'United Church Weighs Next Steps after Internal Report on Forced Adoptions', *The Globe and Mail*, 30 October. Available online: https://www.theglobeandmail.com/news/national/united-church-weighs-next-steps-after-internal-report-on-forced-adoptions/article15177055/ (accessed 20 May 2020).
Castells, M., L. Goh, R.Y.W. Kwok and T.L. Kee (1988), *Economic Development and Housing Policy in the Asian Pacific Rim: A Comparative Study of Hong Kong, Singapore, and Shenzhen Special Economic Zone*, Berkeley, CA: Institute of Urban and Regional Development.
Castillo, G. (2010), *Cold War on the Home Front: The Soft Power of Midcentury Design*, Minneapolis, MN: University of Minnesota Press.
CBC News (2016), 'Canada Discriminates Against Children on Reserves, Tribunal Rules', 26 January. Available online: https://www.cbc.ca/news/indigenous/canada-discriminates-against-children-on-reserves-tribunal-rules-1.3419480 (accessed 20 May 2020).
Çelik, Z. (1997), *Urban Forms and Colonial Confrontations: Algiers under French Rule*, Berkeley, CA: University of California Press.
Chalana, M. (2010), 'Slumdogs vs. Millionaires: Balancing Urban Informality and Global Modernity in Mumbai, India', *Journal of Architectural Education*, 63 (2): 25–37.
Chapman, T. and J. Hockey, eds. (1999), *Ideal Homes? Social Change and Domestic Life*, London: Routledge.

Chawla, D. (2014), *Home, Uprooted: Oral Histories of India's Partition*, New York: Fordham University Press.

Chen, X., L. Wang and R. Kundu (2009), 'Localizing the Production of Global Cities: A Comparison of New Town Developments around Shanghai and Kolkata', *City and Community*, 8 (4): 433–65.

Child, B.J. (2018), 'The Boarding School as Metaphor', *Journal of American Indian Education*, 57 (1): 37–57.

Chokor, B.A. (2005), 'Changing Urban Housing Form and Organization in Nigeria: Lessons for Community Planning', *Planning Perspectives*, 20 (1): 69–96.

Christie, A. and J. Curran (2011), *Clues to Christie: The Definitive Guide to Miss Marple, Hercule Poirot and all of Agatha Christie's Mysteries*, London: HarperCollins.

Cieraad, I., ed. (1999), *At Home: An Anthropology of Domestic Space*, Syracuse, NY: Syracuse University Press.

Cittaslow (2019), 'Cittaslow List'. Available online: https://www.cittaslow.org/sites/default/files/content/page/files/246/cittaslow_list_november_2019.pdf (accessed 17 January 2020).

Clarke, A.J. (2001), 'The Aesthetics of Social Aspiration', in D. Miller (ed.), *Home Possessions: Material Cultures Behind Closed Doors*, 23–45, Oxford: Berg.

Cohen, J.-L. (2013), *Le Corbusier: An Atlas of Modern Landscapes*, New York: Museum of Modern Art.

Cohen, L.A. (1986), 'Embellishing a Life of Labor: An Interpretation of the Material Culture of American Working-Class Homes, 1885–1915', in D. Upton and J. M. Vlach (eds.), *Common Places: Readings in American Vernacular Architecture*, 261–78, Athens, GA: University of Georgia Press.

Cohen, L.A. (2003), *A Consumers' Republic: The Politics of Mass Consumption in Postwar America*, New York: Vintage.

Coleman, L.V. (1933), *Historic House Museums*, Washington, DC: American Association of Museums.

Collins, L. (2011), 'House Perfect: Is the IKEA Ethos Comfy or Creepy?', *The New Yorker*, 3 October. Available online: http://www.newyorker.com/magazine/2011/10/03/house-perfect (accessed 20 May 2020).

Colomina, B. (1999), 'The Lawn at War: 1941–1961', in G. Teyssot (ed.), *The American Lawn*, 134–54, New York: Princeton Architectural Press.

Colomina, B. (2007), *Domesticity at War*, Cambridge, MA: MIT Press.

Comacchio, C. (1999), *The Infinite Bonds of Family: Domesticity in Canada, 1850–1940*, Toronto: University of Toronto Press.

Comacchio, C. (2008), *The Dominion of Youth: Adolescence and the Making of Modern Canada, 1920 to 1950*, Waterloo: Wilfred Laurier Press.

Coontz, S. (1992), *The Way We Never Were: American Families and the Nostalgia Trap*, New York: Basic Books.

Coontz, S. (2011), *A Strange Stirring:* The Feminine Mystique *and American Women at the Dawn of the 1960s*, New York: Basic Books.

Cooper, A. (2008), 'Poor Men in the Land of Promises: Settler Masculinity and the Male Breadwinner Economy in Late Nineteenth-Century New Zealand', *Australian Historical Studies*, 39 (2): 245–61.

Cott, N.F. (1997), *The Bonds of Womanhood: 'Woman's Sphere' in New England, 1780–1835*, 2nd edition, New Haven, CT: Yale University Press.

Cott, N.F. (2009), *Public Vows: A History of Marriage and the Nation*, Cambridge, MA: Harvard University Press.

Coughlan, S. (2009), *The Sleepyhead's Bedside Companion* [e-book], London: Preface Publishing.
Coveney, J. (2000), *Food, Morals and Meanings: The Pleasure and Anxiety of Eating*, London: Routledge.
Cowan, R.S. (1983), *More Work for Mother: The Ironies of Household Technology from the Open Hearth to the Microwave*, New York: Basic Books.
Cowan, R.S. (1985), 'How the Refrigerator Got Its Hum', in D.A. MacKenzie and J. Wajcman (eds.), *The Social Shaping of Technology: How the Refrigerator Got Its Hum*, 202–18, Philadelphia: Open University Press.
Cox, N. and S. Federici (1975), 'Counter-planning from the Kitchen', in N. Cox and S. Federici, *Counter-planning from the Kitchen: Wages for Housework*, 1–16, New York: New York Wages for Housework Committee and Falling Wall Press.
Cox, R. (2006), *The Servant Problem: Domestic Employment in a Global Economy*, London: I.B. Tauris.
Cox, R. (2012), 'Invisible Au Pairs: Gendered Work and Migration Regimes', in R. Sollund (ed.), Advances in Ecopolitics, vol. 10: *Transnational Migration, Gender and Rights*, 33–52, Bingley: Emerald.
Cox, R. (2013), 'The Complications of "Hiring a Hubby": Gender Relations and the Commoditisation of Home Maintenance in New Zealand', *Social and Cultural Geography*, 14 (5): 575–90.
Cox, R. (2014), 'Working on Masculinity at Home', in A. Gorman-Murray and P. Hopkins (eds.), *Masculinities and Place*, 227–40, Aldershot: Ashgate.
Cox, R. (2016), 'Materials, Skills and Gender Identities: Men, Women and Home Improvement Practices in New Zealand', *Gender, Place and Culture*, 23 (4): 572–88.
Crane, S. (2010), 'Mediterranean Dialogues: Le Corbusier, Fernand Pouillon, and Rouland Simounet', in J.-F. Lejeune and M. Sabatino (eds.), *Modern Architecture and the Mediterranean: Vernacular Dialogues and Contested Identities*, 95–110, London: Routledge.
Crane, S. (2013), 'The Shantytown of Algiers and the Colonization of Everyday Life', in K. Cupers (ed.), *Use Matters: An Alternative History of Architecture*, 103–20, London: Routledge.
Creagh, L., H. Kåberg and B.M. Lane, eds. (2008), *Modern Swedish Design: Three Founding Texts*, New York: Museum of Modern Art.
Crenshaw, K. (1989), 'Demarginalizing the Intersection of Race and Sex: A Black Feminist Critique of Antidiscrimination Doctrine, Feminist Theory and Antiracist Politics', *University of Chicago Legal Forum*, 1989 (1): 139–67.
Crepeau, F., D. Nakache, M. Collyer, N.H. Goetz and A. Hansen (2006), *Forced Migration and Global Processes: A View from Forced Migration Studies*, Oxford: Lexington Books.
Cromley, E.C. (1996), 'Transforming the Food Axis: Houses, Tools, Modes of Analysis', *Material History Review/Revue de la culture matérielle*, 44: 8–22.
Cromley, E.C. (2008), 'Bedrooms', in C.A. Mitchell and J. Reid-Walsh (eds.), *Girl Culture: An Encyclopedia*, 173–77, Westport, CT: Greenwood Press.
Crowley, D. (2012), 'From Homelessness to Homelessness', in R. Schuldenfrei (ed.), *Atomic Dwelling: Anxiety, Domesticity and Postwar Architecture*, 277–89, Abingdon: Routledge.
Csikszentmihalyi, M. and E. Rochberg-Halton (1981), *The Meaning of Things: Domestic Symbols and the Self*, Cambridge: Cambridge University Press.

Cumo, C. (2007), *Science and Technology in 20th-century American Life*, Portsmouth, NH: Greenwood Press.

Cunningham, H. (1995), *God and Caesar at the Rio Grande: Sanctuary and the Politics of Religion*, Minneapolis, MN: University of Minnesota Press.

Cupers, K. (2014), *The Social Project: Housing Postwar France*, Minneapolis, MN: University of Minnesota Press.

Cupers, K. (2017), 'Human Territoriality and the Downfall of Public Housing', *Public Culture*, 29 (1): 165–90.

Cushing, P. and T. Lewis (2002), 'Negotiating Mutuality and Agency in Care-Giving Relationships with Women with Intellectual Disabilities, *Hypatia*, 17 (3): 173–93.

Darnell, R. (2008), 'First Nations Identity, Contemporary Interpretive Communities, and Nomadic Legacies', *Arcadia*, 43 (1): 102–13.

Das, V., J.M. Ellen and L. Leonard (2008), 'On the Modalities of the Domestic', *Home Cultures*, 5 (3): 349–71.

Davis, M. (2006), *Planet of Slums*, London: Verso.

Dawes, F.V. ([1973] 1989), *Not in Front of the Servants: A True Portrait of Upstairs, Downstairs Life*, London: Century in association with the National Trust.

de Almeida Abreu, M. (1994), 'Reconstruindo uma história esquecida: Origem e expansão das favelas no Rio de Janeiro', *Espaço & Debates*, 14 (37): 34–44.

de Grazia, V. (2006), *Irresistible Empire: America's Advance Through Twentieth-Century Europe*, Cambridge, MA: Harvard University Press.

Delap, L. (2011), *Knowing Their Place: Domestic Service in Twentieth Century Britain*, Oxford: Oxford University Press.

De Meulder, B., J. Schreurs, A. Cock and B. Notteboom (1999), 'Sleutelen aan het Belgische Stadslandschap', *Oase*, 52: 78–113.

Denhez, M. (1994), *The Canadian Home: From Cave to Electronic Cocoon*, Toronto: Dundum Press.

Descloitres, R., J.-C. Reverdy and C. Descloitres (1961), *L'Algérie des bidonvilles: Le Tiers-Monde dans la cite*, Paris: Mouton & Cie.

Desmond, M. (2016), *Evicted: Poverty and Profit in the American City*, New York: Crown.

Després, C. (1991), 'The Meaning of Home: Literature Review and Directions for Future Research and Theoretical Development', *Journal of Architectural and Planning Research*, 8 (2): 96–155.

di Leonardo, M. (1987), 'The Female World of Cards and Holidays: Women, Families, and the Work of Kinship', *Signs*, 12 (3): 440–53.

di Leonardo, M. (2006), 'There's No Place Like Home: Domestic Domains and Urban Imaginaries in New Haven, Connecticut', *Identities: Global Studies in Culture and Power*, 13 (1): 33–52.

Diller, E. (1996), 'Bad Press', in F. Hughes (ed.), *The Architect: Reconstructing Her Practice*, 74–94, Cambridge, MA: MIT Press.

Donovan, R., A. Williams, K. Stajduhar, K. Brazil and D. Marshall (2011), 'The Influence of Culture on Home-Based Family Caregiving at End-of-Life: A Case Study of Dutch Reformed Family Care Givers in Ontario, Canada', *Social Science and Medicine*, 72 (3): 338–46.

Doshi, S. (2013), 'Resettlement Ecologies: Environmental Subjectivity and Graduated Citizenship in Mumbai', in A. Rademaher and K. Sivaramakrishnan (eds.), *Ecologies of Urbanism in India: Metropolitan Civility and Sustainability*, 225–48, Hong Kong: Hong Kong University Press.

Douglas, M. (1966), *Purity and Danger: An Analysis of Concepts of Pollution and Taboo*, London: Routledge.

Douglas, M. (1995), 'The Idea of Home: A Kind of Space', in A. Mack (ed.), *Home: A Place in the World*, 261–82, New York: New York University Press.
Drazin, A. (2001), 'A Man Will Get Furnished: Wood and Domesticity in Urban Romania', in D. Miller (ed.), *Home Possessions: Material Culture Behind Closed Doors*, 173–99, Oxford: Berg.
Droste, M. (1998), *Bauhaus 1919–1933*, Cologne: Taschen.
Dufaux, F. and A. Fourcaut, eds. (2004), *Le monde des grands ensembles*, Grâne, France: Créaphis.
Ebert, C. (2012), 'Moderate Middle Class Modernism: The Architecture of the West German Bungalow', in S. Herold and B. Stefanovska (eds.), *45+: Postwar Modern Architecture in Europe*, 161–72, Berlin: Institut für Stadt- und Regionalplanung der Technischen Universität Berlin.
Edgell, S. (1993), *Class*, London: Routledge.
Edmond, W. and Fleming, S. (1975). 'If Women were Paid for All They Do', in W. Edmond and S. Fleming (eds.), *All Work and No Pay: Women, Housework, and the Wages Due*, 5–12, Bristol: Power of Women Collective and the Falling Wall Press.
Elias, N. ([1939] 1994), *The Civilizing Process*, vol. 1, *The History of Manners*, Oxford: Blackwell.
Epp, M. (2011), *Mennonite Women in Canada: A History*, Winnipeg: University of Manitoba Press.
European Commission (2016), 'EU Support in Response to the Syrian Crisis', Memo, 4 February, Brussels. Available online: https://ec.europa.eu/commission/presscorner/detail/en/MEMO_16_222 (accessed 20 May 2020).
Evans, D. (2014), *Food Waste: Home Consumption, Material Culture and Everyday Life*, London: Bloomsbury Academic.
Faber, S.T. and H.P. Nielsen (2016), *Remapping Gender, Place and Mobility: Global Confluences and Local Particularities in Nordic Peripheries*, London: Routledge.
Fahr-Becker, G. (2008), *Wiener Werkstaette: 1903–1932*, Cologne: Taschen.
Fallan, K. (2012), *Scandinavian Design: Alternative Histories*, London: Berg.
Fallan, K. and G. Lees-Maffei, eds. (2016), *Designing Worlds: National Design Histories in an Age of Globalization*, Oxford: Berghahn.
Farrugia, D., J. Smyth and T. Harrison (2016), 'Moral Distinctions and Structural Inequality: Homeless Youth Salvaging the Self', *Sociological Review*, 64 (2): 238–55.
Fass, P.S. (2016), *The End of American Childhood: A History of Parenting from Life on the Frontier to the Managed Child*, Princeton, NJ: Princeton University Press.
Fernandes, E. (2011), *Regularization of Informal Settlements in Latin America*, Cambridge, MA: Lincoln Institute of Land Policy.
Fernandes, E. and A. Varley, eds. (1998), *Illegal Cities: Law and Urban Change in Developing Countries*, London: Zed Books.
Finnimore, B. (1989), *Houses from the Factory: System Building and the Welfare State, 1942–1974*, London: Rivers Oram Press.
Fischer, C. (1994), *America Calling: A Social History of the Telephone to 1940*, Berkeley, CA: University of California Press.
Fisher, A.E. (2015), '"This Place Should (Not) Exist": An Ethnography of Shelter Workers and the In-Between', PhD dissertation, University of Toronto, Toronto.
Fishman, R. (1982), *Urban Utopias in the Twentieth Century: Ebenezer Howard, Frank Lloyd Wright, Le Corbusier*, Cambridge, MA: MIT Press.

Fortunati, P. (1975), 'The Housewife', in W. Edmond and S. Fleming (eds.), *All Work and No Pay: Women, Housework, and the Wages Due*, 13–21, Bristol: Power of Women Collective and the Falling Wall Press.

Forty, A. (1986), *Objects of Desire: Designs and Society 1750–1980*, London: Thames & Hudson.

Fourcaut, A. (2000), *La banlieue en morceaux: La crise des lotissements défectueux en France dans l'entre-deux-guerres*, Grâne, France: Créaphis.

Frederick, M. (2003), *Between Sundays: Black Women and Everyday Struggles of Faith*, Berkeley, CA: University of California Press.

Friedman, A.T. (2006), *Women and the Making of the Modern House: A Social and Architectural History*, New Haven, CT: Yale University Press.

Gajendran, R.S. and D.A. Harrison (2007), 'The Good, the Bad, and the Unknown About Telecommuting: Meta-Analysis of Psychological Mediators and Individual Consequences', *Journal of Applied Psychology*, 92 (6): 1524–41. Available online: http://www.apa.org/pubs/journals/releases/apl-9261524.pdf (accessed 20 May 2020).

Galloway, G. (2016), 'Former "Unwed Mothers" Call for Public Inquiry into Forced Adoptions', *Globe and Mail*, 17 May. Available online: https://www.theglobeandmail.com/news/politics/former-unwed-mothers-call-for-public-inquiry-into-forced-adoptions/article30072978/ (accessed 20 May 2020).

Gardner, K. (2002), 'Death of a Migrant: Transnational Death Rituals and Gender among British Sylhetis', *Global Networks*, 2 (3): 191–204.

Garvey, P. (2013), '"Ikea Sofas are Like H&M Trousers": The Potential of Sensuous Signs', *Journal of Business Anthropology*, 2 (1): 75–92.

Garvey, P. (2018), *Unpacking Ikea: Swedish Design for the Purchasing Masses*, Abingdon: Routledge.

Gastaut, Y. (2004), 'Les bidonvilles, lieux d'exclusion et de marginalité en France durant les trente glorieuses', *Cahiers de la Méditerranée*, 69: 2–12.

Gavanas, A. (2004), 'Domesticating Masculinity and Masculinizing Domesticity in Contemporary U.S. Fatherhood Politics', *Social Politics*, 11 (2): 247–66.

Geertz, C. (1973), *The Interpretation of Cultures: Selected Essays*, New York: Basic Books.

Gelber, S.M. (1997), 'Do-It-Yourself: Constructing, Repairing and Maintaining Domestic Masculinity', *American Quarterly*, 49 (1): 66–112.

Gelézeau, V. (2004), 'Les tanji sud-coréens: Des grands ensembles au coeur de la ville', in F. Dufaux and A. Fourcaut (eds.), *Le monde des grands ensembles*, 199–211, Grâne, France: Créaphis.

'Gentrify' (2020), *OED Online*, Oxford University Press (accessed 20 May 2020).

'Gentry' (2020), *OED Online*. Oxford University Press (accessed 20 May 2020).

Ghertner, D.A. (2015), 'Why Gentrification Theory Fails in "Much of the World"', *City: Analysis of Urban Trends, Culture, Theory, Policy, Action*, 19 (4): 552–63.

Giddens, A. (1981), *The Class Structure of the Advanced Societies*, 2nd edition, London: Hutchinson.

Giddens, A. (1984), *The Constitution of Society*, Berkeley, CA: University of California Press.

Giddens, A. (1991), *Modernity and Self-Identity*, Cambridge: Polity Press.

Giles, J. (2004), *The Parlour and the Suburb: Domestic Identities, Class, Femininity and Modernity*, London: Bloomsbury.

Ginsburg, R. (2011), *At Home with Apartheid: The Hidden Landscapes of Domestic Service in Johannesburg*, Charlottesville, VA: University of Virginia Press.

Gleason, M. (1999), *Normalizing the Ideal: Psychology, Schooling, and the Family in Postwar Canada*, Toronto: University of Toronto Press.

Glendinning, M. (2015), 'From European Welfare State to Asian Capitalism: The Transformation of "British Public Housing" in Hong Kong and Singapore', in M. Swenarton, T. Avermaete and D. van den Heuvel (eds.), *Architecture and the Welfare State*, 298–318, London: Routledge.

Glendinning, M. and S. Muthesius (1994), *Tower Block: Modern Public Housing in England, Scotland, Wales and Northern Ireland*, New Haven, CT: Yale University Press.

Global Workplace Analytics and Flexjobs (2017), *The 2017 State of Telecommuting in the U.S. Employee Workforce*. Available online: https://www.flexjobs.com/2017-State-of-Telecommuting-US/ (accessed 12 January 2020).

Goffman, E. ([1959] 1990), *The Presentation of Self in Everyday Life*, London: Penguin.

Goldstein, C.M. (1998), *Do It Yourself: Home Improvement in 20th-Century America*, New York/Washington, DC: Princeton Architectural Press and National Building Museum.

Goldthorpe, J.H., D. Lockwood, F. Bechhofer and J. Platt (1968–69), *The Affluent Worker*, 3 vols., Cambridge: Cambridge University Press.

Gorman-Murray, A. (2011), 'Economic Crises and Emotional Fallout: Work, Home and Men's Senses of Belonging in Post-GFC Sydney', *Emotion, Space and Society*, 4 (4): 211–20.

Gournay, I. (2002), 'Levitt France et la banlieue à l'américaine: premier bilan', *Histoire urbaine*, 5: 167–88.

Graber, J. (2011), *The Furnace of Affliction: Prisons and Religion in Antebellum America*, Durham, NC: University of North Carolina Press.

Grayzel, S.R. (2013), *Women and the First World War*, London: Routledge.

Green, M. and V. Lawson (2011), 'Recentring Care: Interrogating the Commodification of Care', *Social and Cultural Geography*, 12 (6): 639–54.

Green, R.K. and S.M. Wachter (2005), 'The American Mortgage in Historical and International Context', *The Journal of Economic Perspectives*, 19 (4): 93–114.

Greenbaum, A. (2016), 'Finding Solace in a Storage Unit', *The Atlantic*, 9 March. Available online: http://www.theatlantic.com/technology/archive/2016/03/solace-in-a-storage-unit/472890/ (accessed 20 May 2020).

Gregson, N. and M. Lowe (1994), *Servicing the Middle Classes: Class, Gender and Waged Domestic Labor in Contemporary Britain*, London: Routledge.

Grier, K.C. (1988), *Culture & Comfort: Parlor Making and Middle-Class Identity, 1850–1930*, Washington, DC: Smithsonian Institution Press.

Guldberg, J. (2011), '"Scandinavian Design" as Discourse: The Exhibition "Design in Scandinavia", 1954–57', *Design Issues*, 27 (2): 41–58.

Gulyani, S. and D. Talukdar (2008), 'Slum Real Estate: The Low-Quality High-Price Puzzle in Nairobi's Slum Rental Market and its Implications for Theory and Practice', *World Development*, 36 (10): 1916–37.

Gurstein, P. and D. Small (2005), 'From Housing to Home: Reflexive Management for Those Deemed Hard to House', *Housing Studies*, 20 (5): 717–35.

Guyot, K. and I.V. Sawhill (2020), 'Telecommuting will likely continue long after the pandemic', Brookings Institution (blog), 6 April 2020. Available online: https://www.brookings.edu/blog/up-front/2020/04/06/telecommuting-will-likely-continue-long-after-the-pandemic/ (accessed 24 April 2020).

Habermas, J. ([1962] 1991), *The Structural Transformation of the Public Sphere: An Inquiry into a Category of Bourgeois Society*, trans. T. Burger, Cambridge, MA: MIT Press.

Hall, C. ([1973] 1995), 'The History of the Housewife', in E. Malos (ed.), *The Politics of Housework*, 34–58, Cheltenham: New Clarion Press.

Hall, E. (2011), 'Shopping for Support: Personalisation and the New Space and Relations of Commodified Care for People with Learning Disabilities', *Social and Cultural Geography*, 12 (6): 589–603.

Hancock, A.M. (2004), *The Politics of Disgust: The Public Identity of the Welfare Queen*, New York: New York University Press.

Hannemann, C. (2005), *Die Platte: Industrialisierter Wohnungsbau in der DDR*, Berlin: Hans Schiler.

Hanson, M. (2016), 'Robot carers for elderly people are "another way of dying even more miserably"', *The Guardian*, 14 March. Available online: https://www.theguardian.com/lifeandstyle/2016/mar/14/robot-carers-for-elderly-people-are-another-way-of-dying-even-more-miserably (accessed 20 May 2020).

Hård af Segerstad, U. (1961), *Scandinavian Design*, London: Studio.

Hardyment, C. (1995), *Slice of Life: The British Way of Eating Since 1945*, London: BBC Books.

Harloe, M. (1995), *The People's Home? Social Rented Housing in Europe and America*, London: Blackwell.

Harms, H. (1982), 'Historical Perspectives on the Practice and Purpose of Self-Help Housing', in P.M. Ward (ed.), *Self-Help Housing: A Critique*, 17–53, London: Mansell.

Harris, D. (2007), 'Clean and Bright and Everyone White: Seeing the Postwar Domestic Environment in the United States', in D. Harris and D. Fairchild Ruggles (eds.), *Sites Unseen: Landscape and Vision*, 241–62, Pittsburgh, PA: University of Pittsburgh Press.

Harris, D., ed. (2010), *Second Suburb: Levittown, Pennsylvania*, Pittsburgh, PA: University of Pittsburgh Press.

Harris, D. (2013), *Little White Houses: How the Postwar Home Constructed Race in America*, Minneapolis, MN: University of Minnesota Press.

Harris, N. (1999), *Building Lives: Constructing Rites and Passages*, New Haven, CT: Yale University Press.

Harris, R. (1996), *Unplanned Suburbs: Toronto's American Tragedy, 1900 to 1950*, Baltimore, MD: Johns Hopkins University Press.

Harris, R. (1998), 'A Crank's Fate and the Feting of a Visionary: Reflections on the History of Aided Self-Help Housing', *World Planning Review*, 29 (3): iii–viii.

Harris, R. (2003), 'A Double Irony: The Originality and Influence of John F.C. Turner', *Habitat International*, 27 (2): 245–69.

Harris, R. (2012), *Building a Market: The Rise of the Home Improvement Industry, 1914–1960*, Chicago, IL: University of Chicago Press.

Harris, R. and A. Hay (2007), 'New Plans for Housing in Urban Kenya 1939–1963', *Planning Perspectives*, 22 (2): 195–223.

Harris, S. (2013), *Communism on Tomorrow Street: Mass Housing and Everyday Life after Stalin*, Washington, DC: Woodrow Wilson Center Press/Baltimore, MD: Johns Hopkins University Press.

Harrison, D. and J. Taylor (2008), *The New Elite: Inside the Minds of the Truly Wealthy*, New York: AMACOM/American Management Association.

Hart, J.F., M.J. Rhodes, J.T. Morgan and M.B. Lindberg (2003), *The Uncommon World of the Mobile Home*, Baltimore, MD: Johns Hopkins University Press.
Hartman, T. (2007), 'On the Ikeaization of France', *Public Culture*, 19 (3): 483–98.
Hartog, H. (2000), *Man and Wife in America: A History*, Cambridge, MA: Harvard University Press.
Hayden, D. (1976), *Seven American Utopias: The Architecture of Communitarian Socialism, 1790–1975*, Cambridge, MA: MIT Press.
Hayden, D. (1981), *The Grand Domestic Revolution: The History of Feminist Designs for American Homes, Neighborhoods and Cities*, Cambridge, MA: MIT Press.
Hayden, D. (2003), *Building American Suburbia: Green Fields and Urban Growth, 1820–2000*, New York: Pantheon Books.
Hayward, G. (1975), 'Home as an Environmental and Psychological Concept', *Landscape*, 20: 2–9.
Headrick, D.R. (1981), *The Tools of Empire: Technology and European Imperialism in the Nineteenth Century*, Oxford: Oxford University Press.
Hegewisch, A., H. Liepmann, J. Hayes and H. Harmann (2010), 'Separate and Not Equal? Gender Segregation in the Labor Market and the Gender Wage Gap', *Institute for Women's Policy Research Briefing Paper* C377, September 2010. Available online: https://iwpr.org/publications/separate-and-not-equal-gender-segregation-in-the-labor-market-and-the-gender-wage-gap/ (accessed 20 May 2020).
Heidegger, M. ([1954] 1971), 'Building Dwelling Thinking', in *Poetry, Language, Thought*, trans. A. Hofstadter, 143–61, New York: Harper & Row.
Henderson, A. (1992), 'Media and the Rise of Celebrity Culture', *OAH Magazine of History*, 6 (4): 49–54.
Henderson, A. (2005), 'From Barnum to "Bling Bling": The Changing Face of Celebrity Culture', *Hedgehog Review*, 7 (1): 37–46.
Henderson, S.R. (1996), 'A Revolution in the Woman's Sphere: Grete Lihotzky and the Frankfurt Kitchen', in D. Coleman, E. Danze and C. Henderson (eds.), *Architecture and Feminism*, 221–53, New York: Princeton Architectural Press.
Henderson, S.R. (2009), 'Housing the Single Woman: The Frankfurt Experiment', *Journal of the Society of Architectural Historians*, 68 (3): 358–77.
Henderson, S.R. (2013), *Building Culture: Ernst May and the New Frankfurt Initiative, 1926–1931*, New York: Peter Land.
Henderson, T. (2014), 'More Americans Living Alone, Census Says', *Washington Post*, 29 September.
Henthorn, C.L. (2006), *From Submarines to Suburbs: Selling a Better America, 1939–1959*, Athens, OH: Ohio University Press.
Heßler, M. (2009), 'The Frankfurt Kitchen: The Model of Modernity and the "Madness" of Traditional Users, 1926 to 1933', in R. Oldenziel and K. Zachmann (eds.), *Cold War Kitchen: Americanization, Technology, and European Users*, 163–84, Cambridge, MA: MIT Press.
Heynen, H. (2010), 'Belgium and the Netherlands: Two Different Ways of Coping with the Housing Crisis 1945–70', *Home Cultures*, 7 (2): 159–78.
Higman, B.W. (2002), *Domestic Service in Australia*, Melbourne: Melbourne University Press.
Hines, T. (2000), *Irving Gill and the Architecture of Reform*, New York: Monacelli Press.
Hoagland, A.K. (2011), 'Introducing the Bathroom: Space and Change in Working-Class Houses', *Buildings & Landscapes: Journal of the Vernacular Architecture Forum*, 18 (2): 15–42.

Hochhaeusl, S. (2013), 'From Vienna to Frankfurt Inside Core-House Type 7: A History of Scarcity through the Modern Kitchen', *Architectural Histories*, 1 (1): Art. 24. Available online: http://doi.org/10.5334/ah.aq.

Hochschild, A.R. (1983), *The Managed Heart: The Commercialization of Human Feeling*, Berkeley, CA: University of California Press.

Holliday, L.S. (2001), 'Kitchen Technologies: Promises and Alibis, 1944–1966', *Camera Obscura*, December: 1–131.

Hollis, F. (2015), *Beyond Live/Work: The Architecture of Home-Based Work*, London: Routledge.

Holston, J. (2009), *Insurgent Citizenship: Disjunctions of Democracy and Modernity in Brazil*, Princeton, NJ: Princeton University Press.

Hondagneu-Sotelo, P. (2001), *Doméstica: Immigrant Workers Cleaning and Caring in the Shadows of Affluence*, Berkley, CA: University of California Press.

hooks, b. (1984), *Feminist Theory: From Margin to Center*, Boston, MA: South End Press.

hooks, b. ([1990] 2015), 'Homeplace: A Site of Resistance', in b. hooks, *Yearning: Race, Gender, and Cultural Politics*, 41–50, Abingdon: Routledge.

Horne, J.R. (2002), *A Social Laboratory for Modern France: The Musée Social and the Rise of the Welfare State*, Durham, NC: Duke University Press.

Howe, S. (1999), 'Untangling the Scandinavian Blonde: Modernity and the IKEA PS Range Catalogue 1995', *Scandinavian Journal of Design History*, 9: 94–105.

Hurdley, R. (2006), 'Dismantling Mantelpieces: Narrating Identities and Materializing Culture in the Home', *Sociology*, 40 (4): 717–33.

Hurdley R. (2013), *Home, Materiality, Memory and Belonging: Keeping Culture*, Basingstoke: Palgrave Macmillan.

Iacovetta, F., V.J. Korinek and M. Epp (2012), *Edible Histories, Cultural Politics: Towards a Canadian Food History*, Toronto: University of Toronto Press.

Immergluck, D. (2015), *Preventing the Next Mortgage Crisis: The Meltdown, the Federal Response, and the Future of Housing in America*, London: Rowman & Littlefield.

Ingrassia, P. (2013), *Comeback: The Fall and Rise of the American Automobile Industry*, New York: Simon & Schuster.

Inside Self Storage International (2015), London: Informa PLC. Available online: http://www.insideselfstorage.com/digital-issues/2015/10/international-2015.aspx (accessed 20 May 2020).

International Labor Organization (ILO) (2020a),'Who are Domestic Workers'. Available online: https://www.ilo.org/global/topics/domestic-workers/who/lang--en/index.htm (accessed 20 May 2015).

International Labor Organization (ILO) (2020b), 'Ratifications of C189 – Domestic Workers Convention, 2011 (No. 189)'. Available online: https://www.ilo.org/dyn/normlex/en/f?p=NORMLEXPUB:11300:0::NO:11300:P11300_INSTRUMENT_ID:2551460:NO (accessed 20 May 2020).

Isaksen, L.W., ed. (2010), *Global Care Work: Gender and Migration in Nordic Societies*, Lund: Nordic Academic Press.

Isenstadt, S. (2007), 'Four Views, Three of Them through Glass', in D. Harris and D.F. Ruggles (eds.), *Sites Unseen: Landscape and Vision*, 213–40, Pittsburgh, PA: University of Pittsburgh Press.

Jachmann, C. (1992), 'Der IBA-Block 2 in Berlin-Kreuzberg, ein Architektinnenprojekt', *Frauen Kunst Wissenschaft*, 13: 32–38.

Jackson, A. (2006), 'Labor as Leisure – The Mirror Dinghy and DIY Sailors', *Journal of Design History*, 19 (1): 57–67.
Jackson, K.T. (1985), *Crabgrass Frontier: The Suburbanization of the United States*, New York: Oxford University Press.
Jacobs, J.A. (2006), 'Social and Spatial Change in the Postwar Family Room', *Perspectives in Vernacular Architecture*, 13 (1): 70–85.
Jacobs, J.A. (2015), *Detached America: Building Houses in Postwar Suburbia*, Charlottesville, VA: University of Virginia Press.
James, N. (1989), 'Emotional Labor: Skill and Work in the Social Regulation of Feelings', *Sociological Review*, 37 (1): 15–42.
James, S.H. (1995), 'The Master Bedroom Comes of Age: Gender, Sexuality and the C.M.H.C. Competition Series', *Journal of the Society for the Study of Architecture in Canada*, 20 (4): 104–11.
James, S.H. (1996), '"Bedroom Problems": Architecture, Gender, and Sexuality, 1945–63', MA thesis, School of Architecture, McGill University, Montreal.
Jameson, F. (1991), *Postmodernism, or, The Cultural Logic of Late Capitalism*, London: Verso.
Janser, A. (2001), 'New Living: A Model Film? Hans Richter's Werkbund Film: Between Commissioned Work and Poetry on Film', in A. Janser and A. Rüegg (eds.), *Hans Richter: New Living: Architecture, Film, Space*, 16–37, Baden: Lars Müller.
Jarman, J., R.M. Blackburn and G. Racko (2012), 'The Dimensions of Occupational Gender Segregation in Industrial Countries', *Sociology*, 46 (6): 1003–19.
Jenkins, V.S. (1994), *The Lawn: A History of an American Obsession*, Washington, DC: Smithsonian Institution Press.
John, R.R. (2010), *Network Nation: Inventing American Telecommunications*, Cambridge, MA: Harvard University Press.
Johnson, L. and J. Lloyd (2004), *Sentenced to Everyday Life: Feminism and the Housewife*, Oxford: Berg.
Jones, C. and A. Murie (2006), *The Right to Buy: Analysis and Evaluation of a Housing Policy*, London: Blackwell.
Jones, M. (2019), 'The Movement to Bring Death Closer', *New York Times Magazine*, 19 December. Available online: https://www.nytimes.com/2019/12/19/magazine/home-funeral.html (accessed 10 January 2020).
Joselit, J.W. (2002), *The Wonders of America: Reinventing Jewish Culture 1880–1950*, New York: Picador.
Junghanns, K. (1994), *Das Haus für Alle: Zur Geschichte der Vorfertigung in Deutschland*, Berlin: Ernst.
Keane, W. (2003), 'Semiotics and the Social Analysis of Material Things', *Language and Communication*, 23 (3/4): 409–25.
Keane, W. (2005), 'The Hazards of New Clothes: What Signs Make Possible', in S. Küchler and G. Were (eds.), *The Art of Clothing: A Pacific Experience*, 1–16, London: University College London Press.
Keller, J. and C. Dobby (2020), 'Hundreds of Alberta Infections Linked to Meat-Processing Plant', *The Globe and Mail*, 19 April. Available online: https://www.theglobeandmail.com/canada/alberta/article-covid-19-outbreak-in-high-river-linked-to-infections-at-nearby/ (accessed 25 April 2020).
Kelly, B.M. (1993), *Expanding the American Dream: Building and Rebuilding Levittown*, Albany, NY: SUNY Press.
Kelm, M.-E. (1999), *Colonizing Bodies: Aboriginal Health and Healing in British Columbia, 1900–50*, Vancouver, BC: University of British Columbia Press.

Kemeny, J. (1995), *From Public Housing to the Social Market: Rental Policy Strategies in Comparative Perspective*, London: Routledge.

Kiddey, R. and J. Schofield (2011), 'Embrace the Margins: Adventures in Archaeology and Homelessness', *Public Archaeology*, 10 (1): 4–22.

Kilkey, M., D. Perrons and A. Plomien (2013), *Gender, Migration and Domestic Work: Masculinities, Male Labor and Fathering in the UK and USA*, London: Palgrave Macmillan.

Kinchin, J. (2011), 'Passages from *Why I Became an Architect* by Margarete Schütte-Lihotzky', *West 86th: A Journal of Decorative Arts, Design History and Material Culture*, 18 (1): 86–96.

King, A. (1995), *The Bungalow: The Production of a Global Culture*, Oxford: Oxford University Press.

Kirkham, P. (1996), *The Gendered Object*, Manchester: Manchester University Press.

Klassen, P.E. (2001a), *Blessed Events: Religion and Home Birth in America*, Princeton, NJ: Princeton University Press.

Klassen, P.E. (2001b), 'Sacred Maternities and Postbiomedical Bodies: Religion and Nature in Contemporary Home Birth', *Signs*, 26 (3): 775–809.

Klassen, P.E. (2008a), 'Ritual', in J. Corrigan (ed.), *The Oxford Handbook of Religion and Emotion*, 143–61, Oxford: Oxford University Press.

Klassen, P.E. (2008b), 'Practice', in D. Morgan (ed.), *Key Words in Religion, Media and Culture*, 136–47, New York: Routledge.

Klassen, P.E. (2009), *Women and Religion: Critical Concepts in Religious Studies*, vol. 2: *The Politics of Public and Private Religion*, Oxford: Routledge.

Klassen, P.E. (2011), *Spirits of Protestantism: Medicine, Healing, and Liberal Christianity*, Berkeley, CA: University of California Press.

Klassen, P.E. (2012), 'Ritual, Tradition, and the Force of Design', in J. Karolewski, N. Miczek and C. Zotter (eds.), *Ritualdesign. Zur Kultur- und Ritualwissenschaftlichen Analyse »neuer« Rituale*, 327–52, Bielefeld: transcript.

Klassen, P.E. (2016), 'God Keep Our Land: The Legal Ritual of the McKenna-McBride Royal Commission, 1913–1916', in B.L. Berger and R. Moon (eds.), *Religion and the Exercise of Public Authority*, 79–93, Oxford: Hart.

Klassen, P.E. and M. Scheer (2019), *The Public Work of Christmas: Difference and Belonging in Multicultural Societies*, Montreal and Kingston: McGill-Queen's University Press.

Kline, R.R. (2000), *Consumers in the Country: Technology and Social Change in Rural America*, Baltimore, MD: Johns Hopkins University Press.

Klippenstein, F.E. (2011), 'Scattered but Not Lost: Mennonite Domestic Servants in Winnipeg, 1920s–50s', in C.A. Cavanaugh and R.R. Warne (eds.), *Telling Tales: Essays in Western Women's History*, 200–31, Vancouver, BC: University of British Columbia Press.

Kopytoff, I. (1986), 'The Cultural Biography of Things: Commoditization as a Process', in A. Appadurai (ed.), *The Social Life of Things: Commodities in Cultural Perspective*, 64–91, Cambridge: Cambridge University Press.

Krishnan, K. (2009), *From Post-Industrial to Post-Modern Society: New Theories of the Contemporary World*, 2nd edition, Oxford: Wiley.

Kristoffersson, S. (2014), *Design by IKEA: A Cultural History*, trans. W. Jewson, London: Bloomsbury.

Kulić, V., M. Mrduljaš and W. Thaler (2012), *Modernism In-Between: The Mediatory Architectures of Socialist Yugoslavia*, Berlin: Jovis.

Kumar, K. (2009), *Post-Industrial to Post-Modern Society: New Theories of the Contemporary World*, 2nd edition, Hoboken, NJ: Wiley.

Kurien, P. (1999), 'Gendered Ethnicity', *American Behavioral Scientist*, 42 (4): 648–70.

Kurien, P. (2007), *A Place at the Multicultural Table: The Development of an American Hinduism*, New Brunswick, NJ: Rutgers University Press.

Kurlansky, M. (2012), *Birdseye: The Adventures of a Curious Man*, New York: Doubleday.

Labadie-Jackson, G. (2008), 'Reflections on Domestic Work and the Feminization of Migration', *Campbell Law Review*, 31 (1): 67–90.

Laderman, G. (2003), *Rest in Peace: A Cultural History of Death and the Funeral Home in Twentieth-Century America*, Oxford: Oxford University Press.

Laguerre, M. (2016), *The Multisite Nation: Crossborder Organizations, Transfrontier Infrastructure, and Global Digital Public Sphere*, New York: Palgrave Macmillan.

Lane, B.M. (2015), *Houses for a New World: Builders and Buyers in American Suburbs, 1945–1965*, Princeton, NJ: Princeton University Press.

Langdon, P. (1991), 'Lucky Houses: Home Builders in Southern California are Learning to Heed the Chinese Art of Feng Shui', *Atlantic*, November: 146+.

L'Arche International (2020), 'Summary Report from L'Arche International', 22 February. Available online: https://www.larche.org/news/-/asset_publisher/mQsRZspJMdBy/content/inquiry-statement-test (accessed 25 April 2020).

Lasner, M.G. (2009), 'Own-Your-Owns, Co-ops, Town Houses: Hybrid Housing Types and the New Urban Form in Postwar Southern California', *Journal of the Society of Architectural Historians*, 68 (3): 378–403.

Lasner, M.G. (2012), *High Life: Condo Living in the Suburban Century*, New Haven, CT: Yale University Press.

Lauzon, G. (2014), *Pointe-Saint-Charles: L'urbanisation d'un quartier ouvrier de Montréal, 1840–1930*, Montreal: Septentrion.

Laven, C.S. (2014), '4 Ways to Make Housing More Affordable', *World Economic Forum*, 14 November. Available online: https://www.weforum.org/agenda/2014/11/4-ways-to-make-housing-more-affordable/ (accessed 20 May 2020).

Lebergott, S. (2014), *Pursuing Happiness: American Consumers in the Twentieth Century*, Princeton, NJ: Princeton University Press.

Lees-Maffei, G. (2001), 'From Service to Self-Service: Etiquette Writing as Design Discourse, 1920–1970', *Journal of Design History*, 14 (3): 187–206.

Lees-Maffei, G. (2007), 'Accommodating "Mrs. Three-in-One": Homemaking, Home Entertaining and Domestic Advice Literature in Post-war Britain', *Women's History Review*, 16 (5): 723–54.

Lees-Maffei, G. (2010), 'Introduction, War/Post-War/Cold War, 1943–70', in G. Lees-Maffei and R. Houze (eds.), *The Design History Reader*, 129–33, Oxford: Berg.

Lees-Maffei, G. (2014a), *Design at Home: Domestic Advice Books in Britain and the USA since 1945*, Abingdon: Routledge.

Lees-Maffei, G. (2014b), '"Made" in England? The Mediation of Alessi S.p.A.', in G. Lees-Maffei and K. Fallan (eds.), *Made in Italy: Rethinking a Century of Italian Design*, 287–303, London: Bloomsbury.

Lees-Maffei, G. (2016), '"Why then the world's mine oyster": Consumption and Globalization 1851–Now', in P. Sparke and F. Fisher (eds.), *The Routledge Companion to Design Studies*, 445–56, London: Routledge.

Le Hallé, G. (1986), *Les fortifications de Paris*, Paris: Horvath.

Lehmann, J. (2015), 'Alert Bay Residential School Survivors Gather for Demolition Ceremony', *The Globe and Mail*, 18 February. Available online: https://www.

theglobeandmail.com/news/british-columbia/alert-bay-residential-school-survivors-gather-for-demolition-ceremony/article23067233/ (accessed 20 May 2020).

Leinberger, C.B. (2008), *The Option of Urbanism: Investing in a New American Dream*, Washington, DC: Island Press.

Levine, N. (2015), *The Urbanism of Frank Lloyd Wright*, Princeton, NJ: Princeton University Press.

Leslie, D. and S. Reimer (2003), 'Gender, Modern Design and Home Consumption', *Environment and Planning D: Society and Space*, 21 (3): 293–316.

Li, W. (2006), 'Spatial Transformation of an Urban Ethnic Community: From Chinatown to Ethnoburb in Los Angeles', in W. Li (ed.), *From Urban Enclave to Ethnic Suburb: New Asian Communities in Pacific Rim Countries*, 74–94, Honolulu, HI: University of Hawaii Press.

Linklater, A. (2013), *Owning the Earth: The Transforming History of Land Ownership*, New York: Bloomsbury.

Lippert, R. (2011), *Sanctuary, Sovereignty, Sacrifice: Canadian Sanctuary Incidents, Power, and Law*, Vancouver, BC: University of British Columbia Press.

Livio, O. and K.T. Weinblatt (2007), 'Discursive Legitimation of a Controversial Technology: Ultra-Orthodox Jewish Women in Israel and the Internet', *Communication Review*, 10 (1): 29–56.

Lofton, K. (2017), *Consuming Religion*, Chicago, IL: University of Chicago Press.

Long, C. (2009), 'The Origins and Context of Adolf Loos's "Ornament and Crime"', *Journal of the Society of Architectural Historians*, 68 (2): 200–23.

Løvdal, L. (2015), 'Au Pairs in Norway: Experiences from an Outreach Project', in R. Cox (ed.), *Au Pairs' Lives in Global Context: Sisters or Servants?*, 136–54, Basingstoke: Palgrave Macmillan.

Lowe, S. (2011), *The Housing Debate*, Bristol: Policy Press.

Lu, D. (2006), 'Travelling Urban Form: The Neighborhood Unit in China', *Planning Perspectives*, 21 (4): 369–92.

Lupton, E. (1993), *Mechanical Brides: Women and Machines from Home to Office*, New York: Cooper-Hewitt, Smithsonian Design Museum, and Princeton Architectural Press.

Lupton, E. and J.A. Miller (1992), *The Bathroom, the Kitchen, and the Aesthetics of Waste*, New York: A Kiosk Book, distributed by Princeton Architectural Press.

Lutz, H., ed., (2008), *Migration and Domestic Work: A European Perspective on a Global Theme*, Aldershot: Ashgate.

Lutz, H. and E. Palenga-Möllenbeck (2012), 'Care Workers, Care Drain and Care Chains: Reflections on Care, Migration and Citizenship', *Social Politics*, 19 (1): 15–37.

Lutz, J. (2004), *Lest We Forget, a Short History of Housing in the United States*. Berkeley, CA: Energy Analysis Department, Lawrence Berkeley National Laboratory. Available online: https://eta-publications.lbl.gov/sites/default/files/lest_we_forget_a_short_history_of_housing_in_the_united_states_lbnl-4751e.pdf (accessed 20 May 2020).

Lux, M.K. (2001), *Medicine that Walks: Disease, Medicine and Canadian Plains Native People, 1880–1940*, Toronto: University of Toronto Press.

Lynes, R. ([1949] 1980), *The Tastemakers: The Shaping of American Popular Taste*, New York: Dover.

Macdonald, C.L. (2010), *Shadow Mothers: Nannies, Au Pairs, and the Micropolitics of Mothering*, Berkeley, CA: University of California Press.

Mackay, M. (2011), *DIY Home Improvement in New Zealand*, PhD dissertation, Lincoln University, Lincoln, New Zealand.

Mackay, M., H. Perkins and B. Gidlow (2007), 'Constructing and Maintaining a Central Element of Housing Culture in New Zealand: DIY (Do-It-Yourself) Home Building, Renovation and Maintenance', paper presented at *Transformations in Housing, Urban Life and Public Policy Conference*, 30 August–1 September 2007, Seoul, Korea.

MacMillan, A. (2015), 'Why Your Commute Is Bad for You', *CNN.com*, 6 April. Available online: http://www.cnn.com/2015/04/06/health/commute-bad-for-you/ (accessed 20 May 2020).

MacPherson, C.B. (1978), *Property: Mainstream and Critical Positions*, Toronto: University of Toronto Press.

Mahbubani, K. (2013), *The Great Convergence: Asia, the West, and the Logic of One World*, New York: Public Affairs.

Mallett, S. (2004), 'Understanding Home: A Critical Review of the Literature', *Sociological Review*, 52 (1): 62–89.

Malos, E., ed., ([1980] 1995), *The Politics of Housework*, 2nd revised edition, Cheltenham: New Clarion Press.

Mamman, E.A. (2015), 'Slum Housing Conditions and Eradication Practices in Some Selected Nigerian Cities', *Journal of Sustainable Development*, 8 (2): 230–41.

Manalansan, M. (2006), 'Immigrant Lives and the Politics of Olfaction in the Global City', in J. Drobnick (ed.), *The Smell Culture Reader*, 41–52, Oxford: Berg.

Marchetti, S. and A. Venturini (2014), 'Mothers and Grandmothers on the Move: Labor Mobility and the Household Strategies of Moldovan and Ukrainian Migrant Women in Italy', *International Migration*, 52 (5): 111–26.

Marks, L. (1992), '"The Luckless Waifs and Strays of Humanity": Irish and Jewish Immigrant Unwed Mothers in London, 1870–1939', *Twentieth Century British History*, 3 (2): 113–37.

Marsden, S. (2002), 'Adawx, Spanaxnox, and the Geopolitics of the Tsimshian', *BC Studies*, 135 (Autumn): 101–35.

Martin, R., J. Moore and S. Schindler, eds. (2015), *The Art of Inequality: Architecture, Housing, and Real Estate – A Provisional Report*, New York: Temple Hoyne Buell Center for the Study of American Architecture.

Massey, D. (1994), *Space, Place and Gender*, Cambridge: Polity Press.

Matchar, E. (2013), *Homeward Bound: Why Women Are Embracing the New Domesticity*, New York: Simon & Schuster.

Mateyka, P.J., M.A. Rapino and L.C. Landivar (2012), 'Home-Based Workers in the United States: 2010', United States Census Bureau, October. Available online: http://www.census.gov/prod/2012pubs/p70-132.pdf (accessed 20 May 2020).

Matrix (1984), *Making Space: Women and the Man Made Environment*, London: Pluto.

Matthews, G. (1987), *'Just a Housewife': The Rise and Fall of Domesticity in America*, New York: Oxford University Press.

Mattsson, H. and S.-O. Wallenstein, eds. (2010), *Swedish Modernism: Architecture, Consumption, and the Welfare State*, London: Black Dog.

May, E.T. (1988), *Homeward Bound: American Families in the Cold War Era*, New York: Basic Books.

Mayhall, L.E. (1999), 'Domesticating Emmeline: Representing the Suffragette, 1930–1993', *National Women's Studies Association Journal*, 11 (2): 1–24.

McCann, B. (2014), *Hard Times in the Marvelous City: From Dictatorship to Democracy in the Favelas of Rio de Janeiro*, Durham, NC: Duke University Press.

McDannell, C. (1994), *The Christian Home in Victorian America, 1840–1900*, Bloomington, IN: Indiana University Press.

McDonald's Corporation (2015), *McDonald's 2014 Annual Report*, March. Available online: https://corporate.mcdonalds.com/content/dam/AboutMcDonalds/Investors/McDonalds2014AnnualReport.PDF (accessed 20 May 2020).

McGreevy, J.T. (1996), *Parish Boundaries: The Catholic Encounter with Race in the Twentieth-Century Urban North*, Chicago, IL: University of Chicago Press.

McIntyre, N., D. Williams and K. McHugh, eds. (2006), *Multiple Dwelling and Tourism: Negotiating Place, Home and Identity*, Wallingford: CABI.

Mead, G.H. (1934), *Mind, Self and Society from the Standpoint of a Social Behaviorist*, Chicago, IL: Chicago University Press.

Mehta, S.K. (2015), 'Chrismukkah: Millennial Multiculturalism', *Religion and American Culture: A Journal of Interpretation*, 25 (1): 82–109.

Mehta, S.K. (2018), *Beyond Chrismukkah: The Christian-Jewish Interfaith Family in the United States*, Chapel Hill, NC: University of North Carolina Press.

Meier, P. (2018), 'The Swahili House: A Historical Ethnography of Modernity', in S. Wynne-Jones and A. LaViolette (eds.), *The Swahili World*, 629–41, Abingdon: Routledge.

Merish, L. (2000), *Sentimental Materialism: Gender, Commodity Culture, and Nineteenth-Century American Literature*, Durham, NC: Duke University Press.

Milkman, R., E. Reese and B. Roth (1998), 'The Macrosociology of Paid Domestic Labor', *Work and Occupations*, 25 (4): 483–510.

Miller, D., ed. (1995a), *Acknowledging Consumption: A Review of New Studies*, London: Routledge.

Miller, D. (1995b), *Unwrapping Christmas*, Oxford: Clarendon Press.

Miller, D. (1998), *A Theory of Shopping*, Ithaca, NY: Cornell University Press.

Miller, D., ed. (2001), *Home Possessions: Material Culture Behind Closed Doors*, Oxford: Berg.

Miller, D. (2005), *Materiality*, Durham, NC: Duke University Press.

Miller, D. (2008), *The Comfort of Things*, Cambridge: Polity Press.

Miller, J.R. (1996), *Shingwauk's Vision: A History of Native Residential Schools*, Toronto: University of Toronto Press.

Miller, W.C. (1990), 'Scandinavian Architecture during the Late 1930s: Asplund and Aalto Versus Functionalism', *Reflections: Journal of the School of Architecture, University of Illinois at Urbana-Champaign*, 7: 4–13.

Milloy, J.S. (1999), *A National Crime: The Canadian Government and the Residential School System, 1879 to 1986*, Winnipeg: University of Manitoba Press.

Mills, C.W. (1959), *The Sociological Imagination*, Oxford: Oxford University Press.

Mintz, S. and S. Kellogg (1999), *Domestic Revolutions: A Social History of American Family Life*, New York: Simon & Schuster.

Miranda, V. (2011), 'Cooking, Caring and Volunteering: Unpaid Work Around the World', *OECD Social, Employment and Migration Working Papers*, No. 116, Paris: OECD Publications. Available online: http://www.oecd.org/officialdocuments/publicdisplaydocumentpdf/?cote=DELSA/ELSA/WD/SEM(2011)1&doclanguage=en (accessed 20 May 2020).

Mitchell, C. and J. Reid-Walsh, eds. (2008), *Girl Culture: An Encyclopedia*, Westport, CT: Greenwood Press.

Mitchinson, W. (2002), *Giving Birth in Canada, 1900–1950*, Toronto: University of Toronto Press.

Moore, J. (2000), 'Placing Home in Context', *Journal of Experimental Psychology*, 20 (3): 207–17.
Moreton-Robinson, A. (2015), *The White Possessive*, Minneapolis, MN: University of Minnesota Press.
Morgan, D.H.G. (2011), 'Locating "Family Practices"', *Sociological Research Online*, 16 (4): 14. Available online: http://www.socresonline.org.uk/16/4/14.html (accessed 20 May 2020).
Morley, D. (2000), *Home Territories: Media, Mobility and Identity*, Abingdon: Routledge.
Morrison, C.-A. (2012), 'Home and Heterosexuality in Aotearoa New Zealand: The Spaces and Practices of DIY and Home Renovation', *New Zealand Geographer*, 68 (2): 121–29.
Muñoz, I.S. (2020), 'The Coronavirus Pandemic is Making the US Housing Crisis Even Worse', *The Conversation*, 17 April. Available online: http://theconversation.com/the-coronavirus-pandemic-is-making-the-us-housing-crisis-even-worse-136025 (accessed 25 April 2020).
Murdock, G.P. (1949), *Social Structure*, New York: Macmillan.
Murphy, D. (2016), *Last Futures: Nature, Technology, and the End of Architecture*, New York: Verso.
Murphy, K.M. (2015), *Swedish Design: An Ethnography*, Ithaca, NY: Cornell University Press.
Murray, K.B. (2004), 'Governing Unwed Mothers in Toronto at the Turn of the Twentieth Century', *Canadian Historical Review*, 85 (2): 253–76.
Myers, D. and C. Yang Liu (2006), 'The Emerging Dominance of Immigrants in the US Housing Market 1970–2000', *Urban Policy and Research*, 23 (3): 347–66.
Nagengast, B. and G. Meckler (1994), *Heat and Cold: Mastering the Great Indoors: A Selective History of Heating, Ventilation, Air-conditioning and Refrigeration from the Ancients to the 1930s*, Atlanta, GA: American Society of Heating, Refrigerating and Air-Conditioning Engineers.
Nathenson, C. (2013), 'Chrismukkah as Happy Ending? The Weihnukka Exhibition at the Jewish Museum Berlin as German-Jewish Integration Fantasy', *Journal of Jewish Identities*, 6 (1): 57–69.
National Center for Health Statistics (1991), 'Advance Report of Final Divorce Statistics, 1988'. Available online: https://www.cdc.gov/nchs/data/mvsr/supp/mv39_12s2.pdf (accessed 20 May 2020).
Nelson, M.K. (2004). 'How Men Matter: Housework and Self-provisioning Among Rural Single-mother and Married-couple Families in Vermont, US', *Feminist Economics*, 10 (2): 9–36.
Nenonen, S. and K. Storbacka (2018), *Smash: Using Market Shaping to Design New Strategies for Innovation, Value Creation, and Growth*, Bingley: Emerald.
Nepstad, S.E. (2004), *Convictions of the Soul: Religion, Culture, and Agency in the Central America Solidarity Movement*, New York: Oxford University Press.
Neuhaus, J. (2011), *Housework and Housewives in American Advertising: Married to the Mop*, New York: Palgrave Macmillan.
Newland, K. (2016), 'For Every Step Forward on Refugee Protection, Two Steps Back amid Record Displacement', 14 December, Washington, DC: Migration Policy Institute. Available online: https://www.migrationpolicy.org/article/every-step-forward-refugee-protection-two-steps-back-amid-record-displacement (accessed 29 April 2020).
Nicolaides, B. (2002), *My Blue Heaven: Life and Politics in the Working-Class Suburbs of Los Angeles, 1920–1965*, Chicago, IL: University of Chicago Press.

Nicolaides, B. and A. Wiese, eds. (2006), *The Suburb Reader*, London: Routledge.

Noonan, M.C. and J. Glass (2012), 'The Hard Truth about Telecommuting', *Monthly Labor Review*, June: 38–45.

Nuclear Energy Institute (2020), 'World Nuclear Plants in Operation', Washington, DC: Nuclear Energy Institute. Available online: https://www.nei.org/resources/statistics/world-nuclear-power-plants-in-operation (accessed 20 May 2020).

Oakley, A. (1974), *The Sociology of Housework*, Oxford: Martin Robinson.

Oakley, A. ([1974] 1976), *Housewife*, London: Penguin.

O'Brien, J.M. (2010), *Firsting and Lasting: Writing Indians Out of Existence in New England*, Minneapolis, MN: University of Minnesota Press.

Oddy, D.J. (2003), *From Plain Fare to Fusion Food: British Diet from the 1890s to the 1990*, Woodbridge: Boydell Press.

O'Dell, C. (1997), *Women Pioneers in Television: Biographies of Fifteen Industry Leaders*, Jefferson, NC: McFarland.

Ofcom (2015), 'The UK is Now a Smartphone Society', media release, 6 August, London: Ofcom. Available online: https://www.ofcom.org.uk/about-ofcom/latest/media/media-releases/2015/cmr-uk-2015 (accessed 20 May 2020).

Ogata, A.F. (2008–9), 'Building Imagination in Postwar American Children's Rooms', *Studies in the Decorative Arts*, 16 (1): 126–42.

Ohmann, R. (1996), *Selling Culture: Magazines, Markets and Class at the Turn of the Century*, New York: Verso.

Oldenziel, R. (2009), 'Exporting the American Cold War Kitchen: Challenging Americanization, Technological Transfer, and Domestication', in R. Oldenziel and K. Zachmann (eds.), *Cold War Kitchen: Americanization, Technology, and European Users*, 315–39, Cambridge, MA: MIT Press.

Oldenziel, R. and K. Zachmann, eds. (2009), *Cold War Kitchen: Americanization, Technology, and European Users*, Cambridge, MA: MIT Press.

Oliver, P. (1976), *Shelter and Society: New Studies in Vernacular Architecture*, London: Barrie & Jenkins.

Oliver, P. (2003), *Dwellings: The Vernacular House Worldwide*, New York: Phaidon.

Oliver, P., I. Davis and I. Bentley (1981), *Dunroamin: The Suburban Semi and its Enemies*, London: Barrie & Jenkins.

Olson, R. and C. Couchie (2013), 'Returning Birth: The Politics of Midwifery Implementation on First Nations Reserves in Canada', *Midwifery*, 29 (8): 981–87.

Orsi, R.A. (1999), *Gods of the City: Religion and the American Urban Landscape*, Bloomington, IN: Indiana University Press.

Orsi, R.A. (2010), *The Madonna of 115th Street: Faith and Community in Italian Harlem, 1880–1950*, 3rd edition, New Haven, CT: Yale University Press.

Owram, D. (1997), *Born at the Right Time: A History of the Baby Boom Generation*, Toronto: University of Toronto Press.

Pahl, R. (1984), *Divisions of Labor*, Oxford: Wiley-Blackwell.

Pallasmaa, J., ed. (1984), *Alvar Aalto Furniture*, Helsinki: Museum of Finnish Architecture.

Papademetriou, D.G. (2012), 'Rethinking National Identity in the Age of Migration (Transatlantic Council Statement)', *Migration Policy Institute Report*, Washington, DC: Migration Policy Institute. Available online: http://www.migrationpolicy.org/research/TCM-rethinking-national-identity-council-statement (accessed 20 May 2020).

Parissien, S. (2013), *The Life of the Automobile: A New History of the Motor Car*, London: Atlantic.

Parr, J. (1999), *Domestic Goods: The Material, the Moral and the Economic in the Postwar Years*, Toronto: University of Toronto Press.
Parreñas, R. (2001), *Servants of Globalization: Women, Migration and Domestic Work*, Stanford, CA: Stanford University Press.
Parsons, T. (1959), 'The School Class as a Social System: Some of its Functions in American Society', *Harvard Educational Review*, 29 (4): 297–318.
Parsons, T. and Bales, R.F. (1956), *Family, Socialization and Interaction Process*, London: Routledge.
Patel, K. (2013), 'A Successful Slum Upgrade in Durban: A Case of Formal Change and Informal Continuity', *Habitat International*, 40: 211–17.
Penner, B. (2009), '". . .the whole house shook": Mary Poppins and the Modern Home', *Haecceity*, 4 (2): 5–27.
Penner, B. (2013), *Bathroom*, London: Reaktion.
Percy, M.S. (2014), *Not Just a Shelter Kid: How Homeless Children Find Solace*, London: Routledge.
Perkins, H. and D. Thorns (1999), 'House and Home and Their Interaction with Changes in New Zealand's Urban System, Households and Family Structures', *Housing Theory and Society*, 16 (3): 124–35.
Perkins, H. and D. Thorns (2001), 'Houses, Homes and New Zealanders' Everyday Lives', in C. Bell (ed.), *The Sociology of Everyday Life in New Zealand*, 30–51, Palmerston North: Dunmore Press.
Perkins, H. and D. Thorns (2003), 'The Making of Home in a Global World: Aotearoa as an Exemplar', in R. Forest and J. Lee (eds.), *Housing and Social Change: East–West Perspectives*, 120–39, London: Routledge.
Perlman, J. (2010), *Favela: Four Decades of Living on the Edge in Rio de Janeiro*, Oxford: Oxford University Press.
Piketty, T. (2014), *Capital in the Twenty-First Century*, trans. A. Goldhammer, Cambridge, MA: Harvard University Press.
Pilkey, B., R.M. Scicluna and A. Gorman-Murray (2015), 'Alternative Domesticities', *Home Cultures*, 12 (2): 127–38.
Pilkey, B., R.M. Scicluna, B. Campkin and B. Penner, eds. (2017), *Sexuality and Gender at Home: Experience, Politics, Transgression*, London: Bloomsbury.
Pink, S. (2004), *Home Truths: Gender, Domestic Objects and Everyday Life*, Oxford: Berg.
Pino, J.C. (1998), 'Labor in the Favelas of Rio de Janeiro, 1940–1969', *Latin American Perspectives*, 25 (2): 18–40.
Platzer, E. (2010), 'Care Work and Migration Politics in Sweden', in L.W. Isaksen (ed.), *Global Care Work: Gender and Migration in Nordic Societies*, 159–72, Lund: Nordic Academic Press.
Plaut, J.E. (2012), *A Kosher Christmas: 'Tis the Season to Be Jewish*, New Brunswick, NJ: Rutgers University Press.
Potter, D. (1977), 'Trampling the Mud from Wall to Wall', review of *Abigail's Party* in *The Sunday Times*, 6 November: 35.
Pow, C.-P. (2009), 'Neoliberalism and the Aestheticization of New Middle-Class Landscapes', *Antipode*, 41 (2): 371–90.
Powers, A. (2019), *Bauhaus Goes West: Modern Art and Design in Britain and America*, New York: Thames & Hudson.
'PREVI/Lima: Low Cost Housing Project' (1970), *Architectural Design*, 40 (4): 187–205.
Prizeman, J. (1975), *Your House, the Outside View*, London: Hutchinson.

Radforth, I. (2014), 'Collective Rights, Liberal Discourse, and Public Order: The Clash Over Catholic Processions in Mid-Victorian Toronto', *Canadian Historical Review*, 95 (4): 511–44.

Raizman, D. (2004), *History of Modern Design*, Upper Saddle, NJ: Prentice-Hall.

Ramirez, H. and P. Hondagneu-Sotelo (2009), 'Mexican Immigrant Gardeners: Entrepreneurs or Exploited Workers', *Social Problems*, 56 (1): 70–88.

Rao, N. (2013), *House but No Garden: Apartment Living in Bombay's Suburbs 1898–1964*, Minneapolis, MN: University of Minnesota Press.

Rapoza, K. (2013), 'One in Five Americans Work from Home, Numbers Seen Rising Over 60%', *Forbes*, 18 February. Available online: https://www.forbes.com/sites/kenrapoza/2013/02/18/one-in-five-americans-work-from-home-numbers-seen-rising-over-60/#83d536625c1d (accessed 20 May 2020).

Ravetz, A. and R. Turkington (1995), *The Place of Home: English Domestic Environments 1914–2000*, London: Spon.

Ray, R. and S. Qayum (2009), *Cultures of Servitude: Modernity. Domesticity and Class in Modern India*, Stanford, CA: Stanford University Press.

Reaney, P. (2012), 'About One in Five Workers Worldwide Telecommute', *Reuters*, 24 January.

Reid, J. (2010), '"This Room is Yours, Personal!": The Rise and Fall of Middle-Class Decoration Expertise in the Bedrooms of America's Teens, 1900–1985', *Journal of the Canadian Historical Association/Revue de la Société historique du Canada*, 21 (1): 109–29.

Reid, J. (2012), '"My Room! Private! Keep Out! This Means You!": A Brief Overview of the Emergence of the Autonomous Teen Bedroom in Post-World War II America', *Journal of the History of Childhood and Youth*, 5 (3): 419–43.

Reid, S.E. (2005), 'The Khrushchev Kitchen: Domesticating the Scientific-Technological Revolution', *Journal of Contemporary History*, 40 (2): 289–316.

Reid, S.E. (2009), '"Our Kitchen is Just as Good": Soviet Responses to the American Kitchen', in R. Oldenziel and K. Zachmann (eds.), *Cold War Kitchen: Americanization, Technology, and European Users*, 83–112, Cambridge, MA: MIT Press.

Reimer, S. and D. Leslie (2004), 'Identity, Consumption, and the Home', *Home Cultures*, 1 (2): 187–208.

Reimer, S. and P. Pinch (2013), 'Geographies of the British Government's Wartime Utility Furniture Scheme, 1940–1945', *Journal of Historical Geography*, 39: 99–112.

Ribak, R. and M. Rosenthal (2006), 'From the Field Phone to the Mobile Phone: A Cultural Biography of the Telephone in Kibbutz Y', *New Media and Society*, 8 (4): 551–72.

Richardson, J. and A. Ryder (2012), *Gypsies and Travellers: Empowerment and Inclusion in British Society*, Bristol: Policy Press.

Ridgely, S. (2006), *When I Was a Child: Children's Interpretations of First Communion*, Chapel Hill, NC: University of North Carolina Press.

Ritzer, G. (2010), *Globalization: A Basic Text*, Oxford: Wiley-Blackwell.

Robach, C. (2002), 'Design for Modern People', in C. Widenheim (ed.), *Utopia and Reality: Modernity in Sweden, 1900–1960*, 186–201, New Haven, CT: Yale University Press.

Robb Larkins, E.M. (2015), *The Spectacular Favela: Violence in Modern Brazil*, Minneapolis, MN: University of Minnesota Press.

Robertson, H. (1947), *Reconstruction and the Home*, London: The Studio.

Rojas, J. (1991), 'The Enacted Environment: The Creation of Place by Mexicans and Mexican-Americans in East Los Angeles', MA thesis, Massachusetts Institute of Technology.

Romero, M. (2002), *Maid in the USA*, New York: Routledge.

Ross, A. (1999), *The Celebration Chronicles: Life, Liberty, and the Pursuit of Property Value in Disney's New Town*, New York: Ballantyne.

Rothstein, R. (2017), *The Color of Law: A Forgotten History of How Our Government Segregated America*, New York: Liveright.

Rowlands, M. (2005), 'A Materialist Approach to Materiality', in D. Miller (ed.), *Materiality*, 72–87, Durham, NC: Duke University Press.

Rutherdale, R. (1999), 'Fatherhood, Masculinity, and the Good Life during Canada's Baby Boom, 1945–1965', *Journal of Family History*, 24 (3): 351–73.

Rutherdale, M. (2010), *Caregiving on the Periphery: Historical Perspectives on Nursing and Midwifery in Canada*, Montreal/Kingston: McGill-Queen's University Press.

Rybczynski, W. (1986), *Home: A Short History of an Idea*, New York: Viking.

Sand, J. (2005), *House and Home in Modern Japan: Architecture, Domestic Space, and Bourgeois Culture, 1880–1930*, Cambridge, MA: Harvard University Press.

Saunders, P. (1989), 'The Meaning of the Home in the Decade of Owner Occupation', *Housing Studies*, 4 (3): 177–92.

Saunders, P. and P. Williams (1988), 'The Constitution of the Home: Towards a Research Agenda', *Housing Studies*, 3 (2): 81–93.

Scanlon, K. and C. Whitehead (2008), *Social Housing in Europe II: A Review of Policies and Outcomes*, London: London School of Economics and Political Science.

Schlesinger, A.M. ([1946] 1968), *Learning How to Behave: A Historical Study of American Etiquette Books*, New York: Cooper Square and Macmillan.

Schmidt, L.E. (1997), *Consumer Rites: The Buying and Selling of American Holidays*, Princeton, NJ: Princeton University Press.

Schuldenfrei, R., ed. (2012), *Atomic Dwelling: Anxiety, Domesticity and Postwar Architecture*, Abingdon: Routledge.

Schwartz, F. (1996), *The Werkbund: Design Theory and Mass Culture Before the First World War*, New Haven, CT: Yale University Press.

Schwartzel, E. and B. Fritz (2014), 'Fewer Americans Go to the Movies', *Wall Street Journal*, 26 March.

Schweitzer, R. and W.R. Davis (1990), *America's Favorite Homes: Mail-Order Catalogues as a Guide to Popular Early 20th-Century Houses*, Detroit, MI: Wayne State University Press.

Scott, J.W. ([1988] 2000), 'Gender: A Useful Category of Historical Analysis', in J. Rendell, B. Penner and I. Borden (eds.), *Gender Space Architecture: An Interdisciplinary Introduction*, 74–87, London: Routledge.

Scott, P. (2013), *The Making of the Modern British Home: The Suburban Semi and Family Life between the Wars*, Oxford: Oxford University Press.

Scott Brown, D. and R. Venturi (1970), 'Learning from Levittown or Remedial Housing for Architects', unpublished research project, Yale University, New Haven, CT.

Sebastian, M. (2015), 'Martha Stewart Living Omnimedia Sold for $353 Million', *AdAge*, 22 June. Available online: https://adage.com/article/media/martha-stewart-living-omnimedia-sold-353-million/299155 (accessed 17 January 2020).

Seebohm-Rowntree, B. (1910), *Land and Labor: Lessons from Belgium*, London: Macmillan.

Seiler, C. (2009), *Republic of Drivers: A Cultural History of Automobility in America*, Chicago, IL: University of Chicago Press.

Selkurt, C. (2003), 'Design for a Democracy: Scandinavian Design in Postwar America', in W. Halén and K. Wickman (eds.), *Scandinavian Design: Beyond the Myth: Fifty Years of Design from the Nordic Countries*, 59–66, Stockholm: Arvinius.

Sered, S.S. (1986), 'Rachel's Tomb and the Milk Grotto of the Virgin Mary: Two Women's Shrines in Bethlehem', *Journal of Feminist Studies in Religion*, 2 (2): 7–22.

Sered, S.S. (1996), *Women as Ritual Experts: The Religious Lives of Elderly Jewish Women in Jerusalem*, Oxford: Oxford University Press.

Shandler, J. and A. Weintraub (2007), '"Santa, Shmanta": Greeting Cards for the December Dilemma', *Material Religion*, 3 (3): 380–404.

Shen, J. and F. Wu (2011), 'Restless Urban Landscapes in China: A Case Study of Three Projects in Shanghai', *Journal of Urban Affairs*, 34 (3): 255–77.

Shor, F.R. (1997), *Utopianism and Radicalism in a Reforming America, 1888–1918*, Westport, CT: Greenwood Press.

Shove E., M. Watson, M. Hand and J. Ingram (2007), *The Design of Everyday Life*, Oxford: Berg.

Shriver, L. (2010), 'Introduction', in B. Friedan, *The Feminine Mystique*, v–xi, London: Penguin.

Sinclair, R. (2007), 'Identity Lost and Found: Lessons from the Sixties Scoop', *First Peoples Child and Family Review*, 3 (1): 65–82.

Singh, A, N. Iyer and R. Gairola, eds. (2016), *Revisiting India's Partition*, London: Lexington Books.

Skeggs, B. and H. Wood (2009), 'The Transformation of Intimacy: Classed Identities in the Moral Economy of Reality Television', in M. Wetherell (ed.), *Identity in the 21st Century: New Trends in Changing Times*, 231–49, Basingstoke: Palgrave Macmillan.

Sklar, K.K. (1979), *Catharine Beecher: A Study in American Domesticity*, New York: Norton.

Slow Food (2015), 'Slow Food: The History of an Idea'. Available online: https://www.slowfood.com/about-us/our-history/ (accessed 21 April 2020).

Somerville, P. (1992), 'Homelessness and the Meaning of Home: Rooflessness or Rootlessness?', *International Journal of Urban and Regional Research*, 16 (4): 529–39.

Somerville, P. (1997), 'The Social Construction of Home', *Journal of Architectural and Planning Research*, 14 (3): 226–45.

Sörlin, S. (2002), 'Prophets and Deniers: The Idea of Modernity in Swedish Tradition', in C. Widenheim (ed.), *Utopia and Reality: Modernity in Sweden 1900–1960*, 16–25, New Haven, CT: Yale University Press.

Sparke, P. (1995), *As Long as it's Pink: The Sexual Politics of Taste*, London: Pandora.

Spring Rice, M. ([1939] 1995), 'Working-class Wives', in E. Malos (ed.), *The Politics of Housework*, 74–82, Cheltenham: New Clarion Press.

Stansell, C. (2012), *City of Women*, New York: Knopf Doubleday.

Statista, Inc. (2020), 'Number of Mobile Phone Users Worldwide from 2015 to 2020 (in Billions)'. Available online: http://www.statista.com/statistics/274774/forecast-of-mobile-phone-users-worldwide/ (accessed 20 May 2020).

Statistics Canada (2009), 'Dwellings and Family Households, by provinces, 1881 to 1921'. Available online: http://www65.statcan.gc.ca/acyb02/1927/acyb02_19270113013-eng.htm (accessed 20 May 2020).

Statistics Canada (2015), 'Fifty Years of Families in Canada: 1961 to 2011'. Available online: https://www12.statcan.gc.ca/census-recensement/2011/as-sa/98-312-x/98-312-x2011003_1-eng.cfm (accessed 20 May 2020).

Stearns, P.N., P. Rowland and L. Giarnella (1996), 'Children's Sleep: Sketching Historical Change', *Journal of Social History*, 30 (2): 345–66.
Stenum, H. (2010), 'Au Pair Migration and New Inequalities: The Transnational Production of Corruption', in L.W. Isaksen (ed.), *Global Care Work: Gender and Migration in Nordic Societies*, 23–48, Lund: Nordic Academic Press.
Stenum, H. (2015), 'Bane and Boon; Gains and Pains; Dos and Don'ts . . . Moral Economy and Female Bodies in Au Pair Migration', in R. Cox (ed.), *Au Pairs' Lives in Global Context: Sisters or Servants?*, 104–20, Basingstoke: Palgrave Macmillan.
Stevens, M. (2009), *Kingdom of Children: Culture and Controversy in the Homeschooling Movement*, Princeton, NJ: Princeton University Press.
Stieber, N. (1998), *Housing Design and Society in Amsterdam: Reconfiguring Urban Order and Identity, 1900–1920*, Chicago, IL: University of Chicago Press.
Stiefel, B.L. (2014), *Jewish Sanctuary in the Atlantic World: A Social and Architectural History*, Columbia, SC: University of South Carolina Press.
Strasser, S. (1982), *Never Done: A History of American Housework*, New York: Pantheon.
Strathern, M. (1987), 'The Limits of Auto-anthropology', in D. Jackson (ed.), *Anthropology at Home*, 16–37, London: Tavistock.
Stratigakos, D. (2003), 'Women and the Werkbund: Gender Politics and German Design Reform, 1907–14', *Journal of the Society of Architectural Historians*, 62 (4): 490–511.
Stratigakos, D. (2005), 'The Uncanny Architect: Fears of Lesbian Builders and Deviant Homes in Modern Germany', in H. Heynen and G. Baydar (eds.), *Negotiating Domesticity: Spatial Productions of Gender in Modern Architecture*, 145–61, London: Routledge.
Stratigakos, D. (2015), *Hitler at Home*, New Haven, CT: Yale University Press.
Strong-Boag, V. (1991), 'Home Dreams: Women and the Suburban Experiment in Canada, 1945–60', *Canadian Historical Review*, 72 (4): 5–25.
Tharp, B.M. (2007), 'Valued Amish Possessions: Expanding Material Culture and Consumption', *Journal of American Culture*, 30 (1): 38–53.
Thomas, J.B. (2019), 'Domesticity & Spirituality: Kondo Is Not an Animist', *Marginalia*, 8 February. Available online: https://marginalia.lareviewofbooks.org/domesticity-spirituality-kondo-not-animist/ (accessed 25 April 2020).
Tigerman, B. (2015), 'Editor's Introduction', *Design and Culture*, 7 (3): 277–82.
Tinkler, P. and C.K. Warsh (2008), 'Feminine Modernity in Interwar Britain and North America: Corsets, Cars, and Cigarettes', *Journal of Women's History*, 20 (3): 113–43.
Todd, S. (2014), *The People: The Rise and Fall of the Working Class*, London: John Murray.
Tomes, N. (1998), *The Gospel of Germs: Men, Women, and the Microbe in American Life*, Cambridge, MA: Harvard University Press.
Tone, A. (2008), *The Age of Anxiety: A History of America's Turbulent Affair with Tranquilizers*, New York: Basic Books.
Truth and Reconciliation Commission of Canada (2015), 'Truth and Reconciliation Commission of Canada: Calls to Action', Winnipeg: Truth and Reconciliation Commission of Canada.
Tu, J.I. (2015), 'Low pay and long, pricey commute often go hand in hand', *Seattle Times*, 29 August. Available online: http://www.seattletimes.com/business/economy/low-pay-long-pricey-commute-often-go-hand-in-hand/ (accessed 15 May 2020).
Turner, J. (2011), 'John Locke, Christian Mission, and Colonial America', *Modern Intellectual History*, 8 (2): 267–97.

Turner, J.F.C. (1976), *Housing by People: Towards Autonomy in Building Environments*, London: Marion Boyars.
Turner, J.F.C. and R. Fichter, eds. (1972), *Freedom to Build: Dweller Control of the Housing Process*, New York: Macmillan.
Turner, L. (2017), 'The Good Wife: How the Cult of Domesticity Still Reigns in the 21st Century: On the Cost – and Subtle Persistence – of the Cult of Domesticity', *Pacific Standard*, 10 September. Available online: http://www.psmag.com/books-and-culture/the-21st-century-cult-of-domesticity (accessed 20 May 2020).
Tyler, I. (2008), '"Chav Mum, Chav Scum": Class Disgust in Contemporary Britain', *Feminist Media Studies*, 8 (1): 17–34.
U'mista Cultural Centre (2020), 'The History of the Potlatch Collection'. Available online: https://www.umista.ca/pages/collection-history (accessed 10 January 2020).
United Nations (2018), *2018 Revision of World Urbanization Prospects*, New York: United Nations, Department of Economic and Social Affairs. Available online: https://www.un.org/development/desa/publications/2018-revision-of-world-urbanization-prospects.html (accessed 20 May 2020).
United Nations (2019), 'The Number of International Migrants Reaches 272 Million, Continuing an Upward Trend in All World Regions, says UN', New York: United Nations, Department of Economic and Social Affairs. Available online: https://www.un.org/development/desa/en/news/population/international-migrant-stock-2019.html (accessed 29 April 2020).
United Nations Human Settlements Programme (2003), *The Challenge of Slums*, London: Earthscan Publications.
United Nations Population Fund (UNFPA) (2007), *State of World Population 2007: Unleashing the Potential of Urban Growth*, New York: UNFPA.
Upton, D. (1998), *Architecture in the United States*, Oxford: Oxford University Press.
Urbach, H. (1992), 'Peeking at Gay Interiors', *Design Book Review*, 25: 39.
Urbach, H. (1996), 'Closets, Clothes, Disclosure', *Assemblage*, 30: 62–73.
Urban, F. (2011), *Tower and Slab: Histories of Global Mass Housing*, London: Routledge.
Urry, J. (2007), *Mobilities*, Cambridge, UK: Polity Press.
Valentine, M. (1994), *The Show Starts on the Sidewalk: An Architectural History of the Movie Theater, Starring S. Charles Lee*, New Haven, CT: Yale University Press.
Van Caudenberg, A. and H. Heynen (2004), 'The Rational Kitchen in the Interwar Period in Belgium: Discourses and Realities', *Home Cultures*, 1 (1): 23–49.
Van Herck, K. and T. Avermaete, eds. (2006), *Wonen in Welvaart: Woningbouw and woonccultuur in Vlaanderen, 1948–1973*, Rotterdam: 010 Publishers.
von Hoffmann, A. (1996), *Local Attachments: The Making of an American Urban Neighborhood, 1850 to 1920*, Baltimore, MD: Johns Hopkins University Press.
Vollmer, J.L., P.A. Schulze and J.M. Chebra (2005), 'The American Master Bedroom: Its Changing Location and Significance to the Family', *Journal of Interior Design*, 31 (1): 1–13.
Wajcman, J. (2013), *Feminism Confronts Technology*, Cambridge: Polity Press.
Walker, E. (2015), 'The Cleaner's Away: How Can I Survive?', *The Times*, 22 December. Available online: https://www.thetimes.co.uk/article/esther-walker-the-cleaners-away-how-can-i-survive-t3z25pgz6vf (accessed 20 May 2020).
Ward, P. (1999), *A History of Domestic Space: Privacy and the Canadian Home*, Vancouver, BC: UBC Press.
Waste Atlas Collective (2014), *Waste Atlas: The World's 50 Biggest Dumpsites, 2014 Report*. Available online: http://www.atlas.d-waste.com/Documents/Waste-Atlas-report-2014-webEdition.pdf (accessed 20 May 2020).

Weeks, K. (2007), 'Life Within and Against Work: Affective Labor, Feminist Critique, and Post Fordist Politics', *Ephemera*, 7 (1): 233–49.
Weiner, I. (2019), '"And Then! Oh, the Noise! Oh, the Noise! Noise! Noise! Noise!" Or How the Grinch Heard Christmas', in Pamela E. Klassen and Monique Scheer (eds.), *The Public Work of Christmas: Difference and Belonging in Multicultural Societies*, 36–59, Montreal and Kingston: McGill-Queen's University Press.
Weisenfeld, J. (2018), *New World A-Coming: Black Religion and Racial Identity During the Great Migration*, New York: NYU Press.
Weisenfeld, J. and R. Newman, eds. (1995), *This Far by Faith: Readings in African-American Women's Religious Biography*, New York: Routledge.
Werbner, P. (1990), *The Migration Process: Capital, Gifts and Offerings among British Pakistanis*, Oxford: Berg.
White, I.B. (1985), *The Crystal Chain Letters: Architectural Fantasies by Bruno Taut and His Circle*, Cambridge, MA: MIT Press.
Whitney-Brown, C. (2019), *Tender to the World: Jean Vanier, L'Arche, and the United Church of Canada*, Montreal and Kingston: McGill-Queen's University Press.
Wiese, A. (2004), *Places of Their Own: African American Suburbanization in the Twentieth-Century*, Chicago, IL: University of Chicago Press.
Wigley, M. (1992), 'Untitled: The Housing of Gender', in B. Colomina (ed.), *Sexuality and Space*, 327–389, New York: Princeton Architectural Press.
Wilk, C. (1987), 'Furnishing the Future', in D.E. Ostergaard (ed.), *Bent Wood and Metal Furniture 1850–1946*, 153–54, New York: American Federation of the Arts.
Wilk, C. (2006), *Modernism: Designing a New World, 1914–1939*, London: Victoria & Albert Museum.
Willcox, W.F. (1911), 'The Change in the Proportion of Children in the United States and in the Birth Rate in France during the Nineteenth Century', in *Publications of the American Statistical Association*, 12: 490–99. Available online: https://archive.org/details/jstor-2965131 (accessed 20 May 2020).
Williams, C.C. and J. Windebank (2002), 'The Uneven Geographies of Informal Economic Activities: A Case Study of Two British Cities', *Work, Employment and Society*, 16 (2): 231–50.
Wimmelbücker, L. (2012), 'Architecture and City Planning Projects of the German Democratic Republic in Zanzibar', *Journal of Architecture*, 17 (3): 407–32.
Wolf, M. and S. McQuitty (2011), 'Understanding the Do-It-Yourself Consumer: DIY Motivations and Outcomes', *AMS Review*, 1: 154–70.
Woodham, J.M. (1997), *Twentieth-Century Design*, Oxford: Oxford University Press.
Woodham, J.M. (2004), 'Design and Everyday Life at the *Britain Can Make It Exhibition*, 1946: "Stripes, Spots, White Wood and Homespun versus Chintzy Armchairs and Iron Bedsteads with Brass Knobs"', *Journal of Architecture*, 9 (4): 63–76.
World Health Organization (WHO) (2017), *Violence Against Women*, Fact sheet, 29 November. Geneva: WHO. Available online: https://www.who.int/news-room/fact-sheets/detail/violence-against-women (accessed 22 December 2019).
Wright, G. (1980), *Moralism and the Model Home: Domestic Architecture and Cultural Conflict in Chicago, 1873–1913*, Chicago, IL: University of Chicago Press.
Wright, G. (1981), *Building the Dream: A Social History of Housing in America*, New York: Pantheon Books.
Young, I.M. (2005), 'House and Home: Feminist Variations on a Theme', in *On Female Body Experience: 'Throwing Like a Girl' and Other Essays*, 123–54, Oxford: Oxford University Press.

Young, L. (2003), *Middle-Class Culture in the Nineteenth Century: America, Australia and Britain*, Basingstoke: Palgrave Macmillan.
Young-Bruehl, E. (2008), *Anna Freud: A Biography*, New Haven, CT: Yale University Press.
Zarecor, K. (2010), 'The Local History of an International Type: The Structural Panel Building in Czechoslovakia', *Home Cultures*, 7 (2): 217–36.
Zhang, C.Q. (1997), 'Chinese Housing Policy 1949–78: The Development of a Welfare System', *Planning Perspectives*, 12 (4): 433–55.

CONTRIBUTORS

Annmarie Adams, Stevenson Chair in the Philosophy and History of Science, is jointly appointed in the Peter Guo-hua Fu School of Architecture and the Department of Social Studies of Medicine (SSoM) at McGill University in Montreal, Canada. Adams is the author of *Architecture in the Family Way: Doctors, Houses, and Women, 1870–1900* (1996), *Medicine by Design: The Architect and the Modern Hospital, 1893–1943* (2008), and co-author (with Peta Tancred) of *'Designing Women': Gender and the Architectural Profession* (2000).

Rosie Cox is Professor of Geography at Birkbeck, University of London. She has a long-standing research interest in paid domestic labor in the UK, and the organization of reproductive labor more generally. She has written and edited a number of books, including: *The Servant Problem: Domestic Employment in a Global Economy* (2006), *Dirt: New Geographies of Cleanliness and Contamination* (2007, edited with Ben Campkin), *Au Pairs' Lives in Global Context: Sisters or Servants?* (2015), and *As An Equal? Au Pairing in the Twenty-First Century* (2017, authored with Nicky Busch). Her new book, *Home Improvement in the UK and Aotearoa New Zealand*, will be published by Routledge in 2021.

Kenny Cupers is Associate Professor of History and Theory of Architecture and Urbanism at the University of Basel, where he co-founded and leads its new division of Urban Studies. He works at the intersection of architectural history, urban studies, and critical geography. His research focuses on the role of housing in urban and state transformation, the epistemology and geopolitics of modernism, and the power and aesthetics of infrastructure. His book publications include *Neoliberalism on the Ground: Architecture and

Transformation from the 1960s to the Present (2020), *Spaces of Uncertainty: Berlin Revisited* (2017), *The Social Project: Housing Postwar France* (2014), and *Use Matters: An Alternative History of Architecture* (2013).

Pauline Garvey is Associate Professor of Anthropology at Maynooth University, Ireland. Her research interests include material culture and Nordic domesticity, domestic exhibitions (housing theatre) in 20th-century Sweden, design anthropology and the politics surrounding ethnographic collections in Ireland. She is the author of *Unpacking IKEA: Swedish Design for the Purchasing Masses* (2018) and co-editor (with Séamus Ó Síocháin and Adam Drazin) of *Exhibit Ireland: Ethnographic Collections in Irish Museums* (2012). Currently, she is a member of the global team of anthropologists pursuing the ethnographic research project *The Anthropology of Smart Phones and Smart Ageing*, funded by the European Research Council. Since 2013 Pauline has been the editor of the international peer-reviewed journal *Home Cultures: The Journal of Architecture, Design and Domestic Space*.

Rachel Hurdley is Research Fellow in Cultural Sociology in the College of Arts, Humanities and Social Sciences at Cardiff University. Her research interests include the ways that space, things, and people interact in the making of identity, and research methodologies. She is the author of *Home, Materiality, Memory and Belonging: Keeping Culture* (2013). Her work has also appeared in journals including *Sociology* and *Qualitative Inquiry*, and books such as *The Sage Handbook of Cultural Sociology*. Her current research focuses on material cultures of memory. She is also exploring how drawing, rather that writing or filming, affects fieldwork.

Pamela E. Klassen is Professor in the Department for the Study of Religion at the University of Toronto and a Fellow of the Royal Society of Canada. Her most recent books are *The Story of Radio Mind: A Missionary's Journey on Indigenous Land* (2018), *Ekklesia: Three Inquiries in Church and State*, co-authored with Paul Christopher Johnson and Winnifred Fallers Sullivan (2018), and, co-edited with Monique Scheer, *The Public Work of Christmas: Difference and Belonging in Multicultural Societies* (2019). Her digital storytelling project, "Kiinawin Kawindomowin Story Nations" can be found at https://storynations.utoronto.ca/. Among her other publications is the home-focused book, *Blessed Events: Religion and Home Birth in America* (2011). She is now working on a book focused on how gold—as mineral, money, and symbol of divinity—was at the heart of colonial cosmologies of land in the British Empire.

Grace Lees-Maffei is Professor of Design History and Programme Director for DHeritage, the Professional Doctorate in Heritage, at the University of Hertfordshire, UK. Her research investigates the mediation of design including domestic design advice, national identity and globalization. She is author of

Design at Home: Domestic Advice Books in Britain and the USA since 1945 (2014), co-author of *Reading Graphic Design* (2019), co-editor with Kjetil Fallan of *Designing Worlds: National Design Histories in an Age of Globalization* (2016, 2018) and *Made in Italy: Rethinking a Century of Italian Design* (2014), co-editor with Rebecca Houze of *The Design History Reader* (2010), and editor of *Iconic Designs: 50 Stories about 50 Things* (2014, 2020) and *Writing Design: Words and Objects* (2012). She is currently writing *The Hand Book*, and co-editing *Design and Heritage* with Rebecca Houze.

Barbara Penner is Professor in Architectural Humanities at the Bartlett School of Architecture, University College London. Her work consists of interdisciplinary investigations of the intersections between public space, architecture, and private lives. She is author of *Bathroom* (2013) and *Newlyweds on Tour: Honeymooning in Nineteenth-Century America* (2009), and co-editor of *Sexuality and Gender at Home* (2017, with Brent Pilkey, Rachel Scicluna, and Ben Campkin), *Ladies and Gents: Public Toilets and Gender* (2009, with Olga Gershenson), and *Gender Space Architecture: An Interdisciplinary Introduction* (2000, with Jane Rendell and Iain Borden). She has also contributed chapters to *Archi.Pop* (2015), *Globalization in Practice* (2014), and *Use Matters* (2013). She is a regular contributor to the architectural journals *Places* and *Architectural Review*.

Despina Stratigakos is Vice Provost for Inclusive Excellence and Professor of Architecture at the University at Buffalo, State University of New York. Her research explores how power and ideology function in architecture. She is the author of *A Women's Berlin: Building the Modern City* (2008; winner of the DAAD Book Prize of the German Studies Association); *Hitler at Home* (2015), *Where Are the Women Architects?* (2016), and *Hitler's Northern Utopia: Building the New Order in Occupied Norway* (2020). She is currently writing a cultural history of ghost towns from antiquity to the present.

INDEX

Headings in italics are titles of printed or visual media.

Aalto, Alvar 105
The A.B.C. of Etiquette by a Society Lady (1923) 165–6
Abigail's Party (play) 178
Africa 66, 72, 83, 87, 206 n.15
Alexander, Christopher 86
Algeria 83–4
apartments. *See* collective housing
L'Arche homes 202–3
architecture
    feminist 5–6, 145–6, 156
    modernist 1–2, 7–8, 51–4, 66, 71, 75–9, 88, 92–5, 97–100, 101, 108, 146
    postmodernist 71–2, 108
    post-war 8–9, 41–3, 45–6, 49, 51–4, 70–1, 108, 131
    socialist 6–7, 75, 77–8
Austin, Alice Constance 6–7

baby boom 39–40, 43, 70
backstage 54, 147, 167, 173–4, 176–7. *See also* zones
backyards 41–3, 141
bathrooms 43, 45, 51, 53, 55, 59, 154
Bauhaus 3, 76, 95, 101, 110
    furniture 95–8, 102
    kitchens 98–100

bedrooms
    children 40, 43, 45, 46, 49–51, 58–61
    and health 56–8
    inter-war era 54–8
    master 43–9
    postmodern era 59–62
    post-war era 39–54
Belaúnde Terry, Fernando 85–6
Belgium 67, 69, 71, 100
belongings 24, 91–2, 111–12, 159. *See also* consumerism; furniture
    on display 18, 26–34, 35
birth 58, 117, 197–8, 201
blocks. *See* collective housing
Brazil 80, 83, 84, 87
Breuer, Marcel 3, 96–8, 105
Britain
    attitude to housing 34–5, 133, 179
    hospitality 164–5, 168–70, 175–6, 178–9
    housing construction 77, 108
    social structure 38, 164–5
    Utility schemes 101–2, 168, 170
bungalows 66, 71, 72

Canada 55, 59, 186, 187, 198, 200–2, 203–4
Candilis-Josic-Woods 86

capitalism
    consumerism 5, 152–3, 159
    houses as commodities 71, 72–3,
        81, 89
    separation of home and work 139, 145,
        155
    and state aided housing 81, 88–9
celebrities 2–3
chairs 49, 96–8, 104, 105, 111, 150, 151,
    171
Child, Julia 175
children 11, 18, 27, 41–2, 57
    bedrooms 40, 43, 45, 46, 49–51,
        58–60
    and hospitality 162, 164
    indigenous 200–1, 202, 204
    paid childcare 123, 126, 128
    rearing of 5–7, 8, 22, 40, 41, 117, 119,
        134, 140, 146, 190
China 72, 77–8, 80
Christianity 187–8, 190, 191–4, 200, 201
    Christmas 32–3, 189, 195–6
Christie, Agatha 24–5
CIAM (International Congresses of
    Modern Architecture) 76, 85
clothing 44–5, 47, 50, 168, 170
Cold War 3, 77–8, 79, 102, 153, 170–1
collective housing 2, 5, 73–81, 88, 146,
    171
collective living 5–7, 75, 145, 156, 159,
    198, 199, 204
collective ownership 87, 186
colonialism 33, 66, 72, 74, 79, 83, 84, 85,
    88, 111, 186, 200–1, 206 n.15
communities. *See* neighbourhoods
commuting 10–11, 144
construction industry 17, 65, 70, 71, 76,
    77, 88
    prefabrication 74, 75, 76, 78, 110,
        149–50
    standardization 107
    tilt-slab construction 74
consumerism 3–5, 26, 41, 70. *See also*
    belongings
    children 60
    marketing 21–2, 145, 148, 163, 175
    women as consumers 19–21, 48,
        119–20, 152–4, 159, 165
convenience foods 19, 175–8, 179, 183

cooking 116, 167, 169, 179, 182–4, 190
    cookery books 175–6
    as creative event 9, 176–7
Cormier, Ernest 59
Cornell Kitchen 150–2
Covid-19 pandemic 10, 38, 182, 185
CUBEX cupboards 100

David, Elizabeth 175
death 57, 197, 198–9
De Koninck, Louis-Herman 100
de Soto, Hernando 86
dining rooms 55, 121, 141, 162, 165–6,
    170, 177
display 159
    childrens' bedrooms 50–1
    front-stage 147, 167, 174, 176–7
    mantelpieces 18, 27–34, 35
    and women 94, 119
DIY. *See* home maintenance
domestic appliances 9, 19–21, 147–8,
    150–3, 171, 176–7, 184
domesticity, cult of 15–16, 21, 154
domestic work (paid) 9, 114, 121–7, 135,
    167, 171. *See also* housework; home
    as workplace
Du Bois, W.E.B. 37

Eames, Charles and Ray 171, 172
entertainment 9–10. *See also* hospitality
evictions 11, 84

family life 6, 11, 16, 40–1, 197
    inter-war era 8–9, 54–8
    post-war era 41–2
    privacy 43, 53, 72, 92, 140–3, 161–2
family rooms 42
family structure 7, 60, 62, 65, 138–40,
    141, 145, 152
    family size 55, 59
    non-conventional family 7, 41, 51–4, 59
Farnsworth House 52
fast food 6, 183
fatherhood 7, 59, 128, 133–4, 137
Fathy, Hassan 85
favelas 83, 84
feminism 5, 15–6
    architecture 5–6, 145–6, 156
    and housewife role 119–21, 152–60

feng shui 194
First Nations. *See* indigenous peoples
First World War 1, 2, 7, 25, 54, 66, 74, 76, 82, 93, 95, 110, 144
flats. *See* collective housing
food preparation. *See* cooking
formality 9, 165–6
France 63, 69, 71, 76–7, 78, 79, 82, 84, 85, 88, 97, 108
Frankfurt Kitchen 1–2, 9, 75, 99, 100, 102, 149–50, 151–2, 167
Frank, Josef 105
Frederick, Christine 146, 148, 149, 167
Freud, Sigmund 18, 91–2, 111–12, 185
Friedan, Betty 5, 26, 41, 119, 154–5
Friends (TV show) 7
front-stage 54–5, 147, 167, 174, 176–7. *See also* zones
functionalism 3, 19, 22, 77, 104, 105
furniture 24, 91, 92. *See also* belongings
    bedroom 47, 49–50, 103
    chairs 49, 96–8, 111, 171
    modernism 94–8, 101–7, 108, 109, 168–70

garden cities 74
gardens 39, 42–3, 141
Gebhardt, Ernst 98
gender roles 1–2
    employment 121–2, 135, 156. *See also* domestic work (paid)
    in the home 41, 60, 114–17, 134–5, 137–40, 152–5, 159–60. *See also* fatherhood; motherhood
    hospitality 163–4, 167
    religion 189–91
gentrification 188
Germany. *See also* Bauhaus; Frankfurt Kitchen; Werkbund
    homelessness 3
    housing 1–2, 71, 74–5, 77, 78
    squatter settlements 82
GI Bill of Rights (1944) 131
Gilbreth, Lillian 148–9
Gill, Irving 74
Gilman, Charlotte Perkins 121
Ginzburg, Moisei 75
glass house, Connecticut 51–3

globalization 17, 58, 64, 72, 79, 88–9, 109, 114, 122, 125, 135
God Bostad (Swedish National Housing Board) 107
Graves, Michael 108
Gropius, Walter 4, 95, 97, 98, 110
Guide to Easier Living (1950) 171–4

Haus am Horn kitchen 98–9
Havens House 52–4
health 11, 55–8, 66, 84, 96–7, 117, 147–8, 169, 183, 198. *See also* hygiene
high-rise housing 76, 79–81, 108
Hinduism 191, 193, 199
Hitchcock, Henry-Russell 101
Hitler, Adolf 3, 4
Hollyhock House 146
home
    fictional representation 2, 7, 21, 24–6, 35, 50, 60, 119, 137–8, 155, 178
    homeliness 18, 32, 105
    homemaking 5, 119, 156–60, 169, 186, 200
    meaning of 13–18, 33, 36, 37, 67, 110–2, 139, 157–8, 185–6
    as sanctuary 188–9, 191–3
    as workplace 98, 114, 127–8, 144, 190–1. *See also* domestic work (paid); housework
homelessness 3, 11, 13, 34–5, 36, 186–7, 202
home maintenance 115, 128–34
    decorating 154, 159, 163, 169–70, 189–90
home ownership 5, 65, 69, 129
    encouragement by the state 67, 70–1, 79–80, 130–1, 144, 179
    exclusion from 6, 115, 128, 132, 186–7
    and land policies 86–7
homesickness 17–18, 200
homosexuality 51–4, 59
    same-sex couples 7, 56, 159, 191
Hong Kong 79–80
hooks, bell 157–8
Hoover, Herbert 144
hospitality 141, 161–2. *See also* entertainment; formality; informality
    domestic advice books 162–3
    inter-war era 164–8

late twentieth century 175–80
millennials 180–2
post-war era 170–5
Second World War 168–70
hospitals 57–8, 108, 187, 197, 198, 199, 201, 203
households 115, 161–2
family size 55, 59
non-conventional family 7, 41, 51–4, 59, 60, 62
single-person residences 2, 7
house museums 2–3
The House of Single Women (Böhm) 2
houses
low cost 77–8, 79–80, 85–6, 131
single family 22, 64–73, 88–9, 140–7
size 55, 59
standardization 70, 75, 76, 77–8, 107
housework. *See also* domestic work (paid)
domestic appliances 19–21, 147, 150–3, 171
gender roles 5, 21–2, 41, 113–14, 116–17, 119–22, 144–7, 154–5
hidden from view 9, 167, 173–4, 176–7
wages for 156
Howard, Ebenezer 73–4
Hume, Rosemary 175
hygiene 21, 55–6, 144–5, 147, 201. *See also* health

identity 92, 160
children 51
class 5, 43, 72, 119, 132
in homemaking 158–9
male 128, 129, 130, 132–4
mantelpiece displays 24, 27–9
national 37, 64
IKEA 109–10
illness. *See* health
India 80–1
indigenous peoples 186
forced adoption 201–2
midwifery 198
residential schools 199–201, 203–4
industrialization 115–16, 139
of construction 74
modernism 93, 180
and suburbia 65

informality 7, 8–9, 66, 99, 171, 172–3, 180–1
institutions 199–203
International Congresses of Modern Architecture (CIAM) 76, 85
internet 37, 40, 162, 178, 194
social media 60, 181–2
inter-war era 1–3, 19
family life 40, 54–8
hospitality 164–8
housework 116–17, 146–50
housing 69, 74–6, 82
modernism 7–8, 94–5, 101
Islam 191, 198–9

Jachmann, Christine 5
Japan 67
Johansson, Gotthard 107
Johnson, Philip 51–2, 53, 101, 108
Judaism 187, 188, 190, 191, 192, 193
Hannukah 195–7

Kenya 33
Khrushchev, Nikita 3–4, 153
kitchens 147–52, 155
centralized 6, 145, 146
domestic appliances 152–3
Frankfurt Kitchen 1–2, 9, 75, 99, 102, 149–50, 152, 167
hospitality 173–4, 177
kitchen debate 3–4, 153
modernism 98–100
as public zone 9, 54–5

land ownership 65, 86–7, 186
Le Corbusier 66, 74, 76, 111
Levittown, America 70, 71, 131
life cycle of buildings 203
Livermore, Mary 121
living rooms 45, 55, 102, 141
Llano Del Rio 6–7
Loos, Adolf 93, 111

Mad Men (TV show) 44, 119
Magdalene Homes 201
Main Street (Lewis) 25–6
Maison Domino 74
Malmsten, Carl 105
mantelpieces 18, 27–34, 35

marketing 21–2, 48, 102, 109, 145, 148, 154
marriage 41, 117, 139–40, 152–3, 191, 201
    divorce 7, 45, 62
    same-sex couples 7, 159
Mary Poppins (film) 137–8, 154
mass housing 73–81, 108, 206 n.7
materialism. *See* consumerism
maternity homes 201–2
Mathsson, Bruno 104–5
May, Ernst 75, 149, 167
Merivale, Margaret 169–70
Meyer, Adolf 98
middle classes 206 n.1
    family structure 49, 55
    lifestyle 22, 26, 39, 41–2, 44, 51, 54, 58–9, 65, 70, 164–5, 179
    mantelpiece displays 30
    paid domestic work 123, 126–7
    women's movement 5, 119
Mies van der Rohe, Ludwig 3, 52
migrants 3, 37, 71, 77, 193
    paid domestic work 122, 125–7, 190
millennials, hospitality 180–2
Modern Family (TV show) 60, 62
modernism 3, 22, 92–4, 180
    architecture 7–8, 51–4, 66, 71, 75–9, 88, 93–4, 108
    exhibitions of 100–2, 110–11
    furniture 94–8, 101–7, 108
    Ikea 109–10
    kitchens 1–2, 98–100
    mass housing 73, 76
    and women 1–2, 7–8, 52, 92, 94–5, 100, 169–70, 172. *See also* Frankfurt Kitchen
Moore, Charles 108
motherhood 6–7, 39, 41, 55–6, 140
Muche, Georg 98
Museum of Modern Art (MoMA), New York 101
Muslims 191, 198–9
Muthesius, Hermann 167
The Mysterious Affair at Styles (Christie) 24–5

Narkomfin Communal House, Moscow 75
neighbourhoods 11, 71, 80, 85–6, 132, 144, 188
neoliberal policies 79, 86, 87

Netherlands 7–8, 75, 77, 198
Die Neue Wohnung (film) 100
Neufert, Ernst 76
New Urbanism 71
New Zealand 128–30
Nixon, Richard 3–4, 153
Nordic design. *See* Scandinavian design
nostalgia 17–18, 25, 36, 112, 188

occupational segregation 121–2
open plan 8–9, 174, 180
Otte, Benita 98

parlours 8, 47, 55, 57, 141, 147
Passos, Pereira 83
patriarchy 138–40, 144, 152, 154–5, 159, 163
Patten, Marguerite 169
Paulsson, Gregor 103
Peru 85–6, 87
Philippines 78, 126
possessions. *See* belongings
postmodern era 58–62
postmodernism 71–2, 108
post-war era
    domestic advice books 163–4
    family structure 41, 56
    housing 8–9, 70, 76, 108, 131
    kitchens 3–5, 19, 150–5
    lifestyles 41–2, 44–5, 117–19, 170–5
    paid domestic work 124–5
    Scandinavian design 102–7
poverty 5, 11, 23, 73, 82–4, 116
prefabrication 74, 75, 76, 78, 110, 149–50
prisons 187, 199
privacy
    of the home 43, 72, 92, 140–1, 154–5, 161–2
    and social media 181
property developers. *See* construction industry
Proyecto Experimental de Vivienda (PREVI) 85–6
public housing 74–5, 76, 77, 79, 81, 88, 108, 110, 149
public zone 54–5. *See also* front-stage

queer space 51–4

racial differences 85
   meaning of home 157–8
   paid domestic work 125–6, 190–1
   segregation 6, 70, 83, 132
rationing 168–70
refrigerators 19, 21, 147, 150
religion
   domestic labour 191–3
   domestic rituals 189–91
   home as sanctuary 187–8
   Indian residential schools 199–201
   maternity homes 201–2
   rites of passage 197–9
Richter, Hans 100
Rietveld, Gerrit 7–8
Rio de Janeiro 83, 84
rituals 28, 33, 57–8, 189–91
Rosler, Martha 155
Rossi, Aldo 108
Russell, Gordon 101
Russia. *See* Soviet Union

same-sex couples 7, 56, 159, 191
sanctuary 43, 187–8
Scandinavian design 102–7, 109–10
Scheffler, Karl 94
Schröder, Truus 7–8, 146
Schütte-Lihotzky, Margarete (Grete) 1–2, 75, 99, 149–50, 151, 167
scientific management 22, 74, 148–9, 155, 171. *See also* Taylorism
Scott Brown, Denise 71
Second World War
   aftermath 3, 70, 76
   hospitality 168–70
   working women 16, 117, 118, 124
self-help housing 86, 187
   self-built 67, 69, 71
Semiotics of the Kitchen (video) 155
separate spheres ideology 138–43, 155, 191
service hatches 173, 174
sexuality 45, 47, 48, 54, 201
shantytowns 64, 81–8, 206 n.13. *See also* slums
Singapore 79–80, 81
single-family houses. *See* houses
slabs. *See* collective housing
Slow Food movement 183

slums 77, 82, 83, 84, 206 n.13. *See also* shantytowns
social media 60, 61, 62, 162, 181–2
social organization
   by gender 115–17, 121–2, 134–5, 138–41
   influenced by architecture 6–7, 75, 145
   reproduced in the house 41–2, 64, 66, 132–4, 152–5, 156
South Africa 83, 183
Soviet Union 75, 77, 78, 127, 170–1
   kitchen debate 3–5, 153
Spry, Constance 169, 175, 178
squatter settlements 81–8, 206 n.13. *See also* shantytowns
Starck, Philippe 108
state involvement 108
   home ownership 67, 70–1, 79–80, 130–1, 144, 179
   housing construction 73, 74, 75, 76, 77, 79–80, 81, 88, 108
Stewart, Martha 178, 179–80, 182, 184, 189, 206 n.2
Strinning, Nils 107
subdivisions 5, 63–73, 88
suburbia 42–3, 63, 71–3. *See also* subdivisions
   growth of 8–9, 39, 65, 118, 131
   home improvement 130–1
   home ownership 67–71, 143–4
Svenska Slöjdföreningen (Swedish Society of Craft and Industrial Design) 103, 107
Sweden 77, 102, 107, 109, 126, 170
Swedish design. *See* Scandinavian design

Taylorism 21, 22, 74, 148–9, 155. *See also* scientific management
technology 2, 95, 180–1. *See also* internet
   domestic appliances 19–21, 147–8, 150–3, 171, 175
   entertainment 9–10, 60, 181–2
teenagers 42, 51, 60, 164
telecommuting 10–11
telephones 21, 52
televisions 42, 194
Thatcherism 79, 179
Thonet 98
Tocqueville, Alexis de 140
Törten estate 110
Trudeau, Pierre 59

Turkey 67, 84, 87
Turner, John F.C. 86, 87

U'mista Cultural Centre 204
Unité d'habitation 76
urbanization 14, 64, 73–4, 79, 80, 81, 83–4, 87, 115, 126. *See also* shantytowns
USA
    African Americans 6, 69, 70, 132, 158, 190–1, 193, 194
    American dream 4–5, 71, 130–2
    Bauhaus 3, 101
    consumerism 3–5, 21, 26, 48, 70, 119–20, 152–3, 165
    home ownership 5, 65, 70–1, 144
    hospitality 164–5, 179–80
    middle class families 41–5, 55, 70, 153–4
    public housing 79
    religious households 190–8
Utility furniture scheme 101–2, 168, 170

Vanier, Jean 202–3
Vanna Venturi House 146
Venturi, Robert 71, 146
Victorian homes 7, 47, 55–6, 93, 162, 177

Vienna 74–5, 82–3, 93, 95, 112
Villa Savoye 66

Warhaftig, Myra 5
Werkbund 94–5, 97, 100, 103
women *See* consumerism; feminism; gender roles; housework; motherhood; patriarchy; separate spheres ideology
working classes 9, 11, 41, 116–17, 141, 159, 171
    employee housing 73
    home ownership 63, 64, 67, 69–70, 131, 179
    hospitality 164–5
World Bank 86, 87
Wright, Frank Lloyd 8, 66, 146, 205 n.2
Wright, Russel and Mary 171–4

yards 42–3, 141
Young, Iris Marion 158–9

zones 141. *See also* backstage; front-stage
    adult zones 44–5
    open plan 174
    public zones 54–5
    time-based zones 41, 43, 49